Theology within the Bounds of Language

Theology within the Bounds of Language

A Methodological Tour

Garth L. Hallett

Published by State University of New York Press, Albany

© 2011 State University of New York

All rights reserved

Printed in the United States of America

No part of this book may be used or reproduced in any manner whatsoever without written permission. No part of this book may be stored in a retrieval system or transmitted in any form or by any means including electronic, electrostatic, magnetic tape, mechanical, photocopying, recording, or otherwise without the prior permission in writing of the publisher.

For information, contact State University of New York Press, Albany, NY
www.sunypress.edu

Production by Eileen Meehan
Marketing by Anne M. Valentine

Library of Congress Cataloging-in-Publication Data

Hallett, Garth L.
　Theology within the bounds of language : a methodological tour / Garth L. Hallett.
　　p. cm.
　Includes bibliographical references (p.) and index.
　ISBN 978-1-4384-3369-1 (hardcover : alk. paper)
　ISBN 978-1-4384-3370-7 (paperback : alk. paper)
　1. Language and languages—Religious aspects—Christianity. 2. Theology—Methodology. I. Title.

BR115.L25H35 2011
230.01'4—dc22   2010020729

10 9 8 7 6 5 4 3 2 1

Contents

Preface		vii
Chapter 1	The Terrain Ahead	1
Chapter 2	Language and Thought	11
Chapter 3	Linguistic Spectacles	23
Chapter 4	Linguistic Truth	33
Chapter 5	Truth's Norm	45
Chapter 6	The Norm's Feasibility	55
Chapter 7	Making Sense	65
Chapter 8	Sense versus Possibility	73
Chapter 9	Inference and Analogy	81
Chapter 10	Universal Claims (Factual)	91
Chapter 11	Universal Claims (Moral)	97
Chapter 12	Privileged Senses	105
Chapter 13	Defining and Saying What Things Are	117
Chapter 14	The Need of Examples	129
Chapter 15	Important Linguistic Distinctions	137

Chapter 16	Verbal Disagreement	145
Chapter 17	Verbal Agreement	153
Chapter 18	Interfaith Dialogue	165
Chapter 19	Interfaith Identities	175
Chapter 20	Theological Language	187
Chapter 21	Metaphor	197
Chapter 22	Mystery	209
Epilogue		221
Notes		229
Works Cited		245
Index		261

Preface

In *Water Buffalo Theology*, Kosuke Koyama queries the "impressive discussions on methodology" which he has met in the writings of fellow theologians: "How do they know where they are going before they start walking? How can they describe the changing scenery before they see it? What space is there for such unexpected events as the disciples encountered on the way to Emmaus?"[1] The reader need not fear that I shall transgress in any of these ways. Yet at least one fundamental aspect of theological activity, discernible already in Koyama's closing allusion, can be anticipated in advance. The stranger the disciples met spoke with them: "[B]eginning with Moses and all the prophets, he interpreted to them the things about himself in all the scriptures" (Acts 24:27). They, in turn, spoke to one another: "Were not our hearts burning within us while he was talking to us on the road?" (Acts 24:32) Returning in haste to Jerusalem, they heard from those there: "The Lord is risen indeed and he has appeared to Simon" (Acts 24:34). Thereupon, they "told what had happened on the road, and how he had been made known to them in the breaking of the bread" (Acts 24:35). He spoke, they spoke to one another, others conversed with them, they replied—so Christian theology began, and so it has continued ever since: ineluctably linguistic.

In those early exchanges at Emmaus, Jerusalem, and along the road, we see language at the service of truth, of community, and of both together: at the service of truth for the sake of community and at the service of community for the sake of truth. Since then, language has served in both of these ways within Christian theology, and when its role has there been ignored or misunderstood, both truth and community have suffered, often seriously. This is not surprising, for much obscurity surrounds the relationship between language and truth, and the pursuit of truth without due regard for language or understanding of its proper functioning adversely affects the communicative, communitarian aspect of theology. Of modern Western philosophy Thomas McCarthy has observed: "What has been too often ignored and always underanalyzed is the pervasive normativity of social life."[2] The like might be said of theology as a form of social life and of the normativity, or authoritative role, of language in its conduct. Though basic, that role has too often been ignored and too often underanalyzed, even in works of fundamental theology or theological method, where acknowledgment of its importance would be most appropriate and might therefore be expected. The present work is offered as a partial remedy for this neglect.

Much has been written, to be sure, about theology and language. Outside this work's chosen focus, on theological discourse, an ample literature has addressed questions of hermeneutics and biblical interpretation. Inside the focus, a more directly relevant body of theological writing resulted from the "linguistic turn" in philosophy that crested in the middle decades of the last century. However, no previous work closely resembles the present one. My own early *Darkness and Light: The Analysis of Doctrinal Statements*, drawing on a previous study of Wittgenstein's treatment of word meaning and a commentary on his classic *Philosophical Investigations*, comes as close as any but, as the subtitle suggests, focused more on analyzing doctrinal statements than on formulating them. A number of my subsequent works[3] have addressed more fully topics taken up here. However, not only have my thoughts had time to mature, not only do they differ from those in others' writings, but the present work addresses a wider range of issues within its chosen focus than are to be found in previous studies in the same general area of interest.[4] Thus, although in various places I have read or written about most of the matters here discussed, it occurred to me that, rather than leave them scattered here and there, I should bring them together within a single cover and supplement them with some neglected topics. A brief compendium seemed desirable.

It soon became evident, though, that I would not be able to develop these varied materials in strictly systematic fashion, as in a mathematical demonstration or a map of central Manhattan. "Language," wrote Wittgenstein, "is a labyrinth of paths. You approach from *one* side and know your way about; you approach the same place from another side and no longer know your way about."[5] "In teaching you philosophy," he therefore told his students (as they later reconstructed his remarks), "I'm like a guide showing you how to find your way round London. I have to take you through the city from north to south, from east to west, from Euston to the embankment and from Piccadilly to the Marble Arch. After I have taken you many journeys through the city, in all sorts of directions, we shall have passed through any given street a number of times—each time traversing the street as part of a different journey. At the end of this you will know London; you will be able to find your way about like a born Londoner."[6] Although the present quick reconnaissance may not suffice to beget such mastery, still, I like Wittgenstein's comparison. Since language, like London, is not systematic, there is no way to tour it systematically. A given street leads to a lane here, an alley there, a square farther on, and to other streets that meet or cross it. A guide can pass smoothly and without break from the first street into another, or into the lane, the alley, or the square, but not into all at once. After taking one direction, it is necessary to cut back to follow the others. And yet, a guide showing visitors around London can manage without too much confusion, and so, I trust, shall I.

I offer the present tour for interested theologians as well as for students of theology. The sample passages at the end of each chapter, stimulating and broadening reflection on the chapter's themes, should interest both categories of prospective readers. The passages have, in fact, proved helpful to colleagues in locating each chapter within a larger literature and sensing its significance more fully, and have proved handy in classroom instruction. There, once a basis is provided by the text, discussion can take any of the directions suggested by the quotations, according to student interests and preferences. Some passages will agree with the text, while others will disagree; some will lead to related issues, while others will open new perspectives. All can stimulate further reflection and discussion. On offer here, then, is a workbook.

Its practical nature should be noted so as to avoid an unfortunate impression. For the book's focus, understandably, is more on problematic modes of theological discourse than on those which occasion little concern. In this respect it resembles, say, a text of informal logic. There, the many fallacies reviewed, and the unfortunate examples that illustrate them, might impart a jaundiced view of human beings' allegedly rational nature. Here, a similarly negative impression, of theologians and their trade, might arise. For here, too, more benefit will come from attending to problematic than to unproblematic thinking. Here too, accordingly (indeed, especially here), it may be necessary to reassure the reader from the start: the present study does not pretend to offer a balanced survey of theological practice. Positive exposition accompanies critique, and sound sample passages mix with unsound, but, to borrow a saying, those who are well have no need of a physician.

In writing this study, my greatest debt has been to Wittgenstein (specifically, Wittgenstein the philosopher of language, not Wittgenstein the less impressive philosopher of religion), whose thought has influenced philosophical and theological writings of mine on which I have here drawn. I am indebted more immediately to those who have kindly read and commented on these pages: to Gerard Hughes and William Rehg who read the whole work and to Bernhard Asen, Ronald Modras, and James Voiss who read parts of it. My thanks go also to Victoria Carlson-Casaregola for her careful stylistic editing.

Chapter 1

The Terrain Ahead

A tour through the streets and scenes of London: such is the Preface's image, suggesting and suggested by this book's title, *Theology within the Bounds of Language: A Methodological Tour*. What, now, more precisely, is the London in question, the terrain to be reconnoitered? Though the terms *theology*, *language*, and *methodological* provide a general indication of the ground to be covered, the area they collectively encompass is still too vast. Each of these three expressions requires further delimitation.

First, *language* interests theology in various ways, many of fundamental importance; yet not all of them lie within the primary focus of the present work. Here, emphasis will fall on basic questions concerning the use of language rather than its interpretation, on successful discourse rather than on accurate exegesis. This emphasis does not signify exclusion, for the first type of question connects importantly with the second. Deeper understanding of the appropriate use of language brings with it more discerning awareness of how language is in fact employed in discussions or documents we may wish to decipher. Still, in what follows, attention will center primarily on the former sort of question rather than the latter—on linguistic practice rather than linguistic interpretation.

Theology, too—ancient and modern, Eastern and Western, popular and professional—takes in more than this work will attempt to explore. Although most of what is said will apply more broadly, attention will center primarily on Christian theology, from which illustrations and applications will typically be drawn. Though restricted, this focus is nonetheless ample. A recent observer has noted, retrospectively, the "many-faceted richness and vitality of twentieth-century Christian theology," which "has been overwhelming to the point of bewilderment."[1] There has been Catholic, Protestant, and Orthodox theology; European, African, Asian, North American, and Latin American; liberal and conservative;

biblical, dogmatic, kerygmatic, systematic, pastoral, social, and spiritual; confessional and ecumenical; black, feminist, philosophical, ecological, and so forth, with endless variations. Yet common to all these versions and varieties of Christian theology, as to other kinds, has been the use of language. Whether thinking, speaking, or writing, theologians employ a system of signs. And whatever the topics they discuss, they usually wish their statements, using those signs, to have intelligible meaning and to be true. Common, therefore, to the theological enterprise are methodological issues of linguistic practice such as those here addressed. Though much has been written on these questions, they are usually slighted in works of fundamental theology or theological method, and, as already noted, no study has gathered them together in a handy compendium. Such is the aim of the present guide.

Methodology, the category to which this work belongs, captivates few readers. The very word *methodology* has a dry, abstract sound to it. Yet in theology as in philosophy, science, history, and other areas of inquiry, questions of method hold fundamental significance. And in theology more than in most other disciplines, methodological issues with regard to language are among the most fundamental. Or at least some are, and on those this study will focus. Interest will not center on topics such as rhetoric considers, with regard to style, effective argumentation, or the art of persuasion, but on others of a kind whose nature can be suggested, in advance of the many examples to come, by means of a remark of John Macquarrie. "Theology," he has written, "may be defined as the study which, through participation in and reflection upon a religious faith, seeks to express the content of this faith in the clearest and most coherent language available."[2] Here the closing words, "the clearest and most coherent language available," suggest stylistic virtues. "Clarity, clarity, clarity!" insist primers on style. Break up involved, complicated sentences! Make sure relative pronouns have clear referents! Avoid ambiguity! Have mercy on your readers! The present study will not take this tack; it is not a treatise on style. Instead, attention will focus, for example, on issues of the kind raised by Macquarrie's opening five words, "Theology may be defined as." The proposed activity, defining, is linguistic; that much is clear. But here in this quotation as often in theological discussion, the nature and purpose of the activity are less evident. Does the proffered definition aim to capture the existing meaning of the English word *theology*? Does it propose, instead, to fashion a substitute meaning of the term? Or, more interested in theology than in the word *theology*, does it aim to describe all the activities covered by that expression? Or just some of them, or the better ones, or the ones more worthy of serious consideration, or the essence they all share? Without clarification of such questions as these, the "defining" enterprise cannot hope to succeed—assuming that, on closer scrutiny, it still appears worth undertaking.

Reflection at this deeper level can throw further light on all three foci of this study—theology, language, and methodology—and thereby illustrate, and not merely talk about, the direction the study will take.

Theology

In *Meaning and Method*, Anders Nygren declared: "An investigation aimed at getting a clear answer to the question 'What is theology?' and 'What is philosophy?' and clarifying their scientific status is very greatly needed."[3] In Nygren's view, the proper practice of either discipline requires such clarification. Many have thought similarly, specifically about theology and also more generally (consult the passages for further reflection at the end of this chapter). Thus, Wolfhart Pannenberg, for example, has written in a similar way: "Any rational reform of the theology course must be guided by a decision about what theology in fact is and what knowledge and skills a person must acquire to become competent in theology. The crucial question here is what specific subjects make up the essential area of theological enquiry."[4] This sounds reasonable and suitably scientific: How can you teach theology if you don't know what theology is, and how can you teach theology properly if you don't know *precisely* what theology is? In response, rather than specify any essence of theology, we might proffer a sampling of theologies from different times, places, cultures, and schools of thought. This, we might say, is what theology is, specifically, concretely. However, for Nygren, Pannenberg, and like-minded thinkers (whose number, I sense, has declined of late), such a sampling would give no clear or certain indication of what philosophy or theology really is—of its definition, its genuine nature, its essence. And that, they would suggest, is what we need to know, if we wish to proceed scientifically or with overall clarity about what we are doing.

A later chapter will indicate problems for the defining enterprise so conceived. Here, a passage from Wittgenstein's *Philosophical Investigations* can suggest the problems' general nature. "How should we explain to someone what a game is?" asked Wittgenstein. "I imagine," he replied, "that we should describe *games* to him, and we might add: 'This *and similar things* are called "games."' And do we know any more about it ourselves? Is it only other people whom we cannot tell exactly what a game is?—But this is not ignorance. We do not know the boundaries because none have been drawn."[5] Neither have clear, sharp boundaries been drawn for "theology." So what might we still need to know about theology when we know only that these, those, and similar things are called theology? And what importance would that missing knowledge have for the proper conduct of theological inquiry?

According to a common, still influential conception, to many a term there corresponds an essence shared by all and only the members of the class of things covered by the term. An essence of theology, for example, would be shared by all and only the things that people have called theology. It would appear, therefore, in the thought and works of extremely varied thinkers, differing in practically every other respect besides their common classification as theologians: in the topics treated, the questions asked, the answers given, the methods employed, the purposes and audiences envisaged for their inquiries, and so forth. The common essence would be shared by historical, sacramental, pastoral, fundamental, spiritual, systematic, and mystical theologians, and by Protestant, Catholic, Muslim, Hindu, Orthodox, Native American, and other thinkers writing, theologically, on any imaginable topic (family, sport, death, sacraments, grace, evolution, politics, or the City of God).

Accordingly, the shared essence would prescind from all these differences. It would not indicate one area of inquiry rather than another, one type of question rather than another, one verdict rather than another, one method or technique or purpose rather than any other among all those favored by various theologians. For otherwise it would not be common to them all and to their theologies. It would not be a shared essence.

Notice, then, the implications of this conception. Such a bare kernel would offer no guidance on any of these issues, but would pass over each option—of area, question, answer, method, goal—and leave us on our own to decide between alternatives. The nuclear trait or traits shared by all and only theologies would be neutral in every respect that matters for decision, for theologies have differed in every one. To illustrate the point, think again of games, and suppose, for example, that all games had rules. This common fact about them would not dictate what rules to adopt, what games to play, or how to play them. Similarly, suppose, for example, that all theologies made truth-claims. This common fact about them would not indicate what questions to address or what evidence to consider or what conclusions to accept as true. And the like would hold for any trait common to all theologies, whether or not, in addition, the trait belonged to some essence shared only by members of the class of things called theology.

The existence of such an essence looks highly dubious, for reasons, both general and specific, that we shall have occasion to consider. Here, we are concerned with the further question of whether an essence, if found, would offer practical guidance. And the verdict, so far, seems to be clearly negative. An essence of the classical kind we have been considering would just be something possessed in common, not a value, goal, or ideal. Accordingly, it would be neutral with respect to all important options. It would be neutral, first, because it would leave out all points of divergence. It would be neutral, second, because it would favor none of the options it ignored. It would be neutral, furthermore, because what traits it did include would not thereby be shown to be particularly valuable or desirable. They would simply form a common nub (like the uninteresting core that joins the edible leaves of an artichoke).

Perhaps, then, to have the kind of significance often supposed, the question "What is theology?" should be given a different, ideal sense. The essence in question might not be something common to everything *called* theology but to everything *rightly* called theology. However, who or what might validate such a proprietary claim to the label "theology"? Should we consult a Platonic Form of theology, eternal and unchanging in some conceptual heaven? If familiar linguistic usage can be ignored as a test of what counts as theology, what test should replace it? Theologians, like philosophers, often lack answers to questions such as these. Indeed, like philosophers, they may simply declare, in the words of a noted theologian, "what theology really is,"[6] without troubling about linguistic issues of the kind on which this study will focus.

Consider, for example, a couple of sample definitions of theology, chosen not so much for their notable divergence (more disparate ones might have been cited) but for the seriousness with which they are proposed and argued for. In *An Essay on Theological Method*, Gordon Kaufman has written of his "growing conviction that theology is, and always has been, an activity of what I call the 'imaginative construction' of a comprehensive and coherent picture of humanity in the world under God."[7] This is what theology consists in; here is its essence. John Carnes, for his part, after noting critically how freely and variously the term *theology* is applied, has argued for his own definition: theology is "the effort to understand systematically our religious experience."[8] These sound like differing descriptions of what theology is, not recommendations of how it should be conducted, still less of how the word *theology* is or should be applied. However, there is no indication that Kaufman and Carnes, though they both use the word *theology*, are talking about some single entity and describing it differently. Thus, taken descriptively, their accounts may be mere tautologies: the kind of theology they describe is as described. And even as veiled methodological recommendations, these contrasting definitions appear problematic. For it is doubtful that either author would exclude in practice what the other includes in his definition. Kaufman would not oppose the effort indicated by Carnes, to understand religious experience, and neither, for his part, would Carnes oppose the imaginative construction described by Kaufman, of a coherent picture of humanity in the world under God. It is still more doubtful that they view their declarations of what theology "is" as implicit recommendations that the word *theology* be restricted to the variety they describe.

By now, I fear, some readers may be feeling restive. Granted, there may be no single essence of theology. Granted, there may be no single ideal form of theological activity. But surely, here at the start of a work on methodological issues in theology, I should indicate as precisely as possible just what I understand by the word *theology*. Yet why is that? I ask. What sense, on closer reflection, does such a demand have? Suppose, to revert to our earlier comparison, that someone offered to show you around London: Would you insist that the person first define London as precisely as possible? Would you be lost without such a definition? Would the tour somehow fail of its purpose? Hardly, and the like holds for theology. During decades of theological reading and discussion, never, at any moment or in any context, have I discerned any need for a precise definition of the discipline such as many have judged desirable. It would have served no purpose then, and it will serve no purpose here. Chapter by chapter, the reader will know well enough where we are. And if, for instance, we happen to stray over the border from theology into philosophy, no harm will be done, nor will it be necessary to indicate exactly where, if anywhere, that nebulous border lies. (Implicitly or explicitly, to varying degrees, philosophy permeates the whole of theology, for the breadth and depth of philosophy match the breadth and depth of theology.)

I have said enough for the moment to suggest in a preliminary way why my approach to theology will not be "scientific," as that prestigious term has often been understood, and why, instead, I will pay attention to the linguistic considerations that call such aspirations into question. To become attentive to language is to become aware, not only of the possibilities of theology, but also of its limitations. So let me say more about language.

Language

If anything, the term *language* has been still more widely, variously applied—especially in theology—than the term *theology*. It has been said, for example, that "faith is language,"[9] that tradition is language,[10] indeed, quite generally, that "Being that can be understood is language."[11] (One thinks, perhaps, of potatoes, earthquakes, and the stock exchange, all of which can be understood—and wonders.) Amid all this terminological diversity, it seems no more realistic or useful to try to identify an essence of language than to seek an essence of theology. Here, however, for the purposes of the present study, one major instance of this diversity requires attention and emphasis from the start: namely, the distinction between language as *medium* (e.g., the English language that I am here using) and language as *discourse* employing that medium (e.g., my use of the English language to say the things I am saying). As a telephone is not a telephone conversation and a ten dollar bill is not a ten dollar purchase, so the English language, say, is not an utterance, speech, conversation, or treatise employing that language.

Though this distinction between medium and employment is fundamental, its significance is often overlooked. In particular, the distinction and its importance receive slight recognition in theology, where stress typically falls on language as discourse rather than on language as medium of discourse. In the present study, for reasons that will appear, this imbalance will be redressed. Indeed, for clarity's sake, in the following pages (save for some quotations from other writers), the word *language* will always refer to the medium, the system of signs, and not to the linguistic activity conducted by its means. To assure that this distinction is understood and is kept in mind hereafter, it will be well to linger on it a moment longer.

In theological literature, relatively seldom does one encounter the term *language* used with clear reference to just the medium of discourse. Much more frequently the word refers to the uses made of language. When, for instance, Langdon Gilkey speaks of "the theological language of the Church,"[12] or "the realm of discourse called 'religious language,' "[13] he is not referring to the various languages spoken in the Church (French, Latin, Syriac, or the like), nor to those employed in religious discourse. He is speaking of the languages' employment. A similar focus is evident when Rino Fisichella distinguishes "theological language" from "liturgical language," "religious language," "catechetical language," and "pastoral language,"[14] or when Macquarrie writes: "[A]t this point we may draw more sharply the line between theological language and the wider phenomenon of religious language. The latter expression would be used to include such diverse kinds of utterances as praying, praising, exhorting, blessing, cursing, and perhaps many other things besides."[15] Here, as in countless other instances in theological writings, attention centers on the praying, praising, exhorting, and the like—that is, on the utterances, the speech acts, and not on the medium employed in making them.

There is nothing wrong about this application of the word *language*; it is a standard use cited in dictionaries, along with other applications of the term. And the focus represented by these quotations is understandable. After all, theology aims at truth, and languages are not true or false; neither are their words, rules, and conventions. Statements are; utterances are. So attention centers on the utterances. Besides, theologians' interest extends beyond the bare truth of what they say. "Theology," writes Claude Geffré, "can be defined as an attempt to make the already constituted language of revelation more intelligible and meaningful for contemporary man. That language is already an interpretative language and, as a new interpretative language, theology relies on it to develop the meanings of the Christian mystery that are valuable in the present for the Church and society."[16] This new language, notice, is not an improved version of German, English, or the like but a more effective use of whatever tongue is employed. The day will come, predicts Dietrich Bonhoeffer, "when men will once more be called so to utter the Word of God that the world will be changed and renewed by it. It will be a new language, perhaps quite non-religious, but liberating and redeeming."[17] Again, the "new language" Bonhoeffer here envisages is not a replacement for our mother tongues. His focus, appropriately for his message, is on language as discourse, not language as medium.

The explanation of this characteristic emphasis goes deeper than contextual appropriateness or relative importance. For the most part, words resemble spectacles that we look through but seldom at. We need to have such command of whatever language we speak that we are free to attend to the things we say, without figuring out how to say them. Discussion of genetics, investments, politics, or the greenhouse effect—or of God, grace, conversion, baptism, church, or salvation history—may be sufficiently complex without our deliberating just what expressions to use, sentence by sentence, and how. To function efficiently, language must become second nature, and so it does, from infancy.

Inattention to the medium of discourse has still deeper roots. To some extent, speech resembles tennis. Just as proficient players pay little attention to how they make their strokes and much to what strokes they make and where they send the ball, so experienced speakers attend much less to the basics of speech—to the intricacies of syntax and semantics—than they do to what they are saying. There is a difference, however. For many tennis players, there was a time when they received explicit instructions concerning the fundamentals of the game; but for language acquisition there neither is nor can be any comparable process. We cannot be told how to speak before we know any language. (Anne Sullivan could sign "water" as she splashed Helen Keller, and hope she would catch on, but she could not explain to her, in English, the use of the word *water*.) Neither, therefore, can we now call to mind a comprehensive set of instructions, learned long ago, that encapsulate the tactics and techniques of speech. Even the best grammar text takes a great deal for granted. Whether in using language, therefore, or in learning language, our attention is fixed elsewhere—on the topics of discourse or the statements made about them rather than on the rules of the system of signs employed.

It is natural, then, for theologians and others to adopt the perspective they typically do, centered on language as discourse rather than on language as medium. ("The primary job of the theologian," Frederick Ferré rightly remarks, "is not to philosophize about his language but to use it.")[18] Furthermore, for the most part, on most occasions and in most contexts, words can indeed take care of themselves. If, occasionally, expressions are ambiguous, we can indicate the intended sense (as I did above for "language"). If they are not sufficiently precise for our purposes, we can sharpen them. Where necessary, we can fashion new ones. Otherwise, we can get on with the business at hand. We can report the weather, describe the party, explain the explosion, predict the election's outcome, or what have you. Yet in theology, as also in philosophy, this customary stance, centered on the message rather than the medium, can veil serious problems. Examples in this introductory chapter—for instance, with regard to the definition of theology and the need for such a definition—suggest already how significant these problems may be. However, only much fuller illustration, of the kind to be offered hereafter, can possibly remedy the vicious circle that otherwise threatens: not reflecting seriously on our linguistic medium, we may see no reason to do so; seeing no reason to do so, we may not do so. Thanks to this self-perpetuating merry-go-round, difficulties in dire need of attention may not receive it.

The natural fixation that I have been explaining reflects, and has helped to perpetuate, a major feature of Western thought. Languages were long viewed, and sometimes still are, as mere codes, needed to communicate thoughts from mind to mind but having no life of their own. (What semantic complexity or social, cultural richness does Morse Code reveal?) In this conception, meaning and truth reside in the thoughts expressed, not in their arbitrary linguistic expression. That, then, is where attention has turned: to thought and its objects far more than to words and the languages to which they belong. The next chapter, reflecting much recent thinking, challenges this conception of the relationship between language and thought. Language has far more significance for meaning and truth than the traditional viewpoint recognized or permitted to appear at all clearly or forcefully.

For Further Reflection

1. "The most prolegomena to theology can appropriately do is provide readers an advance description of the enterprise. Even this cannot be a pre-theological beginning, for every attempt to say what sort of thing theology is implies material theological propositions, and so is false if the latter are false"[19] (Robert Jenson).

2. "We can describe an important feature of the service which the community should expect from theologians as 'faith seeking *a new language.*' Christians express their faith through worship, preaching, teaching, pastoral care and social action. Theologians, more than other groups, have the task of testing, criticizing and revising the language which—in all these activities—the community uses about God and the divine revelation communicated through Jesus Christ"[20] (Gerald O'Collins).

3. "Because the method of a science is dependent upon its nature, the method of moral theology cannot be determined without taking exact account of the nature of theology in general and of moral theology in particular"[21] (M. Labourdette).

4. "A primary responsibility of metareligious thought that aims at being comprehensive and critical is to determine as *generally* and, at the same time, as *precisely* as possible what it is that we are thinking about. That is, one of the first and most important tasks of philosophy of religion must be to supply an adequate definition of 'religion' "[22] (Frederick Ferré).

5. "Tillich, like Luther before him, suggests another way of distinguishing theological issues from other issues: a theological issue is one that concerns us ultimately. Only those issues are theological that deal with a matter of ultimate concern, such as our relation to God and each other, the possibility and nature of redemption, and the meaning of our lives"[23] (Owen Thomas and Ellen Wondra).

Chapter 2

Language and Thought

In *Dynamics of Theology*, Roger Haight identifies common characteristics that are "so essential to human existence as such that they serve as transcendental bonds of unity and communication." He writes:

> For example, all human beings desire to know and all think, understand, and make judgments; all human beings are contingent and must face death; all are in history and must face the future and the question of their ultimate destiny; all human beings experience suffering which can call into question the meaningfulness of existence itself; because of the radical freedom that constitutes a reflective human spirit, all are open to the possible experience of transcendence; all are religious in the radical sense of having to decide what is of ultimate importance and concern.[1]

Haight might have cited language as a further such "bond of unity and communication," shared by all human beings of normal abilities. And many would add that not only when we speak and write but also when we "think, understand, and make judgments," we do so linguistically: language is not only an instrument of human communication but is the characteristic medium of human thought. This view represents a major shift from earlier conceptions and one that calls for close scrutiny, since its implications affect the whole of theology (not to mention other disciplines) in fundamental ways.

A Dialectical Development

"Concepts and ideas," notes Hilary Putnam, "were always thought important; language was thought unimportant, because it was considered to be merely a system of conventional signs for concepts and ideas (considered as mental entities of some kind, and quite independent of the signs used to express them)."[2] In classic expression of this mentalistic viewpoint, the famed Port Royal *Logic*, for instance, states: "To say that a written or spoken word means such and such is to say only that our minds entertain the meaning, that is, the idea connected with that word whenever we hear or see the word."[3] Words, in this view, have no life of their own; all meaning and truth reside in the nonlinguistic thoughts they express. Subsequently, the pendulum swung far in the opposite direction. Already in the nineteenth century, Friedrich Schleiermacher could assert that "there are no thoughts without speech,"[4] and more recent thinkers, including some theologians, have concurred. Thus, for Georges Tavard, "No one thinks without words."[5] For John Macquarrie, "Whatever man does beyond the most elementary biological reactions, he makes use of language. Even when he is doing nothing overtly, his thoughts are formed by language."[6]

This stress on language as the medium of human thought has owed much to the later Wittgenstein. However, after flirting momentarily with the idea that "[t]hinking is operating with language,"[7] Wittgenstein took a more balanced stance. While recognizing that there is such a thing as nonlinguistic thought, which can be given verbal expression,[8] he nonetheless maintained: "When I think in language, there aren't 'meanings' going through my mind in addition to the verbal expressions: the language is itself the vehicle of thought."[9] This pregnant remark raises a question of great interest and importance for all discourse and inquiry, especially theological: might those same thoughts—the ones expressed in words—be entertained some other way? Might they be had nonlinguistically?

To sense the significance of this query, try the following test. Pick out any sentence or clause so far in this chapter—say, "All human beings desire to know," "Words have no life of their own," or "More recent thinkers, including some theologians, have concurred." Now do this: have the same thought, nonlinguistically. Do it without words. If, as I expect, you have no idea how even to begin, or if, having made the attempt, you at least have serious doubts whether what you did, nonlinguistically, really had the same meaning as the words, you may appreciate the importance of language for thought. For, instead of citing the sentences in the preceding paragraphs, I could have substituted those in this whole chapter, this book, or any other work of theology—indeed, those in any other work on any other topic. Try random statements in the morning paper; try "An earthquake hit Sumatra last night" or "Stocks climbed higher today."

Language and Thought 13

If, in fact, every thought expressed in any scriptural passage, patristic saying, conciliar pronouncement, or theological utterance, in any work or document, is linguistic and can be entertained, by humans, in no other, nonlinguistic form, the implications for the conduct of theology are of fundamental significance, and will have to be examined. First, though, it will be necessary to consider more attentively whether such is in fact the case, and, if so, why.

Linguistic Thoughts

Selecting a sample passage for scrutiny, let us not pick an abstract, deeply abstruse specimen. Let us not, for example, try to think "The Word was made flesh" or "The Father and I are one" without the words. For such utterances, success looks too unlikely. However, consider even Luke 23:33: "When they came to the place that is called The Skull, they crucified Jesus there." For a statement such as this, doubtless we can at least form a few appropriate images. And if we were very good at mental picturing and were up on pertinent details, we might do better. We might imagine Roman soldiers, suitably attired, for the pronoun "they," some hilly terrain for "The Skull," and our favorite representation of Jesus for the name "Jesus"; and, putting all these images together, we might perhaps form a mental snapshot of the scene. Yet, could we then run off a mental movie, step by step, of Jesus being crucified? And would the movie be a faithful nonlinguistic rendering of Luke 23:33? Hardly. Not only would countless details be missing. Not only would all the details included, without any likely exception, be inaccurate in their portrayal of the actual event. But the mental representation would be narrower and more detailed than the meaning of the text. Luke's words do not say how many soldiers there were, what they looked like, what they wore, how they performed their task, using what instruments, with how many strokes, etc. However, let it pass; all this suggested imagining is, of course, pure fantasy. No such mental movie, in full color, accompanies the saying, writing, reading, or hearing of a sentence such as Luke's. And even if it did, it would not be a full, faithful rendering of the utterance's meaning, any more than even the most realistic book *illustration* is a faithful *translation* of any sentence or passage in the book. For example, even the most accurate, complete mental representation of external appearances for "they" and "Jesus," in Luke's text, would leave out most of what constitutes a human being (mind, heart, muscles, bones, inner organs, etc.).

From such an example and such a critique, it is clear why many thinkers of the past had recourse to abstract intellectual likenesses, not concrete sensible images, for the content of the thoughts that supposedly accompany and generate our utterances. It is hopeless to suppose that we can accurately imagine each step in Jesus' crucifixion; but if, despite their differences, all acts of crucifying shared a common essence, and if we could form an abstract mental likeness of that essence, and if the word *crucify* communicated that likeness from mind to mind, then we might have no need of questionable details: perhaps we could accurately think everything the word *crucify* expresses. Perhaps, when we wrote or read the word *crucified*, we could think that abstract, stripped-down thought and nothing else, and therewith entertain the word's full meaning, nonlinguistically.

Yet, even on these very generous assumptions, what about the rest of the sentence? What about the pronoun "they," the place name "The Skull," or the personal name "Jesus"? Is there an essence of each soldier, of the place, or of Jesus, capable of abstract representation? To avoid such complications as these, and to probe the heart of the essentialistic conception of language, thought, and world, let us shift to a different, simpler example. Suppose a person says, "Snow is white." Here, in this utterance, there are no proper names or pronouns requiring mental matching, but just two general terms, a noun and an adjective, joined by the copula "is." So now, if there is an abstract essence common to all snow and an abstract essence common to all whiteness, perhaps we can represent both essences mentally, join them, and thereby achieve the mental equivalent of "Snow is white." Perhaps this is what passes through the mind of a person who says these words and of a person who hears them.

Perhaps. It depends, fundamentally, on whether there are such essences to be detected, represented, and communicated. The noted analytic philosopher G. E. Moore, for one, apparently believed at one time that there are. Musing to himself in his *Commonplace Book*, Moore remarked:

> This character wh[ich] we express by "is a shade of blue," is, of course, something which is common to all shades of blue—something which they have "in common." Some people seem loth to admit that they have anything "in common." And of course this character is not "in common" to both of 2 blue shades, in the sense that it is a part or constituent of both.... Obviously this character also is not identical with any shade which possesses it, nor yet with any other shade of colour that we *see*. It is not similar in shade to any shade that we *see*. So that, if it is "seen" at all, it is only in a completely different sense.[10]

With similar emphasis, Moore affirmed: "*All* the shades we *see* occupy some position in the colour octahedron; but 'blue,' in the sense in which many of the shades in the octahedron are 'blue,' occupies *no* position in it: therefore it is not seen."[11]

What all shades of blue have in common is something that can be truly said of all of them. For example, they are all members of the disjunctive class (cobalt *or* aquamarine *or* turquoise *or* . . .) designated by the common term *blue*. Or, they all belong to a continuum of shades labeled "blue" and bordered roundabout by colors that bear other labels ("purple," "mauve," "black," etc.). This disjunctive membership, or position within a linguistically defined continuum of shades, is not, to be sure, something that can be "seen." Neither, however, is it something of which one might form an abstract mental likeness. I can form no such likeness of disjunction as such, much less of this particular disjunction with all its constituent shades. Talk of abstraction suggests leaving out the sensible particulars, but to leave out the shades of blue that form the continuum or disjunctive class of blues would be to leave out the sensible content of the concept "blue." In Wittgenstein's comparison, it would be like stripping an artichoke of its leaves in search of the real, essential artichoke and concluding that, since no single leaf constitutes the essence, the essence is invisible and intangible and can only be captured by an intellectual likeness. Thus, recourse to inner resemblance works no better, I suggest, for general terms such as "blue" and "red" than it does for "they," "the place named The Skull," or "Jesus" in Luke 23:33. Language does not function in the way supposed.

In comparison with the skimpy imagining that can and sometimes does accompany our words, the cognitive content that the words communicate—what speakers know and hearers learn—is enormously rich. When typical English-speakers hear and learn that something is blue, they know that it falls somewhere within the blue spectrum. And they know with equal immediacy that it is not (or not to the same extent) green, red, purple, orange, or any other color that does not fall within that spectrum. They know, furthermore, the difference between the object's being blue and its merely appearing blue (say by reason of the light or the spectacles worn). Nowadays, in addition, when they hear, for example, that the sky is blue, they are likely to pick up some scientific information about the sky and the light rays that pass through it. There is no need to determine, if we could, how much of all this belongs to the "meaning" of the utterance "The Sky is blue." This is what the words communicate, and no fleeting representation in the mind of the speaker or hearer could possibly capture it all, nonlinguistically. What holds for this sample holds generally. Most other concepts—"climate," "city," "corporation," "astronomy," "human being"—are richer and more complex than the concept "blue." And no single mental likeness captures an essence common to all and only members of any such class.

This can be said with assurance for several reasons, which I shall here develop. The development, though brief, is necessarily complex; and some readers, sensing no need to be convinced, may wish to skip over it. However, I must at least sketch the case against essences mirrored by mental likenesses, for this model, long favored, is the most plausible way to conceive equivalence between linguistic and nonlinguistic thoughts. The critique makes three main points, which I have highlighted for ease in following the train of thought.

First, no such essences have in fact been detected. Formulas are sometimes proposed as characterizing all and only members of some class designated by a general term. But the formulas seldom if ever do so accurately; and even if they did, they would not thereby demonstrate the existence of an essence, capable of being captured by some single mental likeness.[12] To illustrate the difference between single defining formula and single essence, consider a fanciful example. There is, let us suppose, an English word "brank," that the dictionary accurately defines "right bank." If it be asked in what sense of "bank" (economic or topographical) a brank is a bank and in what sense of "right" (opposed to "left" or opposed to "wrong") it is right, the answer is "Both." The imagined concept, established by usage, so decrees. Though this example is fanciful, its message is clear: we should not be overly impressed in the unlikely event that some equally accurate defining formula was discovered for any actual concept. That remarkable coincidence of conceptual borders would not demonstrate the uniformity of whatever fell within the coinciding borders.

Second, not only has no all-and-only essence been detected, of a kind that might be captured in some single mental likeness, but *the reasons alleged for supposing that, nonetheless, such essences surely exist look unsound.* The only such argument that I have heard with my own ears is the one suggested early on by Plato. "Well, then," asks Socrates in the *Republic,* "shall we proceed as usual and begin by assuming the existence of a single essential nature or Form for every set of things which we call by the same name?"[13] Shifting the focus from the things to the names, we might ask, "Shall we assume that names do and must function in this way—to pick out single, invariant essences?" How might this be shown? Gottlob Frege's words sound like a possible reply. "Signs," he wrote, "would hardly be useful if they did not serve the purpose of signifying the same thing repeatedly and in different contexts, while making evident that the same thing was meant."[14] This claim of Frege's might be variously understood. Without stretching, we might take it as verified, say, by "blue": to say that something is blue is to say "the same thing" about it, namely that it falls somewhere within the indefinite borders of the concept "blue." Similarly, it could be admitted that, in a sense, the imagined word *brank* repeatedly signifies the same thing: it signifies that a thing so described belongs to the disparate collection of things that are banks and are right, in either sense of "bank" and either sense of "right." Thus, unless it is taken more essentialistically, Frege's demand appears vacuous. But if it is so understood, there is no reason to accept his claim and, upon further reflection, every reason not to.

For, *third*, not only has no all-and-only essence of the pertinent kind, representable by a single mental likeness accompanying a word, been detected; not only are the reasons for supposing the existence of such essences, matched one to one with words, unsound; but *their existence would require a most unlikely restriction of linguistic usage to some single, constant content, despite various analogies, contexts, purposes, and speaker tendencies, tugging the word this way and that*. Language, naturally and reasonably, functions very differently. Its concepts tend to spread, diversify, and become diffuse. Take Wittgenstein's example, "number":

> Why do we call something a "number"? Well, perhaps because it has a—direct—relationship with several things that have hitherto been called number; and this can be said to give it an indirect relationship to other things we call the same name. And we extend our concept of number as in spinning a thread we twist fibre on fibre. And the strength of the thread does not reside in the fact that some one fibre runs through its whole length, but in the overlapping of many fibres.[15]

Staying with mathematics, think of the concept "circle." We apply the word strictly to ideal figures never seen or drawn. We also apply the term less strictly, to circles traced in the sand or on a blackboard, whose every point is not perfectly equidistant from a central point. And we use the same word to refer to literary circles, arguments that go in circles, circles of friends, and the like. Still, it might be objected, when we use the word with mathematical strictness, doesn't it then designate an essence? Perhaps; but why, then, is it so difficult to conceive that essence nonlinguistically?

Much more could be said to confirm and explain the thesis that no thought linguistically expressed can be had nonlinguistically. But further details might obscure the general drift of the argument, which goes as follows. It has been supposed that linguistic thoughts translate nonlinguistic thoughts. These latter could hardly consist of sensible images, for such images are too skimpy and inaccurate for equivalence. (Luke 23:33 doesn't say that the soldiers, the crucifix, the action, the place, or Jesus looked precisely like *that*.) The only plausible way to conceive the equivalence of nonlinguistic thoughts with linguistic would be by means of essences captured by mental likenesses and expressed by words. But even for general terms (as distinct, say, from proper names such as "Jesus" and "The Skull"), and even for general terms as simple as "blue," no such essences are discernible. Neither do any sound reasons suggest that such essences exist. Rather, their postulated connection with linguistic usage—their rigid, invariant connection with individual words—makes their existence appear unlikely. Given the evident fluidity of speech, it is implausible to suppose that the speakers of any language, resisting all contrary influences, consistently restrict their application of terms to all-and-only essences of the requisite kind.

Theological Thoughts

All of this applies generally, in theology and elsewhere. Linguistic thoughts—those expressed linguistically—are not mere translations of nonlinguistic thoughts. This is not to deny the existence of nonlinguistic thoughts. Such there surely are. People can, for instance, think nonlinguistically about a painting they are doing, about rearranging the furniture, or the like. However, these are not theological thoughts. And the question now to be considered—one with perhaps still broader, more radical implications for the conduct of theology—is whether there are any other *theological* thoughts besides the linguistic variety. The ineluctably linguistic nature of any and every thought encountered in theological discourse is, if valid, a sufficiently momentous thesis. But if there can be no theological thoughts of *any other, nonlinguistic kind*, the significance of language for theological inquiry becomes still more unmistakable.

An intriguing passage in Wittgenstein's *Philosophical Investigations* raises this very issue:

> William James, in order to shew that thought is possible without speech, quotes the recollection of a deaf-mute, Mr. Ballard, who wrote that in his early youth, even before he could speak, he had had thoughts about God and the world.—What can he have meant?—Ballard writes: "It was during those delightful

rides, some two or three years before my initiation into the rudiments of written language, that I began to ask myself the question: how came the world into being?"

Wittgenstein finds this puzzling:

> Are you sure—one would like to ask—that this is the correct translation of your wordless thought into words? And why does this question—which otherwise seems not to exist—raise its head here? Do I want to say that the writer's memory deceives him?—I don't even know if I should say *that*. These recollections are a queer memory phenomenon,—and I do not know what conclusions one can draw from them about the past of the man who recounts them.[16]

Here, the preceding discussion can help. It suggests that we distinguish between these two questions: (1) Did Ballard's account give a "correct translation" (as Wittgenstein puts it) of Ballard's earlier wordless thoughts into words? Could it do so? This is our previous query. (2) Could Ballard have had nonlinguistic religious thoughts that are now aptly recounted or expressed, though not translated, in words? This is our new question.

The difference between apt expression and accurate translation can be suggested by an anecdote. One Sunday, his wife could not accompany Calvin Coolidge to church. When he returned, she asked the notoriously taciturn president what the minister had preached about. "Sin," Coolidge replied. "Yes, Cal, but what did he say about sin?" his poor wife insisted. So Cal amplified: "He was agin' it." Although this reply did not translate any one of the preacher's remarks, or all of them combined, it may have faithfully communicated their general drift. So we wonder: May something similar have occurred in Ballard's case? Did he perhaps have nonlinguistic thoughts about God and the world and later express them verbally?

With regard to such thoughts as he reported, consider a possible comparison. People familiar with ducks and with rabbits can see Jastrow's famed duck-rabbit drawing now as a duck and now as a rabbit, wordlessly. (In one case, the protruding appendages are an open bill, in the other case, they are ears.) Similarly, might not Ballard, familiar with making and with things made, see the world as something made, likewise wordlessly? I would not exclude the possibility. However, I suggest that it has slight relevance for theological method. Manifestly, we who possess language can have such thoughts linguistically, about

God, creation, and the like. And the questions and problems, addressed in coming chapters, that such linguistic thoughts occasion, cannot be clarified by unclear surmises about hypothetical nonlinguistic thoughts on the same topics. On the contrary, the issues can be addressed more clearly and effectively by focusing on linguistic thoughts of the kind that occur in theological discourse. If the nonlinguistic thoughts cannot be expressed in words, they cannot be discussed in words. If they can be so expressed—publicly, communicably, we can discuss them as thus verbalized. Surmises about the possibility of having the verbal thoughts nonlinguistically would not clarify the subject of discussion but would only lead, fruitlessly, to puzzlement such as Wittgenstein expressed. The question, for instance, "Can we think about creation nonlinguistically?," would throw no light on the meaningfulness or truth of our linguistic thoughts about creation, but would only complicate discussion needlessly. For, as the previous section stressed, the linguistic thoughts are not translations of nonlinguistic thoughts in which their meaning and truth reside.

Implications

Let us return, then, to that earlier, more general thesis, that thoughts expressed linguistically cannot be entertained nonlinguistically. I have done as proposed and considered whether such is, in fact, the case and, if so, why. Some readers may have felt no need of proof, while others may view my remarks as insufficiently full and detailed. To these latter I concede that, for reasons I will later suggest, theses as general and significant as this one are not likely to be airtight. With ingenuity, we might perhaps imagine some exception to the stated rule. However, as I will also suggest, rare exceptions do not affect the general validity of a rule, and its general validity is what makes this present thesis (the nonequivalence of nonlinguistic thoughts with linguistic) methodologically important.

Its significance can be suggested through a comparison. As previously remarked, many have viewed public language as though it were a mere code, instrumentally convenient but having no life of its own; all meaning and truth have lain in the thoughts translated by the code. In this conception, the transition from thought to speech has appeared to pose no more problem than, for instance, the transition from English to Morse Code: one just needed to know the pertinent rules of substitution. Think, then, of Morse Code. If there is any ambiguity in a message, it is not the fault of the code. If there is any unclarity or incoherence in a message, it is not the fault of the code. If there is any falsity or distortion or misrepresentation in a message, again, the code is not to blame. Meaning and truth reside elsewhere, in the original utterance. That is why Morse and other codes have received so little attention in philosophy, theology, or scientific inquiry. They can largely be ignored. But suppose it were discovered that this is all wrong—that the supposed codes are not in fact codes, that they do not translate anything but operate on their own. What an astonishing reversal that would be!

Such is the reversal here indicated. It does not signify that we speak without thinking. It does not mean that our thinking is reduced to sensible images. But it does mean that both our thinking and our speaking function very differently than was long and widely supposed. When, for example, we compare shades of blue to see whether they share some simple, invisible essence, we do more than view or imagine the shades; yet we form no mental likeness of the essence we fail to discover. Neither does the word *blue* serve to indicate that nonexistent abstract entity or to express the missing likeness. Such an example, illustrating fundamental misconceptions about speech, thought, and reality, suggests already one of the major implications of the shift from language as a mere code to language as a complex form of life. A code does not powerfully shape, or misshape, our conceptions of reality. But, as the next chapter will indicate, language can and repeatedly does so influence our thinking. This is not the only implication of this chapter's discussion, or even the most important one, but it does have methodological implications for theology that can profitably be examined at this point.

For Further Reflection

1. "The purpose of a fish trap is to catch fish and when the fish are caught, the trap is forgotten. The purpose of a rabbit snare is to catch rabbits. When the rabbits are caught, the snare is forgotten. The purpose of the word is to convey ideas. When the ideas are grasped, the words are forgotten. Where can I find a man who has forgotten words? He is the one I would like to talk to"[17] (Chuang Tzu).

2. "There is validity in pointing out there must be something in common between religions in order for them to be recognized by the same term itself and be distinguished from other cultural dimensions"[18] (Alan Race).

3. "Universals arise solely from the fact that we avail ourselves of one and the same idea in order to think of all individual things which have a certain similitude; and when we comprehend under the same name all the objects represented by this idea, that name is universal. For example, when we see two stones, and without thinking further of their nature than to remark that there are two, we form in ourselves an idea of a certain number which we term the number of two; and when afterwards we see two birds or two trees, and we observe without further thinking about their nature, that there are two of them, we again take up the same idea which we had before, which idea is universal; and we give to this number the universal name 'two' "[19] (René Descartes).

4. "My imaginary skeptic is getting a little nervous:

When I think, I think in English (or Chinese, or whatever). So how can thought be different from language?

My response is that the language we hear in our heads while thinking is a *conscious manifestation* of the thought—not the thought itself, which isn't present to consciousness"[20] (Ray Jackendoff).

5. "Consider for example the proceedings that we call 'games.' I mean board-games, card-games, ball-games, Olympic games, and so on. What is common to them all?—Don't say: 'There *must* be something common, or they would not be called "games'—but *look and see* whether there is anything common to all.—For if you look at them you will not see something that is common to *all*, but similarities, relationships, and a whole series of them at that. To repeat: don't think, but look!"[21] (Ludwig Wittgenstein).

Chapter 3

Linguistic Spectacles

For the most part, I have suggested, words resemble spectacles, which we look through but seldom look at. And, for the most part, there is nothing wrong with that. We don't suppose for a moment that the things we see have the shapes of the spectacles through which we view them. Neither, if the spectacles are dark, do we suppose that everything we gaze at through them is dark. We are not duped. So we leave the spectacles on our noses, and keep looking through them. Our linguistic spectacles, however, are not nearly so innocuous. Strong evidence indicates that they not only shape our conceptions of reality but also misshape them, in fundamental ways, as spectacles do not. And they do so more in theology than in most other areas. I will start with the shaping, then pass to the misshaping, citing theological illustrations and suggesting their methodological significance.

Linguistic Shaping

In the eighteenth century, Johann Herder pioneered a theme that has since been variously orchestrated by Wilhelm von Humboldt, Edward Sapir, Benjamin Lee Whorf, and others. According to Herder, language "determines the boundary and the outline of all human cognition."[1] According to Whorf, "We dissect nature along lines laid down by our native languages."[2] For Sapir, the forms of language "predetermine for us certain modes of observation and interpretation"—indeed, "no matter how sophisticated our modes of interpretation become, we never really get beyond the projection and continuous transfer of relations suggested by the forms of our speech."[3] A people's language, it is suggested, shapes their *Weltanschauung*, their worldview.[4]

For theological method, with its concern for truth, the key question raised by all this talk of shaping, boundaries, outlines, forming, and the like is the one suggested by the analogy of spectacles. In a weak sense, the shape of spectacles does of course affect the shape of what we see: circular frames impose circular boundaries, oblong frames impose oblong boundaries, and so forth. But no one supposes that the things thus seen have these shapes. Similarly, some rulers measure objects in feet, others in meters, but no one supposes that these different measures affect the length of the objects measured. So, too, some words embrace more, some less; some cut finely, some crudely; some slice reality this way, some that. But do any of these differences affect the way we suppose the realities described are in themselves, independently of our words? And do our resulting conceptions, therefore, not only differ but conflict—the circular ones, as it were, contradicting the oblong?

Theorists sometimes veer toward this assessment. Whorf, for instance, writes that, given "the linguistic systems in our minds," "no individual is free to describe nature with absolute impartiality."[5] And, contrasting a tensed, "temporal" language such as English with a "timeless" language such as Hopi, he writes: "What are to English differences of time are to Hopi differences in the kind of validity."[6] If this is aptly stated, it seems that at least one of the descriptions must be wrong, for the same realities cannot satisfy both of these characterizations, as time differences and as kinds of validity. However, Whorf's illustrations suggest that it would be less misleading to say that in the same situation, speakers of the different languages describe the situation differently, with no more suggestion of disagreement than in the case of measurements in meters versus measurements in feet. One group describes a man's running as having occurred in the past, the other group describes it as being remembered; one group describes a man's running as future in time, the other group describes it as being expected; and so forth. There is no disagreement. Thus, in terms of our original figure, Whorf's examples do not suggest that those who view the world through circular frames see it as circular and those who view it through oblong frames see it as oblong, and therefore disagree about the world's shape.

And yet, as Wittgenstein put it, we often do "predicate of the thing what lies in the method of representing it."[7] Language often does distort our conceptions of reality, and often does so notably.

Linguistic Deception

In simple illustration, recall Moore's account of blues. In Wittgenstein's terms, Moore predicated of the varied shades of blue what lay in the mode of representing them. Viewing the many shades through the single word *blue*, he inferred a single essence common to them all. Wittgenstein had a similar example in mind when he wrote: "A *picture* held us captive. And we could not get outside it, for it lay in our language and language seemed to repeat it to us inexorably."[8] The particular picture in question was his earlier conception of propositions or assertions (in German, *Sätze*). These might be still more varied than the shades of blue, but Wittgenstein had discerned a single essence common to them all: "The general form of propositions is: This is how things stand."[9] Of this former claim of his Wittgenstein remarked: "That is the kind of proposition that one repeats to oneself countless times. One thinks that one is tracing the outline of the thing's nature over and over again, and one is merely tracing round the frame through which we look at it."[10] Thus, Wittgenstein had earlier declared that his *whole* task consisted "in explaining the nature of the proposition"[11]—notice, "the" nature of "the" proposition, both in the singular, as the single word suggested. Such is the power of words.

In Moore's case, the single word *blue* conjured up an invisible essence where there was none. In Wittgenstein's case, the single word *proposition* (*Satz*) obscured the diversity of the utterances thus labeled. Though some of the things so named do function in the way described, simply reporting "how things stand," others do not. The apology "I'm sorry" does not. Neither does the declaration "I pronounce you man and wife," nor the umpire's shout "You're out." "But how many kinds of sentence [*Sätze*] are there?" the later Wittgenstein queried. "There are *countless* kinds," he replied: "countless different kinds of use of what we call 'symbols,' 'words,' 'sentences.' "[12]

Already in his youthful classic, the *Tractatus Logico-Philosophicus*, Wittgenstein had expressed some awareness of language's power to deceive through misleading surface similarities. "In everyday language," he warned, "it very frequently happens that the same word has different modes of signification, and so belongs to different symbols—or two words that have different modes of signification are employed in propositions in what is superficially the same way."[13] For example, he noted, the single word *is* has three distinct modes of signification: as the copula (e.g., in "The day is sunny"), as a sign for identity (e.g., in "The president is Obama"), and as an expression for existence (e.g., in "Troy is no more"). "In this way," Wittgenstein observed, "the most fundamental confusions are easily produced (the whole of philosophy is full of them)."[14] If anything, Wittgenstein's warning is still more apposite in theology.

There, the same sample expression can illustrate his warning. In recent times as in the past, Christian theologians have employed "is" and its variants or equivalents with still greater freedom than Wittgenstein's threefold distinction indicates. They have done so, for instance, in speaking of Jesus. As formerly Origen did not hesitate to say that Jesus *is* the Gospel, or that he *is* the Kingdom in person, so in our day Karl Rahner has spoken of "the *salvific* event which Jesus Christ himself *is*."[15] For Walter Kasper, "Jesus is nothing but the incarnate love of the Father and the incarnate response of obedience."[16] For Emile Mersch, Jesus is God's "decree that is realized and, we may say, incarnated."[17] In Christ, "the alliance between God and men becomes the very person of the Man-God."[18] "The redemption is not an abstract concept or theory. It is a Person who is intensely alive."[19] Indeed, for Mersch, "The Church is Christ,"[20] "Christ is . . . everything,"[21] "He is all, all in all; for He is God."[22] In such subject-predicate pairings as these, the linking verb *is* hardly signals some single, invariant relationship.

Yet from early on, theme after major theme of Christian theology has been profoundly affected by a simplifying conception with regard to "is" (or variants) similar to Moore's with regard to "blue" or young Wittgenstein's with regard to "proposition." Here, too, a single word has revealed its power. Time and again it is assumed, when not explicitly declared, that there is just one kind of identity, namely, the strict kind that obtains, say, between George Washington and the first president of the United States: whatever holds for one term of the identity statement must hold for the other term; there can be no difference between them. (If Washington was born in Virginia, the first president was born in Virginia; if Washington was more than six feet tall, the first president was more than six feet tall; and so forth.) As operative in much theological reasoning, this supposition may be compared to the default setting in a computer. If no contrary command is entered, the computer automatically formats copy a given way (single spacing, one inch margins, Times Roman font, or the like). The strict-identity supposition functions similarly in the thought of many thinkers, on many topics. Here, staying with the example of Jesus' identity, I will offer just one important illustration of the general syndrome,[23] and, still more broadly, of language's power to mislead.

If the identity expressed by such statements as "Jesus is God" or "Jesus is the Second Person of the Holy Trinity" is strict, admitting no distinction or difference, apparent contradiction results. How can beings so different, human and divine, be strictly, indiscernibly identical? With respect to the Incarnation, three solutions—three alternative ways of responding—have often been proposed.

1. *Limit Jesus' Humanity.* In former times, this solution is represented, for example, by Saint Hilary. "The man Christ Jesus," he

wrote, "the only-begotten God, by flesh and the Word both Son of Man and Son of God, assumed the true man according to the likeness of our manhood without departing from being God."[24] Reading into this explicit premise an implicit strict-identity reading of "being God," Hilary concluded (in R. P. C. Hanson's partial summation):

> Christ could not have been afraid; he could not have been "sorrowful unto death." He could not have seriously asked that the cup should pass from him. The utterance "My God, my God why hast thou forsaken me?" could not have meant any consciousness of the absence of God's presence. The cross represented no weakness and no disgrace. In short "although suffering was inflicted on the body, yet it did not introduce the quality of pain into the body." . . . "Sorrowful unto death" meant sorrowful in such a way that death would terminate the sorrow. Jesus was omniscient because he was God. He was sad not for himself but for his apostles. The bloody sweat was no sign of weakness. He did not need any comfort. And so Hilary continues to the end of the tenth book . . .[25]

More recently, Thomas Morris has made Hilary's implicit premise explicit: in Jesus, the identity between God and man (or, more precisely, between the second person of the Trinity and the man Jesus) must indeed be strict. However, there is no compelling reason, Morris has argued, to suppose that all the ways in which human beings are, in fact, limited—say with respect to knowledge, power, and goodness—pertain to the very nature of humanity. Thus, for example, although most people do not exist before their conception and birth, that may be just a trait human beings happen to share, not an essential, necessary property.[26] This solution of Morris's, avoiding contradiction by diminishing Jesus' humanity, has led one reviewer to comment: "If the only constituents of the human nature Christ takes on are those properties essential to human beings but not incompatible with any divine properties, what I share with Christ as regards human nature seems rather meager."[27]

2. *Limit Jesus' Divinity*. The alternative solution is to limit Jesus' divinity rather than his humanity. "I am unable," wrote Gottfried Thomasius, a classic representative of this approach, "to hold both things firmly together, namely the full reality of the divine and human being of Christ (especially the full truth of his naturally human development of life) on the one hand, and on the other hand the full unity of his divine-human person, without the supposition of a self-limitation of the divine Logos coincident with the incarnation."[28] Treating the unity of

human and divine as an irresolvable mystery would not "hold both things firmly together," whereas having the transcendent Word become less transcendent avoids "inner contradiction" and brings the two terms of the human-divine polarity into closer proximity. Nonetheless, Thomasius explains, God does not thereby cease to be God. For the divine attributes willingly surrendered (omnipotence, omnipresence, omniscience) are relative and nonessential, whereas those retained (absolute power and freedom, eternity, absolute holiness, truth, love) are immanent and essential.[29] As Morris pares away inessential human attributes, so Thomasius—driven by the same strict-identity assumption—pares away inessential divine attributes.

3. *Deny the Identity.* To others, even this desperate trimming of inessential properties on one side or the other has appeared inadequate. "The question, then," writes John Hick, "is whether it makes coherent sense to hold that Jesus Christ had both all essential divine and all essential human attributes, so as to be both fully God and fully man. On the face of it, this does not make sense. For how could anyone have both divine omniscience and human ignorance, divine omnipotence and human weakness, divine goodness and human temptability, divine omni-presence and a finite human body?"[30] Thus, for Don Cupitt, to declare that the eternal God and a historical man—"two beings of quite different ontological status"—are identical is simply unintelligible.[31] For Hick, as for Spinoza, such an assertion is comparable to "This circle is a square."[32] For John Knox, it is "impossible, by definition, that God should become a man."[33] The question, however, here as in the previous alternatives, is whether the impossibility lies in the definition of "God" and "man" or, instead, in the rigid understanding of such terms as "is" and "become."

Once this recurring assumption of strict identity is dropped, the solution of Cyril of Alexandria, reflected in the Council of Chalcedon, becomes available. God is fully God and man is fully man, but the nature of their union in Jesus transcends our understanding. While stressing its mysteriousness, Cyril found a glimmer of understanding in what John McGuckin terms "Cyril's most recurring image of the union of godhead and humanity in Christ."[34] We humans are constituted, Cyril suggests, by the mysterious union of body and soul. The soul is not the body, nor the body the soul; each retains its own nature. Nonetheless, the union between them is so intimate, so close, that a single individual results, of whom we readily predicate both physical and spiritual properties. One and the same person, formed of body and soul, possesses both intelligence and lungs. One and the same individual both laughs and rejoices, sits and meditates. To deny any of these ascriptions, or to restrict them to just the soul or just the body would be to question the closeness of the union that binds body and soul. This is how it is, Cyril suggests, for the single individual formed by the hypostatic union. Using the name "Jesus" for that one, composite individual, we can say that Jesus is divine. Using the name "God the Son" for that same individual, we can say that God suffered and died. But this mode of speech—this "communication of idioms"—implies no confusion between the human and divine terms of the relation, any more than the corresponding mode of speech implies confusion of body and soul in the single human composite.[35]

Neither Christian scripture nor Christian tradition precludes this solution. Neither indicates, in general or in detail, that the hypostatic union must be a relation of strict identity.[36] Indeed, many a familiar New Testament passage strongly suggests the contrary (e.g., Romans 8:24: "It is Christ Jesus who died, yes, who was raised, who is at the right hand of God, who intercedes for us"). And a comparison such as Cyril's clearly indicates that he did not feel so constrained. Whence, then, this recurring, powerful assumption, forcing thought this way and that, to dodge apparent contradiction? Were this an isolated instance, we might wonder. But countless comparable cases, in theology and elsewhere, suggest one important answer. It is the same answer as for Moore and young Wittgenstein. It is the one Wittgenstein warned about, specifically with regard to "is": the power of the word. The single word suggests a single reality—in this instance a single form of identity, of one thing "being" another.

Thus, there are those who, hearing the suggestion that the man Jesus is not strictly identical with God or the second person of the Trinity, suppose that Jesus' divinity is being denied—as though the assertion of his divinity had a perfectly clear, unmistakable sense and was only epistemologically, not semantically, problematic. Cyril and the Council of Chalcedon took more seriously the need to try to understand, as best they could, a doctrine they recognized as deeply mysterious. We are not puzzled when, for instance, someone is said to sing the notes in a score. We do not wonder, "How can sung notes be identical with written notes?" Such a saying is clear enough, as is its difference from many another assertion of identity. But the sense of such a statement as "The Father and I are one" is far from evident; so, filling the vacuum, we may too readily assume the simplest sort of identity with which we are familiar—namely, strict identity, permitting not the slightest discrepancy between one referent and the other. Unnoticed and unchallenged, this default setting may rigidly fix the saying's sense. All else is heresy!

I might expand on this single, representative example. Then, moving out in concentric circles, I could proffer other, varied theological examples, first with regard to the word *is* and near-equivalents, then with regard to the similar, simplifying effect of other terms, then with regard to still more varied illustrations of language's power to deceive.[37] There could then be no doubt about the need to take this widespread phenomenon very seriously and to consider ways to counter it. However, in the present quick reconnaissance I will stop here and reflect on the examples given. How, in our simpler, nontheological illustrations, did language succeed in duping Moore and Wittgenstein? What remedy can therefore be proposed in these and similar instances, including those in theology?

The Remedy

Reflecting on his own experience—his search for a single general form of propositions and of language—Wittgenstein suggested the comparison we have already encountered: "Consider for example the proceedings that we call 'games.' I mean board-games, card-games, ball-games, Olympic games, and so on. What is common to them all?—Don't say: 'There *must* be something common, or they would not be called "games"'—but *look and see* whether there is anything common to all."[38] So, too, don't just *assume* that there must be something common to all propositions. Don't just *assume* that there must be something common to all blues. Don't just *assume* that there must be something common to all identities. But look and see. Pay attention to the words' actual mode of employment.

"One cannot guess how a word functions," Wittgenstein observed. "One has to *look at* its use and learn from that. But the difficulty is to remove the prejudice which stands in the way of doing this. It is not a *stupid* prejudice."[39] Surely the author of the *Tractatus*, Wittgenstein's chief target, was not stupid, and he did show some awareness of the duplicity of language, for instance with regard to "is"; but that younger self of his does not seem even to have been tempted to examine how German-speakers employ expressions such as "Name," "Satz," and "Sprache" or how English-speakers employ expressions such as "name," "statement," and "language." What would be the point? He was interested in the nature of names, statements, and language, not in the vagaries of German or English usage.

The great remedy for such linguistic insouciance—characteristic of so many thinkers, including many theologians—is to raise the question of *truth*. Can truth be achieved without any contribution from the words used to state it? Could Wittgenstein, for example, expect to say true things about the nature of names, propositions, language, or anything else if he ignored the words he employed ("name," "proposition," "language," etc.) and their meanings in the language he spoke? Could he truly declare what all names or propositions are or what language is if the words he used were differently employed, for different things, in the language he used to make his claims? The traditional view considered in the last chapter (of which Wittgenstein's *Tractatus* offered its own refined version) looked to the mind for meaning and truth; speech was derivative, a mere epiphenomenon. The critique of that position suggests, as a still more important ramification than the present discussion, the need to consider the claims of language as a determinant of truth. Somehow, it seems, our utterances achieve truth more on their own than was long supposed—more independently of the thoughts that may accompany them. How they do so is the question we must now consider.

For Further Reflection

1. "In Arabic, in Sanskrit, or in German, for instance, we perceive—*through* these languages, as it were, through lenses—different realities"[40] (Michael von Brück).

2. "Language can, very generally, be seen as an attempt to organize and classify our patterns of experience. If so, then it follows that the language which we inherit from society has the leading role in forming our world-view"[41] (Michael Barnes).

3. "The social sciences argue that our language about God both expresses the ultimate values of the community and serves as a model for human behaviour and social structure. According to the feminist critique, describing God as 'He,' even when insisting that He is not male, has this simultaneous dual function of expressing and impressing"[42] (Susannah Heschel).

4. "What, after all, is the basis for comparing talk of one who is both God and man to talk of a square circle? Certainly a square circle is a contradiction in terms. The terms 'square' and 'circle' are precisely defined terms, and their logical incompatibility is obvious from the definition. But 'God' and 'man' are far from being such tightly defined concepts.... Who are we to say that the essence of God is such as to rule out the possibility of his

making himself present in the created world as a human being, while in no way ceasing to be the God he ever is?"[43] (Brian Hebblethwaite).

5. "Another example: although creation is not really a process of change, it seems to be so according to our mode of understanding, for we imagine and understand the same thing as existing both before and after its creation; and since the manner of signification follows the manner of understanding, we also signify creation as if it were a change"[44] (Gregory Rocca).

6. "The point is that language molds and, in a way, restricts the mental process. The mold consists of the native language, which is an accumulation of the knowledge of a given nation, knowledge that corresponds to that nation's experience, living conditions, and character. Language is 'a form of science, a form not only in which but also in accordance with which, thoughts are shaped.' In the process of upbringing we come to know ideas through the intermediary of words. We think in language. Thinking is nothing but speaking. Hence every nation speaks the way it thinks and thinks the way it speaks"[45] (Adam Schaff, on J. G. Herder).

Chapter 4

Linguistic Truth

Theology seeks truth, but it does not explain what truth consists in. That is a task for philosophy. Since this may appear a bold claim, let me suggest, in a preliminary way, the thinking behind it. Theology, philosophy, science, mathematics, and the like make statements that are true or false; and it is the business of each discipline, drawing on its own resources, to assess the statements' truth. However, are the true statements such, each time, in a different sense of the term *true*—one sense for theology, another for philosophy, another for science, still another for history, and so forth—and must theology discern the distinctive sense the term has in its own domain? Unlikely. On the contrary, then, are all true statements true in much the same sense of the term, and, amid all the different disciplines, does it fall to theology to detect that single, universal sense, and so to determine what makes philosophical, scientific, mathematical, and other statements, as well as its own, to be true? Hardly. Again, will theology (still drawing on its transcendent source or sources) determine how the truth of statements relates to the truth of the beliefs that the statements verbally express? Indeed, can theology answer any of these meta-queries, about its own and other disciplines' conceptual capacities? The answer each time is the same. Here, as often, theology needs input from philosophy.

True, such reliance may occasion misgivings; for philosophers have often erred in their accounts of truth, and their errors have had serious implications for theology. However, the remedy, as usual, is not to dismiss the contribution of philosophy but to make it better, more reliable. Thus, despite passing references to theology, supplemented by passages for further reflection, this chapter on language and truth will be more heavily philosophical than usual. Theological applications and implications will follow throughout the book, but first the nature of truth—this prime value, this basic, pervasive goal of theology—will have to be clarified, and its relationship to language.

Truth was long viewed as consisting primarily in mental correspondence with reality: true thoughts represent things as they are, false thoughts represent them as they are not, and true utterances translate the true thoughts into communicable signs. Linguistic truth is secondary, derivative. Chapter 2 indicated why thinkers in recent times have had trouble discerning what the alleged mental correspondence might consist in. William James's difficulties are typical. He writes:

> The popular notion is that a true idea must copy its reality. Like other popular views, this one follows the analogy of the most usual experience. Our true ideas of sensible things do indeed copy them. Shut your eyes and think of yonder clock on the wall, and you get just such a true picture or copy of its dial. But your idea of its "works" (unless you are a clock-maker) is much less of a copy, yet it passes muster, for it in no way clashes with the reality. Even tho [sic] it should shrink to the mere word "works," that word still serves you truly; and when you speak of the "time-keeping function" of the clock, or of its spring's "elasticity," it is hard to see exactly what your ideas can copy.[1]

A more linguistic account might obviate such difficulties. If, for instance, a statement about the spring's elasticity is true, the thing called a "spring" resembles the kind of things called "springs," and the thing described as "elastic" resembles the kind of things described as "elastic." There is no need to conjure up mental duplicates. Once this turn to language is taken, the sense in which truth might involve resemblance or "correspondence" looks clearer and less problematic.

The Oxford philosopher John Austin spelled out an account of this linguistic kind. To answer the question "What is truth?" he first consulted varied applications of the word *true*. "We say (or are said to say) that beliefs are true, that descriptions or accounts are true, that propositions or assertions or statements are true, and that words or sentences are true: and this is to mention only a selection of the more obvious candidates."[2] The primary application of the word, Austin argued, is not to mere sentences, whose truth value may vary from utterance to utterance, nor to beliefs or abstract propositions, but to statements, in the sense of individual utterances or speech acts. "A statement is made and its making is an historic event, the utterance by a certain speaker or writer of certain words (a sentence) to an audience with reference to a historic situation, event or what not."[3] For such utterances to do their job, there must be a stock of symbols of some kind (the "words"), something other than the symbols (the "world") which the symbols are used to communicate about, and two sets of conventions relating the symbols to the world: *demonstrative* conventions that allow people to indicate what they are talking about and *descriptive* conventions that allow them to describe it. Applying this distinction to the query "When is a statement true?," Austin replied: "A statement is said to be true when the historic state of affairs to which it is correlated by the demonstrative conventions (the one to which it 'refers') is of a type with which the sentence used in making it [the statement] is correlated by the descriptive conventions."[4] To illustrate: in the presence, say, of a cat stretched on a mat, I pick out this "historic state of affairs" and say, "The cat is on the mat." Demonstrative conventions connect my statement with the cat and the mat, and the relationship of these two things, the cat and the mat, is of a kind conventionally described as one thing being "on" another. So my statement is true. Granted, the agreement with past linguistic practice may not be perfect. The cat's position on the mat may not match exactly the position of other cats on other mats, or more generally, of other things described as being "on" other objects. Nonetheless, Austin explains, the historic situation picked out by the true utterance "is sufficiently like those standard states of affairs" with which the sentence used in making the utterance is correlated by the descriptive conventions.[5] What degree of likeness counts as sufficient, Austin did not specify. He just sketched and defended this general account of what makes statements true.

Despite its notable merits, Austin's analysis also has serious limitations. Two are of special interest for theology. First, critics have noted the narrowness of Austin's account. It is not clear, for example, how his analysis applies even to simple cases of negation. If I say, truly, "The cat is on the mat," there is no problem identifying the historic state of affairs I have described: there is the cat lying on the mat. However, suppose I look at the mat and see no cat there, or spot the cat on the sofa, and deny that the cat is on the mat. "With what type of state-of-affairs (chunk of reality)," inquires Peter Strawson, "is the sentence 'The cat is not on the mat' correlated by conventions of description? With a mat *simpliciter*? With a dog on a mat? With a cat up a tree?"[6] What is more, as Strawson also notes, though a negative utterance such as "The cat is not on the mat" at least employs demonstrative conventions, not all statements do. "Existential statements don't, nor do statements of (even relatively) unrestricted generality."[7] (Think of "Cats exist" or "All cats are animals.") Neither, as Geoffrey Warnock observed, do "analytic statements, or theorems in logic, or in mathematics," yet we often call them "true."[8]

To accommodate a wider variety of statements, we might take a cue from Wittgenstein's suggestion that, on many occasions, when we speak of a word's meaning we are speaking of its "use in the language." This can be equated, roughly, with the conventions governing the word's application (the sort of thing cited in a dictionary), and these conventions are most varied (think of "sugar," "sleep," "circular," "hello," "if," "forever," "maybe," "amen," "infinite"). So broader coverage than in Austin's formula results if we suggest that, for a statement to be true, its use of terms must agree with the terms' established uses (established either by custom or, on occasion, by stipulation). Now Strawson's and Warnock's countercases occasion no difficulty. "The cat is not on the mat" satisfies this test, and so, for instance, does "No part is greater than the whole" or "Three plus five equals eight." In their varied ways, all satisfy the stated condition. All use their terms in accordance with the terms' established uses in the language. However, though the test they thus meet may be a necessary condition of truth, as it stands it is not a sufficient condition; for even false statements employ expressions in keeping, to some extent, with their established uses. They are at least grammatical, or at least sufficiently grammatical to qualify as false. How full, then, or of what kind, must the agreement be to guarantee *truth*?

Here we encounter Austin's second problem, the one he acknowledged but left dangling when he explained: "[F]or a statement to be true one state of affairs must be *like* certain others, which is a natural relation, but also *sufficiently* like to merit the same 'description,' which is no longer a purely natural relation."[9] In many respects, raccoons resemble cats and carpets resemble mats; so what makes it true to say that a cat is on the mat but false to say a *raccoon* is on the mat or that a cat is on the *carpet*? How close must the resemblance be? Austin offered no indication. However, these simple examples suggest a possible reply: the requisite resemblance is relative to the rest of language. Each of these things—cats, raccoons, mats, carpets—has its own name. And the names may be stretched, indeed may be stretched considerably, but not if they trespass on the territory occupied by competing expressions. Raccoons should not be called cats, carpets should not be called mats. To accommodate these considerations, reflected in the use of the word "true," I have proposed the following "Principle of Relative Similarity" (PRS for short): "A statement is true if, and only if, its use of terms resembles more closely the established uses of terms (whether standard or stipulated) than would the substitution of any rival, incompatible expression."[10]

This formula is still rough. For instance, it accepts but does not explicate the notion of greater or less similarity between things,[11] or the notion that some expressions (e.g., "cat" and "raccoon") are mutually incompatible whereas others (e.g., "cat" and "animal") are not. It does not sharply delimit what varieties of utterances count as "statements." Nonetheless, the principle looks roughly right. It strikes a balance between excessive rigidity and excessive permissiveness. Thus, on the one hand, despite considerable similarities, for the cat on the mat it rules out "A *raccoon* is on the mat," "The cat is on a *carpet*," or "The cat is *under* the mat." "Cat," "mat," and "on" successfully compete with "raccoon," "carpet," and "under." On the other hand, despite great dissimilarities, the formula does not rule out our saying, for example, that computers play "chess." There may be no board or pieces or moving of pieces, but for the activity in question "chess" comes closer than does "checkers," "poker," "pinochle," or any other competing expression.

Still, do these suggested definitional borders of "true" coincide with those of the word's customary application in the language? How exactly or adequately does PRS mirror familiar usage? Consider this case. I draw a figure on the blackboard. I am inclined to call it a "wavy circle" or a "circle with wavy borders," for it is the figure one could generate by drawing two concentric circles then joining them by a wavy line. This wavy figure resembles a circle more than it resembles a triangle, octagon, square, or ellipse. "Circle" comes closest. So is it true to say, as the Principle of Relative Similarity would suggest, that I drew a circle on the board? Not at all clearly. So yes, the principle is only roughly right. And we shall have occasion to scrutinize its credentials more closely when we come to consider metaphorical and figurative speech. However, the principle's many merits suggest that it may reliably be accepted as a general rule of thumb in theology as elsewhere. For the most part and on most occasions, truth will be achieved if our use of terms resembles their established uses (familiar or stipulated) more closely than would the substitution of any rival, incompatible expression.

Anticipating fuller development in coming chapters, I will here briefly suggest some of this formula's attractive features.

Stability. A mere sentence (e.g., "It's raining") may be true on one occasion, false on another. Or, with a shift in the meaning of the words it contains, the sentence may be true at one time, false at another. But a statement, in the sense Austin cited, of an "historic event, the utterance by a certain speaker or writer of certain words (a sentence) to an audience with reference to a historic situation, event or what not," never changes its truth value. If, in the midst of a downpour, using present-day English, someone says, "It's raining," the statement is true, and its truth will be unaffected by the use of the same words on some other, drier occasion, or by future shifts in the meaning of the word *raining*. A century or millennium hence, that utterance at that moment will still qualify as a true statement.

Objectivity. Nonetheless, in comparison with truth as accurate mental picturing, PRS truth may appear "relativistic." Hearing all this talk about resemblance between "word uses," a reader may feel that reality has been slighted. "It all depends on language." However, notice that the same complaint does not arise, for example, with regard to measurements in feet versus measurements in meters. These, too, are relative—relative to the system of measurement employed. But the measurements thus made, in feet or in meters, may be perfectly objective. The table *is* four feet long. The room *is* four meters long. Similarly, "It's raining" may be as objectively true as "Il pleut," "Il piove," or "Es regnet," despite the dependence of each utterance's truth on the language employed—English, French, Italian, or German. To say that the utterance's truth depends on language is not to say that it depends *only* on language.

PRS truth is also objective in a second sense. It has been said that for statements of faith, "it is not meaningful to state that they are true 'in themselves,' if by 'in themselves' is meant to ignore the fact that they have to be understood by someone, in order to be—in this interpretation—true."[12] PRS takes a more objective view of truth, less dependent on how speakers or hearers happen to interpret the words of a statement. The utterance "It's raining," for example, may be true regardless of whether, or how, some individual hearer understands it. All it takes is drops of water falling roundabout from clouds. Together with the language spoken, they verify the statement. The like holds for theological utterances ("God exists," "Jesus died for us," "All will be judged," etc.). Regardless of who interprets them or how, the utterances' use of terms may resemble more closely the established use of terms than would the substitution of any rival, incompatible expression.

If language as medium is not distinguished from language as discourse, as in chapter 1, PRS may nonetheless appear relativistic or subjective. It may seem that whatever people agree in asserting counts automatically as true. If all say that ghosts exist, the statement is true; if all say that the Earth is flat, that statement is true; and so on. For in each such case, does not the use of terms agree with their customary, widespread use in the language? In a sense it does, but not in the requisite sense: not in the word-by-word, language-wide sense intended and required by the Principle of Relative Similarity. Thus, no matter how often or widely it is repeated, such an assertion as "The Earth is flat" clearly disagrees with the established use of its constituent expressions in the language as a whole—for instance, with the use of the word *flat* in countless, varied assertions about tables, plains, plates, roofs, terraces, and so forth. Our planet is not *that* shape, regardless of how many people say that it is. If the whole population said it was, the whole population would be wrong. Truth is not a mere matter of opinion.

Comprehensiveness. Utterances of many kinds—historical, mathematical, scientific, philosophical, theological, etc.—qualify as true, and PRS accommodates them all, with their own terms and their own use of familiar terms. In physics, "mass" functions differently than it does in colloquial conversation (e.g., "mass confusion"); in geometry, "square" functions differently than it does in geography (e.g., "town square"); in botany, "root" functions differently than it does in mathematics (e.g., "square root"). Such are the "established uses," varying from context to context, by which the truth of utterances is judged in their respective "language-games."

Centrality. Austin was right, I believe, in regarding the truth of utterances as primary and the truth of sentences, propositions, judgments, thoughts, beliefs, and the like as secondary and derivative. There is no telling, for example, whether a *sentence* (e.g., "It's raining") is true apart from its use on some occasion, in an utterance. Spoken on one occasion, the sentence may be true; spoken on another occasion, it may be false. Again, there is no telling whether a *belief* is true apart from the truth of the words that state it. Believing it is raining, someone says, "It is raining," and a single test establishes the truth both of the belief and of the statement. For reasons suggested in chapter 2, that test is not mental, but linguistic. The speaker does not picture the drops, their motion, their source, their chemical composition, and get it all right, but the words spoken do get it right. The condition here called "raining" resembles, in all these respects, the condition thus named by speakers of the English language on countless occasions.

Realism. Not surprisingly, when people habituated to traditional accounts of truth hear all this talk about "use" and "established uses" and the correspondence between them, they are wont to inquire: "But what about the *facts*? What about *reality*?" They are thinking, for instance, of the rain—the actual precipitation—that verifies "It's raining." The answer to this objection is that PRS embraces not only the present rain, but also innumerable previous showers for which people have used the same verb. *This* stuff resembles all that *other* stuff. Thus, the principle takes in far more rain, not less, than did traditional mentalistic accounts, which focused only on the rain reported. And the like holds for all other descriptions of reality whose truth PRS acknowledges.

The principle's realism has a further aspect. Even the most realistic mental representation of rain would not resemble rain as closely as rain resembles rain. But such is the correspondence PRS highlights. The condition called raining on this occasion resembles the condition called raining on previous occasions, as the creature called a cat resembles the creatures called cats, the mat on which it is stretched resembles the things called mats, and so forth. And, for truth, in each such instance the resemblance must be closer than it would be for any competing expression. So PRS decrees.

Flexibility. Despite this constraint of closer resemblance, PRS is very flexible. The Earth may no longer be viewed as the center of the planetary system and still be called the Earth. Atoms may be split and still be called atoms. Chess may be played by computers (without board or pieces or moving of pieces) and still be called chess. Divine love, life, power, and knowledge may differ greatly from human and still be called love, life, power, and knowledge. All such extensions PRS approves, subject to the condition that the terms employed successfully compete with all rival, incompatible expressions. Coming chapters will note the fundamental significance of this PRS flexibility for theological discourse.

Meaning. They will also cite PRS in response to the complaint, common some decades back, that the theological use of expressions lacks meaning. Typically, the accusation stressed truth-conditions as indicators of meaning. How, it was asked, can we know what a statement means unless we understand what would make the statement true or false? And, given the huge disparity between God and human paradigms, how can we understand what would make it true to say, for example, that God acts, loves, or knows? PRS, specifying what typically makes any statement true, furnishes a response. If, for instance, despite great differences, the divine reality spoken of resembles human activity more closely than it does human passivity or inactivity, or resembles human love more than it does human hatred or indifference, or resembles human knowledge more closely than it does human ignorance, conjecture, confusion, or uncertainty, then it is true to say that God acts, loves, or knows. The term "act," "love," or "know" comes closer than any competing expression.

Importance. From the PRS account, with its strong, world-world correspondence (cats with cats, mats with mats, etc.), we can sense the importance of truth and why human beings have valued it so highly. Just as there would be no nature without laws of nature, but a chaos in which no living being could survive, so without symbolic regularity, there would be no symbolism, no world of language in which *animal symbolicum* could survive. The most crucial type of symbolic regularity, without which government, science, literature, business, education, medicine, philosophy, theology, and indeed our whole society and culture would vanish, is the variety and degree of regularity called "truth"—the kind that PRS spells out. Without it, humankind as we know it would not exist.

Normativity. PRS, then, can be recognized, not only as an interesting, possibly accurate analysis of the concept "true," but as a norm of predication: when making statements, we should, as a rule, employ words in the way described. Our use of terms should resemble their established uses more closely than would the substitution of any rival, incompatible expression. This norm, which will receive fuller attention in the next chapter, is still more important than the analysis that suggests it, and its validity is independent of the analysis's accuracy. The analysis might be flawed—the word *true* might not function in the way described—and the norm might still be sound. Indeed, the dependence goes the other way. If the norm is valid, then the analysis should conform to it. And so it does, for this is in fact how the word *true* is used in the language—for this kind and degree of correspondence.

Validity. Thus, the Principle of Relative Similarity passes, roughly, the same test as does "It's raining" or "The ice is thick." Statements of the kind described by PRS are the ones we call true, and for that reason. Not that we are reflectively aware of this explanation of our so describing them. But the characteristics PRS picks out are the kind we typically know or believe about a statement when we call it true, and are the ones that account for our calling it true. If, for instance, we acknowledge the statement "It's raining" as true, we do so because we know or believe the things PRS mentions: the state of the weather, the meanings of the words employed, and the fact that "raining" comes closer than would "snowing," "sleeting," or any other rival expression. Thus, PRS meets its own test, as the corresponding norm of predication requires that it should.

Other merits of the principle might be cited besides these, but enough has already been said to suggest the principle's significance not only for statements about cats, mats, ice, or the weather, but for discourse generally, in any area of inquiry, including theology. Chapter 2 argued the irreducibly linguistic nature of linguistic thoughts, and mentioned implications of this fact. The power of language to shape and misshape our conceptions of reality, examined in the last chapter, is one such implication, but we have now examined a still more important one. If the mental representations that utterances supposedly translate do not account for utterances' truth, what does? How is truth achieved? How does language manage on its own? Here, I suggest in first summation, is how it does so: the Principle of Relative Similarity. Here, too, revealed by this principle, is the reason why truth deserves its traditional preeminence as the chief requisite of predication. Here, accordingly, is the starting point for many subsequent developments. Coming chapters will scrutinize this basic principle more closely, test it, refine it, apply it, and trace its ramifications throughout theology.[13]

Scrutiny of the principle can begin already here with the passages for reflection below, which merit special attention. A glance at PRS's historical setting can highlight their significance. Often, human thought on some important, complex topic does not arrive straightway at an adequate conception but passes, dialectically, through successive stages, in which an initial account gets things partly right and partly wrong, a reaction rejects the right along with the wrong, and a final solution sorts things out, synthetically, retaining the truth in both prior positions and eliminating the error. Thesis, antithesis, synthesis—such is the movement chapter 2 noted with regard to thought (viewed as nonlinguistic, then linguistic, then finally both); and such is the movement this chapter has now brought to light with regard to truth.

The traditional thesis position was right in characterizing truth as correspondence, in the straightforward sense of similarity, but wrong in supposing that the similarity holds between likenesses in the minds of believers or speakers and the things they believe or speak about. Critics were right, for reasons chapter 2 detailed, to reject such imagined truth-making movies in the mind but wrong to discard correspondence along with them. The present chapter's analysis agrees with the thesis position in accepting truth as correspondence, agrees with the critics in rejecting the mentalistic account of such correspondence, and combines both these partial truths in a new synthesis, summed up in the Principle of Relative Similarity. The triad is now complete.

For the most part, however, present-day philosophers and theologians do not view matters this way. It appears that, implicitly or explicitly, most occupy some variant of the antithetical, anti-picturing position. The variants are too many to consider here, but they all have this in common: not only do they reject truth as mental correspondence; not only do they do not replace mental correspondence with linguistic correspondence; but, like James, they do not envisage, assess, or respond to any such synthetic solution as PRS. The sample passages below are an invitation to such comparative assessment. Do they agree with the Principle of Relative Similarity? Should they? The coming chapter will argue that they should. The PRS analysis of what makes our statements true indicates how we ought to make them. The analysis merits acceptance as a norm.

For Further Reflection

1. "If we ask, for example, what makes the sentence 'The moon is a quarter of a million miles away' true, the only answer we come up with is that it is the fact that the

moon is a quarter of a million miles away"[14] (Donald Davidson).

2. "[Bultmann] is arguing that every true theological statement must itself be a confessional utterance. Theological speech is part of the event of faith and only as such can it possess meaning and truth. A theological statement is a performative utterance in which the believer witnesses to his or her existence as determined by God"[15] (David Fergusson).

3. "Consider, for example, the following proposal as recently advanced by George Lindbeck. When the crusader in the pitch of battle cries '*Christus est Dominus*' [Christ is Lord], and when this cry is used by the crusader to authorize his cleaving the skull of an infidel, then in such circumstances, Lindbeck argues, the utterance '*Christus est Dominus*' is false. The usage of the utterance would so contradict its correlative form of life as to falsify the utterance itself"[16] (George Hunsinger).

4. "The nature of truth is never established only in systems of true statements about God, man and the world, never only in a series of propositional truths, as opposed to which all others are false. Truth is always at the same time a *praxis*, a way of experience, enlightenment and proven worth, as well as of illumination, redemption and liberation"[17] (Hans Küng).

5. "God is not a person like us who could listen to what we say and see what we do. Our scriptures do sometimes describe him in this way, though, because those texts are designed to convey the truth to those who find it impossible to accept in its pure form. They require it to be dressed up in imaginative language"[18] (Oliver Leaman).

6. "It does not seem to be an absurd supposition that there may be something which human concepts simply cannot describe at all, if it is so different from anything we know that we are at a loss to know how to describe it"[19] (Keith Ward).

Chapter 5

Truth's Norm

If the Principle of Relative Similarity accurately states what makes most statements true and if, for the most part, our statements should be true, then we should typically make them in the way the principle describes: our use of words should resemble more closely the established uses of words than would the substitution of any rival, incompatible expression. From the analysis of what makes statements true there follows this prescription for how to fashion them. Now, though this inference may look evident, easy, and hardly worth stressing, it merits emphasis, for several reasons.

First, however accurate the analysis and however prestigious the expression analyzed, PRS's account of one standard application of the English word *true*—namely, its application to statements, rather than to beliefs, propositions, sentences, etc. (which require a different, related analysis)—has incomparably less importance than does a corresponding norm of predication, enjoining that words be used in the manner described. That norm, if valid, holds for all linguistic discourse and all languages, past, present, and to come, and its validity is unaffected by the existence or nonexistence of the English language or of the English term *true*.

Second, the analysis might be wildly inaccurate and the norm might still be perfectly valid. Suppose, for example, as some have suggested, that the word *true* does not describe statements, beliefs, or propositions, but simply endorses them (e.g., one person says "It's too risky" and another agrees by saying "That's true"). PRS might still stand up as a norm, if not as an analysis. That is, it still might be highly advisable, when making statements, to employ words in ways that resemble more closely the established use of words than would the substitution of any rival, incompatible expression.

Third, the opposite is also conceivable: the analysis might be accurate but the norm invalid. For it might turn out that truth, if thus analyzed, does not warrant the authority and prestige it has traditionally been accorded. "If that is what truth amounts to," some might say, "then so much the worse for truth. It should not determine our use of words." As we shall see, objections have, in fact, been raised that have this implication.

The transition, then, from analysis to norm is momentous. How can it be made? For reasons that chapter 4 suggested and subsequent chapters will confirm, one can sense that truth-correspondence of the kind described by PRS embodies important values, values that explain and justify the traditional prestige of truth. There is such a thing as stating matters as they really are (the snow *is* deep, the sun *is* bright), and there is nothing deeply mysterious about how it is done: PRS typically explains it. There is such a thing as communicating how matters are, and there is nothing mysterious about that, either: without any need of mental likenesses or their transferal from mind to mind, PRS typically explains it. There is value, furthermore, both in getting things right, for the sake of whatever purposes we may have, and in accurately, effectively communicating how things are—whether the things in question be the weather, the greenhouse effect, or salvation history.

I therefore agree with Roger Hazelton's stress on the importance of truth in theology:

> A truth-claim is bound up in any act or statement of Christian faith, so inextricably that it must be deemed a part of faith itself. It may be implicit as in a prayer or explicit as in a creed. It may be more like an assurance than an assertion, more *fiducia* than *assensus*. The point is that such a claim is always present, whether faith takes the form of proclamation, celebration or obedient enactment. . . . To suppose otherwise is to refuse to deal with faith on its own terms, to take it seriously as faith.[1]

Prayer, for example, without belief in God, is not prayer to God. And belief in God is belief that God really exists, as stated in a creed. The one who prays believes that the creedal statement is *true*.

In the present work, discussion will continue to center, in Hazelton's terms, on assertion rather than assurance and on proclamation rather than celebration or obedient enactment. For such is theology's focus, and theology and its methodology are here our concern. Within this focus, the most fundamental methodological norm is the one which privileges truth and which, if the Principle of Relative Similarity is accepted as basically correct, takes that account of truth as broadly normative. In theological statements, as in others, the use of terms should typically resemble the established use of terms more closely than would the substitution of any rival, incompatible expression. Language should exercise this authority, as a codeterminant of truth, along with the reality described.

On the whole (with reservations that chapter 21 will note at the appropriate moment), I believe that the resulting norm is neither too lax nor too rigid. Remarks of C. S. Lewis can illustrate this balance. "Most of my generation," he writes, "were reproved as children for saying that we 'loved' strawberries, and some people take a pride in the fact that English has the two verbs *love* and *like* while French has to get on with *aimer* for both. But French has a good many other languages on its side. Indeed it very often has actual English usage on its side too."[2] There is no point in arguing with such usage, PRS would say. If you like strawberries enough, you can say you love them, and you will be telling no lie. The language you speak will back you, and you will be understood perfectly well. If, on the other hand, you claim (as one noted author has) that any things that in any way attract one another love one another, and that, accordingly, artichokes, pebbles, and atoms love one another, PRS will demur. You have stretched the term too far. Here, denying love conforms better with established usage, which withholds the term *love* from mere gravitational pull.

Despite its virtues, in the history of thought, if not in popular practice, PRS's norm, and more generally the authority of language as a determinant of truth, has largely been either ignored or resisted. Chapter 1 cited multiple reasons why such a norm, drawing attention to language, might be ignored. For the most part, I suggested, words resemble spectacles which we look through but seldom at. We need to have such command of language that we are free to attend to the things we say, without figuring out how to say them. So we seldom advert to the language we speak as codetermining the truth of everything we say.

Mark Twain makes the same point with sly humor in his tale of Adam and Eve. According to Twain, when Adam couldn't think of a name for one of the animals, he appealed to Eve for help. "What name shall I give to this animal?" "Call it a horse," answered Eve. "But why a horse?" "Well," replied Eve, "it looks like a horse, doesn't it?" The laugh is on us, as well as on Eve. Gazing through the language we speak at the things we speak about, we readily suppose that the things have names all on their own, regardless of us and our linguistic usage. After all, a horse is a horse, whatever we choose to call it. Yet, *pace* Eve and such commonsense truisms, the things we speak about do not carry verbal labels on their own: we attach them. And if we attach the right label in the language we are speaking, the result is a true utterance. For example, we describe the frisky quadruped as a horse.

In the present chapter, it remains to indicate why the authority of language has not only been ignored but has also been strongly resisted.

Sources of Resistance

Sources of the massive resistance to language's authority can be listed under two principal headings: rivals, competing with language, and objections, born, I believe, of misunderstandings. I will note a couple of major instances under each of these two headings and will suggest why, in my view, they do not justify rejection of PRS (typically not envisaged or encountered by those who hold contrary views) as a guide to predication.

Rivals

Historically, language's chief rival has been the one chapter 2 noted. Truth, it was long thought, resides primarily in nonlinguistic thought; words are mere code. To determine the meaning and truth of verbal assertions, you must consult the mental representations they express. Now, if chapter 2 is right, language never does function in the way supposed. Mental representations do, of course, sometimes accompany our speaking, but they are at best mere sketches. They do not adequately capture what is said, nor do they accompany every word, nor do those in the mind of the reader or hearer match those in the mind of the writer or speaker. To determine the truth of utterances, we must therefore look elsewhere—to the language employed and the established uses of its expressions.

Nowadays, a different rival, namely theoretical ambition, poses a greater obstacle to the acceptance of language's authority. In illustration, recall Nygren's queries in chapter 1. "What is philosophy?" he asked, and, "What is theology?" PRS would reply that (even without analogical stretching of the terms) philosophy is what speakers of the language typically call philosophy and theology is what they typically call theology; and people apply these terms freely and variously to a wide variety of specimens. This, that, and the other are examples of philosophy. This, that, and the other are examples of theology. Someone of Nygren's mentality would find this response unacceptable. Salt water, fresh water, polluted water, and muddy water—all these, he might suggest, are called water. But that does not prevent scientists from seeking and identifying the chemical ingredient that makes them all water. Why should theologians proceed any differently? What is to prevent them, too, from being scientific? If everyday expressions and their meanings are too varied and indefinite for scientific purposes, they can be refined, as in the natural sciences. As the term *water* can be restricted scientifically to pure H_2O, so the term *theology* can be restricted to pure theology—that is, to whatever makes theology theology. Theologians can aspire to discover the essence of theology as scientists aspired to discover the essence of water, and succeeded.

Now, where does this parallel go wrong? In its supposition, first, of theological kinds (theology, grace, revelation, faith, etc.) comparable to natural kinds (water, copper, protein, etc.), and in its supposition, second, of a conceptual process comparable to chemical analysis that can detect the true nature of each such kind. Putnam has aptly characterized this mentality in his comments on G. E. Moore's *Principia Ethica*: "Moore writes as if there were an *object*, 'the concept Good,' that one could pass about, inspect under a microscope, perhaps take to pieces (be careful not to break it!). The word, on this view, is only a convenient if accidental label for this object. Once we have had our attention called to the object, we can simply forget about the word and concentrate on the object."[3] If, however, a concept—for instance, the concept "theology"—is determined by linguistic practice, and linguistic practice neither reveals nor is guided by any essence of theology, conceptual analysis will not yield a result of the kind desired. To champion such an essence, therefore, a "scientific" thinker will have to disregard linguistic usage and the authority of language. Such disregard has been common in theology as elsewhere.

Nygren's search exemplifies one species of theoretical ambition, but there are others. The sort of definition essentialists aspire to would delineate sufficient and necessary conditions of membership in the class to be defined (e.g., theology). It would indicate what set of properties all members of the class and only members of the class possess. Often, however, as we shall see in chapter 10, theorizing may limit itself to making universal claims about what property or properties *all* members of a class possess (e.g., "The existence of the tremendous transcendent reality that we name GOD is the foundation of all religion in all ages and among all peoples")[4] or what property or properties *only* members of a class possess (e.g., "Long-term commitment is the only kind of commitment that is possible").[5] This is just a sampling. Theoretical aspirations take many forms in theology as elsewhere, and in theology more than in many other disciplines these aspirations tend to conflict with the authority of language, which, if consulted, would severely limit them.

In a listing of major competitors for language's authority, some would be sure to add a third: "reality." "This," writes John Mackie, "is the basic problem for linguistic philosophy, to decide whether it is concerned with grammar or metaphysics, with language or the world."[6] One or the other: make your choice. Such a remark reflects a common misunderstanding. When linguistic philosophers enjoin attention to language as well as to reality, they are often taken to be interested only in language. Thus, Bertrand Russell, for example, wrote disparagingly of "linguistic philosophy, which cares only about language, and not about the world."[7] To turn to language, it is thought, is to turn away from reality. So, back to reality and away from language! Such criticism ignores the fact that no reality, by itself, dictates its own description. Reality and language, *together*, determine the truth of our assertions. They do not compete for authority.

Objections

Another chief objection to acceptance of language's authority can be stated as follows. The Principle of Relative Similarity enjoins respect for the established use of words—for example, for what people call philosophy or what people call theology. But what makes all these people right? If everybody agrees in saying something, are they automatically infallible? No, but agreement in the language they speak must be distinguished from agreement in the individual opinions they express in that language. The language—for instance, English—is neither right nor wrong, neither true nor false. It is just an instrument of communication, and, whatever the language being spoken, PRS backs it for that reason: successful communication. The individual opinions expressed, however, even if widely or universally accepted, may be right or wrong, and their widespread acceptance does not suffice to win PRS's approval. For the established use of terms to which PRS appeals is not their use in any one assertion, however frequently made or widely accepted, but their use in the language as a whole, on various occasions and in widely varied utterances.

Consider again the last chapter's simple illustration. Many people once believed and said that the Earth is flat. Suppose they all agreed, without exception. By PRS's test, they would still be mistaken. For the established use of "flat" in the English language (and of equivalents or near-equivalents in other tongues) is much broader than any one assertion. The term *flat* is applied to floors, roofs, tables, plateaus, and so forth. The dictionary reminds us of this general usage when it says, for example: "flat: having a horizontal surface without a slope, tilt, or curvature." Spheres do not qualify. But the Earth is spherical. So those who said the Earth is flat were wrong; their statement was false. Their use of words did not resemble the established use of words as closely as would the substitution of the rival expression *spherical*.

This may sound dogmatic, but notice: flat-earthers would themselves accept the dictionary definition as an accurate account of established usage. No alien sense of "flat" is being foisted on them. And they would agree that if the earth does not satisfy that familiar, shared definition, then the earth does not qualify as flat. They would just disagree about whether it satisfies the definition.

A passage from Nygren's *Meaning and Method* can illustrate the relevance, as well as the importance, of this first clarification:

> Once I have defined a term, logic demands that according to the law of identity I should stick to the meaning given in the definition throughout my entire argument. For if I begin to use the term—feeling perhaps that the definition is not quite right—now in one sense, now in another, the result can only be confusion. Consistency demands that I stick to the definition until it has been duly corrected. But what has this to do with truth? My sticking to the definition will, of course, if the definition is wrong, result in no truth whatever.[8]

Here, differently expressed, the conflation just warned against reappears. If it is a word meaning I have established when "I have defined a term," the stipulated meaning is neither right nor wrong and will, of itself, have no effect on truth. I can use it to make true statements or false. Furthermore, logic does not demand that I stick to it but communication does. If I use the word now in one sense now in another, the result, as Nygren notes, can only be confusion. If, instead, I have not defined a word but have made a factual claim of some sort, then the claim may be true or false, and neither language nor communication requires that I stay with it. The conflation here exemplified, of neutral word meanings and non-neutral factual claims, takes endlessly varied forms. That is why I have dwelt on it.

But now a further objection surfaces. Are word meanings really neutral? Are languages neutral? Look again at the dictionary, for instance under "water." The first entry in my dictionary reads: "A clear, colorless, odorless, and tasteless liquid, H_2O, essential for most plant and animal life and the most widely used of all solvents." Notice all these assertions about the appearance, analysis, role, and utility of water. Where, then, here and in similar instances, is the alleged "neutrality" of word meanings? The answer lies in PRS and can be illustrated from a historical example.

It was once believed that atoms could not be split. Then they were. Scientists did not thereupon conclude that there were no atoms, but rather that atoms could be split. For their prior belief did not rigidly define the word *atom*. It was as flexible as PRS indicates and its corresponding norm prescribes. "Atom" still came closer than any rival, incompatible expression, so continued to be used, to say, "Atoms can be split." And so it would be for water if scientists ever discovered that their analysis was mistaken and water was not H_2O as supposed. They would not deny that water had ever existed but would use the same term, "water," to say, "Water is not H_2O." "Water" would still be the right word to use; it would satisfy the Principle of Relative Similarity.

Thus, as Wittgenstein observed, we use words without a *fixed* meaning. For example,

> the name "Moses" can be defined by means of various descriptions.... But when I make a statement about Moses,—am I always ready to substitute some *one* of these descriptions for "Moses"? I shall perhaps say: By "Moses" I understand the man who did what the Bible relates of Moses, or at any rate a good deal of it. But how much? Have I decided how much must be proved false for me to give up my proposition as false? Has the name "Moses" got a fixed and unequivocal use for me in all possible cases?—Is it not the case that I have, so to speak, a whole series of props in readiness, and am ready to lean on one if another should be taken from under me and vice versa?[9]

From examples such as these it can be seen in what sense words and their meanings are neutral, indeed doubly neutral. They are neutral, first, because they are not statements and therefore are not true or false. They are neutral, second, because they are not rigidly defined by the beliefs of speakers and hearers, however widespread the beliefs may be. Words are not so used, in fact, and should not be so used, for effective communication.

Let these first objections and replies suffice for now; the chapter is already sufficiently complex. Among difficulties still to be addressed, it may help to signal one well in advance. The preceding pair of objections, failing to recognize the neutrality of language, question the *sufficiency* of PRS as a test of truth. The Principle appears too permissive, too lax. If enough people agreed, the Principle might approve a statement such as "The Earth is flat." So goes the complaint, now answered. On the other hand, as a *necessary* condition of truth, PRS might appear too restrictive, rather than too permissive. The principle may be right in resisting the statement "Atoms love one another," but what, for instance, of "The Lord is my rock"? Shouldn't PRS or its corresponding norm of predication leave room for the metaphorical stretching of expressions? Perhaps theology is not the place for such utterances, or perhaps they do not qualify as "true," but, whatever the verdict on these debatable issues, surely the utterances may be apt, surely they are legitimate? With other questions pressing for attention, I can leave these ones for later. One reason I can do so is that in theological writings metaphorical utterances such as "The Lord is my rock" are relatively rare in comparison with nonmetaphorical (though often analogical) utterances. Another is the benefit that eventual attention to metaphor may derive from antecedent consideration of other basic issues raised by the present discussion.

For Further Reflection

1. "[C. H. Dodd's] chief concern had been to show that 'the strain of tradition recovered from the Fourth Gospel is capable of being compared with other strains, corroborating or supplementing them, correcting them or being corrected by them, and of being in the end, perhaps, integrated into a consistent picture of the facts as they were handed down by the first witnesses.' Strangely, in this concluding statement Dodd is less clear and precise than is normally the case. How can 'facts' be handed down? How can 'facts' be integrated into a *picture*?"[10] (F. W. Dillistone).

2. "We must therefore stick to the original, obvious meaning. The name *Christians* was given at Antioch (Acts xi.26) to 'the disciples,' to those who accepted the teaching of the apostles. There is no question of its being restricted to those who profited by that teaching as much as they should have. There is no question of its being extended to those who in some refined, spiritual, inward fashion were 'far closer to the spirit of Christ' than the less satisfactory of the disciples. The point is not a theological or moral

one. It is only a question of using words so that we can all understand what is being said. When a man who accepts the Christian doctrine lives unworthily of it, it is much clearer to say he is a bad Christian than to say he is not a Christian"[11] (C. S. Lewis).

3. "Particularly influential in direct ways has been Tillich's way of mediating between the Christian tradition and modern culture in a theology of culture. Perhaps his influence is shown to be most pervasive in widespread understandings of the words 'religion' and 'religious.' It has become commonplace to say that any human activity (e.g., works of art, institutions, broadly shared moral standards, various practices) that exhibits an 'ultimate concern' is *for that reason* 'religious' "[12] (David Kelsey).

4. "Ogden and those who follow his lead seek to demonstrate the necessity of faith and of its objective ground, God, thereby showing the logical impossibility of atheism. By defining faith as 'our ineradicable confidence in the final worth of our existence' and God as 'whatever it is about this experienced whole that calls forth and justifies our original and inescapable trust,' Ogden comes as close as one can to providing an adequate defense of God's prevenience through an argument for *homo religiosus*"[13] (Ronald Thiemann).

5. "We presuppose that a term 'x' means 'y' in another language, and translate accordingly. But dictionaries originated for the most part in the 19th century and do not convey eternal wisdom itself, only the state of knowledge and the philosophy, anthropology, cosmology, and political situation of the 19th century. Even if we constantly improve the dictionaries, the problem still remains that in each translation we convey our metaphysical, anthropological, and theological tradition"[14] (Michael von Brück).

Chapter 6

The Norm's Feasibility

To the theoretical objections of the last chapter a practical objection may be added. The PRS-based norm says to take established word uses as our guide—either ordinary, familiar word uses such as dictionaries cite or, on occasion, ones personally stipulated for the occasion. In either alternative, there might seem to be no problem doing as required; for we can hardly be ignorant of uses we ourselves have stipulated, and are we not masters of our mother tongues? Yes, but very unreflective masters. For Wittgenstein was right: "Man possesses the ability to construct languages capable of expressing every sense, without having any idea how each word has meaning or what its meaning is—just as people speak without knowing how the individual sounds are produced."[1] Although this assessment may sound extreme, even philosophers who have troubled to scrutinize language have given divergent accounts of even basic, familiar expressions. And most language users are not linguistic philosophers. Thus, to the advice to heed established word use, the reply may be, "Easier said than done." "How," one writer queries, "ought one to determine what this ordinary use is, *e.g.* in a case of doubt? What ought one to do—to *ask* people? *Any* people? Or only the competent ones? And who is to decide who is 'competent'—the leading circles of society, the experts in language, the writers just in vogue? And supposing there are people generally considered competent—what if they disagree?"[2]

"What ought one to do?" The query is both a challenge to the proposed PRS norm of predication and an invitation to methodological clarity. Since the challenge takes varied forms, so too does the response. Each of the following case studies illustrates a different form of practical difficulty and a suitably different way to deal with it.

The Opacity of Common Usage: "True"

We have already encountered one notable instance of experts disagreeing about the use of even familiar expressions. For some, the term *true* applies properly or primarily to sentences, for others to utterances, for others to beliefs, for others to abstract thoughts or propositions. For some the term has one descriptive content, for others another, and for others the content varies according to the things called true (sentences, utterances, propositions, beliefs, etc.). Again, for some the word *true* describes, for others it merely signals assent, for still others it functions now one way, now the other. Disagreement is nearly total concerning this common expression. How unrealistic it may therefore appear to enjoin conformity to the "established uses" of words." *What* uses?! Rather than throw up our hands too readily in despair and dismiss PRS's norm as impractical, let us examine more closely this particularly interesting, troublesome, important—and instructive—example.

As we have seen, for Austin, to say an utterance is true is to describe it: it is to say that "the historic state of affairs to which it is correlated by the demonstrative conventions (the one to which it 'refers') is of a type with which the sentence used in making it is correlated by the descriptive conventions." Peter Strawson disagreed. The term *true*, he argued, serves to *assert*, not to *describe*. Granted, we may respond "That's true" after hearing an utterance, and we may therefore suppose that "true" describes the utterance. However, consider such a statement as "It is true that the general health of the community has improved (that *p*), but this is due only to the advance in medical science." On the use of "true" at the start of this sample statement, Strawson commented:

> It is not necessary that anyone should have said that *p*, in order for this to be a perfectly proper observation. In making it, I am not talking *about* an actual or possible speech-episode. I am myself asserting that *p*, in a certain way, with a certain purpose. I am anticipatorily conceding, in order to neutralize, a possible objection. I forestall someone's making the statement that *p* by making it myself, with additions. It is of prime importance to distinguish the fact that the use of "true" always glances backwards or forwards to the actual or envisaged making of a statement by someone, from the theory that it is used to characterize such (actual or possible) episodes.[3]

In defense of his descriptive analysis, Austin had cited other, different verbal specimens—"His closing words were very true" and "The third sentence on page 5 of his speech is quite false"—that more readily lend themselves to his interpretation.[4] Thus, some evidence points one way, some the other. There is no need, however, to declare this Austin-Strawson debate a draw. It appears that "true," like many another concept, is bipolar, and that Austin had hold of one pole and Strawson had hold of the other. For an illuminating comparison, consider the "performative" utterances that Austin made famous. Typically, the utterance "I forbid you," "I thank you," or "I order you" is an act of forbidding, thanking, or ordering, not the description of such an action; whereas "He forbade me," "She thanked me," or "You ordered me" does describe the action named. The verbs *forbid*, *thank*, and *order* have these different, but tightly related uses, some descriptive and some not. Similarly, "It is true that *p*" does not describe any utterance, whereas "He spoke true words" does.[5] Continuing the comparison, we can see that, just as the nondescriptive occurrences of a verb such as "forbid" do not preclude a description of forbidding, so, too, the nondescriptive occurrences of "true" do not preclude a description of truth. For both terms have a descriptive as well as a nondescriptive use. Austin may have been one-sided in the evidence he considered, but that does not invalidate his account in the way Strawson alleged.[6]

What, then, in the light of this example, can we say in reply to the objection that recourse to the authority of language is not feasible? An initial response can go as follows:

1. Often, it is true, consultation of language offers no "quick fix." As nonlinguistic issues may be difficult and complex, so may linguistic. Given the labyrinthine complexity of human languages, this should come as no surprise.

2. However, even when a verdict is not obvious, as here, an answer may be possible. Language may be a maze in which we often lose our way, but it is also a maze from which we can sometimes find an exit.

3. As the present example testifies, finding a way out may be important. On the strength of his one-sided, inadequate analysis, Strawson rejected any descriptive account of truth, such as PRS, and any norm based on it, such as the one we have been assessing in this and the previous chapter.

4. Fortunately, not all cases are as difficult as this one. Problems may arise not so much from consulting established word use as from ignoring it. Consider, for instance, what Gerhard Ebeling says on the same subject of truth.

"Wherever language is doing what it is its nature to do," he first observes, "its ultimate obligation is to the truth alone, and it is by the truth that it must be tested."[7] So, we may wonder, are questions, prayers, commands, cheers, jeers, and exclamations all true or false? Or is truth their "ultimate obligation," the test they must all pass? In what sense must such utterances pass a test of *truth*? "If we dare to take a further step," Ebeling replies, "and characterize as decisively as possible the concept of truth as it is related to life, the definition on which we light may sound extremely banal, but the longer we think about it, the more significance it takes on: The one thing that is true is love."[8]

There are various things I might be tempted to say about this definition, but certainly not that it is banal. I might note with Ebeling himself how words "undergo a process of inflation and lose their value. They are made to carry more and more meaning, lose definition, and finally come to mean everything and nothing."[9] So it is here. One reason for Ebeling's own inflation of the concept "true" seems evident: when he thought long and lit on his definition, he did not consult the established use of the English word *true* or of any German equivalent. By that test, there are problems with his saying that love is true, and still more with his saying that love alone is true. When we call sentences, statements, beliefs, propositions, and the rest true or false, we are not mistaken; we have the backing of language.

In this instance, the clash with the established use of the word is evident. For Ebeling here stands alone, idiosyncratically, in conflict with established usage. If, however, many other theologians said the same or similar things, we might start to wonder whether their numerous assertions established a contrary usage and whether a principle such as PRS was any longer applicable. It might seem, in Wittgenstein's words, that "Anything—and nothing—is right."[10] In illustration, consider a different example.

The Opacity of Theological Usage: "Act"

This comparison sometimes seems apt: theology is like a porous blotter; when words fall on it, they spread, blur, and lose their shape. What use, then, is a norm of linguistic correspondence—even one as flexible as PRS—that looks to the "established use" of words for guidance? *What* established use? *Whose* use?

Talk of "acts" strikingly illustrates this new problem, arising, not from conflicting accounts of familiar word usage, or inattention to it, but from the vagaries of usage begotten by such inattention, especially in theology. Thus, consider, for example, a passage such as the following:

> Theologians, recognizing the complexity and intrinsic unity of the act of faith, distinguish in it the following basic dimen-

sions: faith as knowledge of revealed truth (believing in God who reveals himself in Christ: "*fides quae creditur*"); faith as trusting obedience to God and as a personal encounter with him: "*fides qua creditur*" (believing God, the formal structure of faith): in this sense faith is the disposition for justification and ordination to final salvation in the beatific vision, that is, to participation in the life of the glorious Christ (the salvific and eschatological dimensions of faith).[11]

Most theologians, it seems, have little problem with such talk of "acts." Yet notice what this "act of faith" is here identified with: knowledge, belief, obedience, an encounter, a disposition, an ordination. Each of these terms, one might think, should count as a competitor with "act." If, for instance, faith is a disposition, it is not an act. However, such is the verdict when PRS takes common usage as its standard, whereas widespread theological usage, oblivious of such a norm, is far more fluid. Thus, the preceding quotation might occasion no misgivings in an author who could write: "Few are the acts whose value simple direct insight suffices to establish. They would be restricted to acts such as 'love and honor and pity and pride and compassion and sacrifice.' "[12] I recall one man who, when queried, maintained that his belief in the location of New York City was indeed an act he had been performing, uninterruptedly, for the last forty years. Such, I suggest, is the power of the verbal form—the "active" form—that the verb *believe* shares with "beckon," "berate," "beat," and the like. Belief, too, is taken for an act. But all verbs have an active form—yes, even "exist." So a contemporary theologian takes this final step in the expansion of "act":

> Action in its most general sense refers to existence, in this case human existence. Human existence is action. But action denotes a human existence always in act; it is a dynamic existing. Like the term existence itself, action is analogous; existence takes many forms, and the action that is human existence unfolds at a variety of levels. Beyond the sheer act of existing, the human person acts biologically and psychologically; knowing is action; willing is action; doing this or that is action. When action is fully human, when it is mediated by conscious intelligence, action is scarcely distinct from freedom in act.[13]

I find all this unfortunate. One does not have to be a stickler for precision (PRS is not), to feel that once the term *act* applies to anything that can be expressed by an active verb, it has lost all power of discrimination and is ready to be scrapped. But words such as "act" and "action" are handy if properly used. Can they somehow be salvaged?

Regrettable though the suggestion may sound to some, I think the only remedy is the one Wittgenstein recommended. "What *we* do," he wrote, "is to bring words back from their metaphysical to their everyday use."[14] In everyday language, a disposition is not an act. Neither, I would say, is knowledge or belief an act. To many, this may seem less clear. (Isn't believing something people *do*? Isn't existing, sleeping, or growing old something people *do*?) So let me suggest, less dogmatically, that once we look beneath the surface similarity between "believe" and "beckon," "know" and "calculate," "grow old" and "grow radishes," "exist" and "exhale," and so forth, the less inclined we will be to apply the label "act" to anything and everything expressed by an active verb. "Say what you choose," wrote Wittgenstein, "so long as it does not prevent you from seeing the facts. (And when you see them there is a good deal that you will not say.)"[15]

The example I have chosen may convey a discouraging impression of theological discourse and of the prospects for PRS in theology. So let me acknowledge that this sample is extreme, even in theology. Most of the expressions theologians employ do not become quite as amorphous as has "act." And even when this or that individual writer or speaker loosens them considerably, the loosening is not language-wide or theology-wide. Since such limited loosening does not reshape the expressions' "established use," PRS can still apply. Besides—and here is a further point to dwell on—even when there is no verdict, that fact itself is a verdict. When neither of two rival candidate expressions approximates more closely to established word use than does the other, PRS rejects them both. Neither satisfies the principle's requirements. An outstanding example with which to illustrate this possibility is the ongoing debate about fetal status.

Fuzzy Borders: "Person," "Human Being"

The dispute exemplifies the following syndrome: (1) Conceptual borders are blurred; no term in any language differentiates so precisely between instances and non-instances that in-between cases, conceivable or actual, are excluded. (2) Borderline cases are not only conceivable, but exist for many concepts. Actual items fall between purple and blue, rain and sleet, bushes and trees, tables and desks. (3) However, the vast majority of the things we identify fall clearly inside or outside of the conceptual borders drawn loosely but effectively by usage. The rain clearly is rain;

the plane clearly is a plane; the prediction clearly is a prediction; the person clearly is a person. (4) This fact begets in those who do not reflect on language—thus, in most people—the assumption that answers exist for all such questions. If we cannot tell whether something is rain, a plane, a prediction, or a person, the fault must lie in us and not in the language we speak. (5) Accordingly, when discussion does focus on a borderline case, we assume that an answer exists. (6) If, in addition, the answer looks important, we seek it, give it, argue for or against it. Hence, for example, the question of fetal status—which appears, literally, to be a matter of life and death—has elicited endless debate.

This very fact indicates what verdict PRS would give. In the broad, in-between zone where people disagree, neither side has the backing of language. For some, a human genetic code, or possession of a human soul, suffices to constitute a person or human being, regardless of the stage of physical development. For others, fairly full development is necessary—say, "a human form, so that it has a nervous system, a heart and circulatory apparatus, and indications of human shape."[16] Others require something more than physical development. The embryo, fetus, and newborn of the human species, it has been said, "do not really become functionally human until humanized in the human socialization process. 'Humanity is an achievement not an endowment.' "[17] These examples are merely suggestive, for the variations are many.[18] Some disputants draw the line at one place, others at another place; some for one reason, others for another. But usage draws no such borderline. Each implicit redefinition of "person" or "human being" departs from the vagueness of the familiar, everyday concept, that embraces Thomas Edison and Flannery O'Connor, on one side, excludes gorillas and unfertilized ova, on the other, but has nothing to say about embryos or fetuses.

As noted, I have chosen this dramatic example to illustrate a simple point: when neither of two rival answers—for example, neither the assertion nor the denial of the fetus' humanity or personhood—agrees more closely than the other with established word usage, neither satisfies PRS; and when PRS permits no answer pro or con, that itself suffices for a verdict: we should not give either answer, pro or con. We should, for instance, neither assert nor deny that the fetus is a person or a human being. Thus, an apparent limitation on PRS is not a limitation: the principle can give a verdict even when it can give no verdict. That is, it can give a verdict *against* both alternatives when it can give no verdict *for* either alternative.[19]

These brief, focused remarks may seem to do slight justice to an important, complex issue. So let me note that chapter 16 will revisit the same example from a different point of view.

Collectively, this chapter's examples demonstrate how serious the difficulties for application of PRS's norm sometimes are. However, the word *sometimes* merits emphasis. Few words have occasioned as much confusion and disagreement as has the word *true*. Few words have become quite as amorphous in theological literature as has the word *act*. Few conceptual borders have provoked as much disputation as have those for *person* and *human being*. And even in such instances as these, the practical problems in applying the norm do not impugn its validity, for the alternative to its acceptance is the sort of Babel these examples illustrate.

For Further Reflection

1. "One of the chief things which we mean, by saying we have *minds*, is, I think, this: namely, that we perform certain mental acts or acts of consciousness. That is to say, we see and hear and feel and remember and imagine and think and believe and desire and like and dislike and will and love and are angry and afraid, etc. These things that we do are all of them mental acts—acts of mind or acts of *consciousness*: whenever we do any of them, we are conscious of something"[20] (G. E. Moore).

2. "Seeing in any case is more than the registration of a surface. It is a penetration yielding some sense of the other's structure, so that the experiencing of another is never merely visual or auditory or tactile. We see the features and comprehend the humanity at the same time. Look at the fetus, say the anti-abortionists, and you will see humanity.... The proponent of abortion is invited to consider the organism kicking the mother, swimming peacefully in amniotic fluid, responding to the prick of an instrument, being extracted from the womb, sleeping in death. Is the kicker or swimmer similar to him or to her? Is the response to pain like his or hers? Will his or her own face look much different in death?"[21] (John Noonan).

3. "With almost everything they say, the fanatics against abortion show that they will not, or cannot, face the known facts of this matter. The inability of a fetus to say 'I' is not merely a lack of skill; there is nothing there to

which a pronoun could properly refer. A fetus is not a person but a *potential* person"[22] (Charles Hartshorne).

4. "There has been widespread agreement that two separate issues are really at stake in the debate over the determination of death. The first question is essentially philosophical, conceptual, and ethical: Under what circumstances do we consider a person dead? The question is asked in several ways. What are the necessary and sufficient conditions for a person to be alive? What is the essential characteristic of persons such that its loss can be said to constitute death?"[23] (Robert Veatch).

5. "The three basic principles of classical logic are the principles of identity, noncontradiction, and excluded middle.... The principle of excluded middle affirms that any statement is either true or false. The three principles are important in that they provide necessary conditions for meaningful and intelligible thinking and discourse on any subject whatsoever"[24] (Harold Netland).

Chapter 7

Making Sense

Chapter 5 noted one major upshot of the Principle of Relative Similarity, which chapter 6 further assessed: the principle, identifying what makes statements true, can and should guide our predication. This is how we should speak. Now we can note another important ramification: by specifying the truth-conditions of utterances, the principle can largely allay misgivings concerning the meaningfulness of theological discourse.

From early times, Christian thinkers have acknowledged that God largely transcends our knowledge and our words. In the last century, philosophical critics went farther. Talk about God, they repeatedly asserted, does not make sense. Kai Nielsen's complaints are typical:

> We cannot understand what it would be for such a being to act and thus to be loving, merciful or just, for these predicates apply to things that *a person does*. But we have no understanding of "a person" without "a body" and it is only persons that in the last analysis can act or do things. We have no understanding of "disembodied action" or "bodiless doing" and thus no understanding of "a loving but bodiless being."[1]

Clearly, we cannot understand these things in the sense of imagining them; but "understand" is not synonymous with "imagine." As one writer has observed, "Whether I can imagine it or not, a thousand-sided polygon, an animal that's a cross between a walrus and a wasp, and a color different from any we have ever seen, are *all logically possible*; we need not stop to ask whether we can *imagine* them."[2] How and in what sense, though, can such hypotheses, and those Nielsen cites, be "understood"? How can Nielsen and like-minded critics be answered?

The traditional response relies on analogy. Using "love" as illustration, one writer describes this appeal as "an attempt to find a position between the two extremes; in speaking about God and man the term 'love' is to be used neither in two absolutely different senses nor in one exactly identical sense, but in an analogical sense, which is to say that one love is *similar* to the other, where 'similar' means neither 'absolutely different' nor 'absolutely identical.' To be similar is therefore to combine sameness and otherness, continuity and discontinuity in a peculiar way."[3] Reference to "one exactly identical sense" sounds problematic (confer chapter 2), but let it pass for now. The indicated scheme is roughly this: on one side stands "univocal" predication (e.g., "human being" predicated of Galileo and Einstein); on the other hand stands "equivocal" predication (e.g., "club" predicated of a weapon and a social entity); and between them slips analogical predication (e.g., "loving" predicated of humans and of God).

Thus, Aquinas, for example, insisted that terms such as "good" and "wise" are not predicated univocally of God and of humans, but analogously. God's goodness and wisdom far transcend those of creatures, yet the resemblance between the created and divine analogs suffices to legitimate application of the same terms to God as to creatures. "Thus God is called wise," Aquinas explains, "not simply because he begets wisdom but because, insofar as we are wise, we imitate to some extent the divine source of our wisdom."[4] This account is still current. Thus, Norris Clarke, for example, in replying to Nielsen, has stressed "the principle, handed down to St. Thomas by both the Neoplatonic and the Aristotelian traditions, that *every effect must in some way resemble its cause*. In a word, every causal bond sets up at the same time a bond of intrinsic similarity in being."[5] Hence, God's creatures resemble their creator, and creaturely predicates can be applied to him.

Evidently, though, not just any kind or degree of similarity warrants such predicates' application, or else we would have to say that the creator of trees is a tree, the creator of mice is a mouse, and so forth. But once we try to indicate more precisely the nature and degree of the requisite similarity, no account that fails to mention rival, alternative expressions can succeed. Even close similarity may fail the test of truth if it is not "relative similarity"—that is, the kind specified by PRS. Thus, crimson may closely resemble scarlet and might be called scarlet were it not for the competing claim of the rival term *crimson*. Trees may closely resemble bushes and might be called bushes were it not for the competing claim of the rival term *tree*. And so it is quite generally. The requisite similarity cannot be stated absolutely, as close, distant, or in-between; it must be stated relative to the language at large and what terms occupy what parts of the semantic landscape. Where concepts cluster thickly, as for colors, similarity must be close. Where no concepts come close, as for God, similarity may be looser. In either case, PRS suggests, in order for a statement to be true its use of terms should resemble more nearly the established use of terms than would the substitution of any rival, incompatible expression.

In diverting illustration, consider the case of my niece Laura. When, at the tender age of two, she first saw the Gulf of Mexico, she exclaimed, "Big bathtub!" Bathtubs she knew, and sinks, buckets, and the like, but neither oceans nor lakes nor ponds nor swimming pools. So of the terms she was acquainted with, "bathtub" came closest. She realized, of course, that this expanse of water and its receptacle differed notably from the familiar ones at home; the ones she now gazed on were enormous. Still, given the limited verbal means at her disposal, her choice of words was apt. The only trouble was that, unknown to her, English possesses a whole series of terms in successful competition with "bathtub." "Pool" and "pond" come closer to what she saw, "lake" still closer, "ocean" and "bay" closer still, and "gulf" closest of all. Hence, despite the increasing similarity between their referents and the Gulf of Mexico, "bathtub," "pool," "pond," "lake," "ocean," and "bay" do not qualify as true or apt descriptions of that body of water, whereas "gulf" does. Only "gulf" satisfies the suggested requirement.

Here, quickly sketched, we can recognize a dialectical development. The traditional account of analogy allowed theological discourse too much leeway; Nielsen and others have allowed it too little leeway; and PRS strikes a balance between them. Sheer similarity does not suffice, it is true; but relative similarity does suffice. (As we shall see in the next chapter, Nielsen himself has need of some such principle as PRS.) The following points suggest more fully, now, the interest of this PRS solution.

1. Realistically, the solution does not rely on mental representation of the divine, so avoids a chief difficulty for the theological use of language. In the long-dominant tradition examined in chapter 2, verbal signs express the conscious contents of speakers' minds and beget similar representations in the minds of hearers. But whose representations can keep pace with the assertions of theology? Who can represent to themselves the transcendent realities of which such assertions speak? In the account just sketched, there is no such need. For the truth of theological assertions, it suffices that the realities described, however transcendent, bear sufficient resemblance to realities customarily thus described in the language—that is, that they satisfy the Principle of Relative Similarity.

2. This PRS solution is realistic in another sense: it conforms with the understanding of believers. For instance, it fits hand in glove with the type of theological analysis most favored through the centuries,

combining affirmation with negation and transcending them. Implicit in the "affirmative way" of traditional theology is the conviction that the word employed—"simple," "wise," "good," "powerful," "caring," or the like—is somehow legitimate. Implicit in the "negative way" is recognition that the word's legitimacy does not derive from close similarity. All that is missing from these traditional two ways is a clear grasp of what kind and degree of similarity would suffice. Such understanding is not adequately achieved or expressed by asserting, as in the "way of eminence," that divine simplicity, wisdom, goodness, or the like is higher or more perfect: it must be higher or more perfect *simplicity, wisdom,* or *goodness*. The same word must apply. And it does if PRS is satisfied.

3. In this account, the theological use of language is not as "queer," "odd," or idiosyncratic as many have supposed. N. H. G. Robinson's remarks exemplify their claims. "Linguistic analysis," he writes, "has been of service to the systematic theologian by making him more acutely aware of the problematical character of his accustomed language which, perhaps by reason of his main preoccupation, he may be prone to use without a due sense that it is a very odd language indeed."[6] Reliance on analogy does not make it odd. As Robert Capon has pointed out, "When I say my dog knows the way home from the other side of town, I am making just as full a use of analogy as when I say the Lord knows all things eternally. True enough, there is not as much temptation to think of my dog as a little four-legged man as there is to think of God as a big invisible one, but the same rules apply."[7] Specifically, I suggest, the PRS rule applies, in theology as elsewhere. It is satisfied by true theological statements as it is satisfied by talk of animals "knowing," computers playing "chess," or autistic savants silently, mysteriously "calculating" the date of the third Thursday in August, 2117.

4. As analogy is not a peculiarity of theological discourse, neither is it a peculiarity of just certain privileged expressions. "Our language," it has been said, "contains a set of terms whose syntactic structure leaves them free to be used in ways that outstrip our present settled idiom."[8] This elasticity, PRS suggests, characterizes all nouns, verbs, adjectives, adverbs, and prepositions in a language such as English, and other types of expression in other languages. It applies not only to favorites such as "good," "wise," and "know," but also to "chess," "rain," "is," "in," and "saucer" (as in "flying saucer"). The Principle of Relative Similarity holds for a whole language.

5. PRS's reliance on similarity can meet a recurring challenge.[9] Imperfect similarity, it is said, means partial similarity, and partial similarity means partly the same and partly different. But the sameness can be stated univocally, so there is no need for analogy. Thus, analogy reduces

to univocity, with all its problems for theological discourse. Several responses can be made to this objection. One is to note that imperfect similarity need not be analyzable in this dyadic fashion, part the same and part different. There is, for example, no discernible sameness in the resemblance between one shade of red and another; yet they do resemble each another, and do so more than they resemble shades of green or gray. And the like holds in many other instances (violin notes versus trumpet notes, roughly circular figures versus triangular, etc.). Furthermore, even where there is exact resemblance, there is no name for the identical trait. Two objects—say, a sweater and a book—may be precisely the same shade of red, but there is no name for that precise shade ("scarlet," "crimson," "rose," and the like just cover a narrower range of shades than does "red"). Furthermore, even where one precise similarity is detectable in an overall resemblance, that need not be the whole reason for applying the same term to the resembling things. Two people, for example, may both be called "healthy," and, though differing somewhat in their weight, bone density, pulse rate, and other pertinent respects, they may both have identical cholesterol readings; but that single trait, by itself, does not explain their both being called "healthy." Finally, and most importantly, even if, improbably, the overall resemblance between God and creatures included some such sameness amid all the diversity, that trait and its existence would not be discernible by us, so could not be named, even if, improbably, some term existed with which to pinpoint it.

In short, the objection is far too simplistic, whereas PRS can readily accommodate all this diversity. Even if we have no way of discerning any sameness amid the difference, indeed even if there is none, there can still be resemblance, and the resemblance may be greater than for any rival expression, and the term applied may therefore be the right one.

6. PRS not only clarifies but also modifies the familiar tripartite scheme: univocal, equivocal, and analogous. Recall the quotation above assigning analogical predication a position between two extremes: "[I]n speaking about God and man the term 'love' is to be used neither in two absolutely different senses nor in one exactly identical sense." No terms in natural languages, subject as they are to the Principle of Relative Similarity, have "one exactly identical sense." None are confined to some single, sharp, defining essence (see chapter 2). All are flexible, and the principle suggests how flexible they are. People play "chess" with boards and pieces, or by mail, or in their heads, or with computers; and now computers can play chess with computers. Noting just the two extremes in this continuum—"chess" applied to people's playing, with boards and pieces, on the one hand, and to computers'

playing, without boards or pieces, on the other—we might term the first application "univocal" and the other "analogical." But at no point in such stretching of a term does any clear demarcation indicate where "univocity" ceases and "analogy" begins.

7. Some may find PRS too nebulous, while others may find it too definite. Yet, on reflection, the principle may satisfy both the dogmatically and the mystically inclined. The former may be reassured by the fact that relative similarity may be close, the latter by the fact that it may be distant. Thus, "life" believed to exist on far-off planets may be just like that on ours, or it may surpass the wildest fancies of science fiction. A bee's "image" of a flower may be just like ours, or it may be so dissimilar that, were we made aware of it, we would have difficulty recognizing it even as an image, let alone the image of a flower. God's love and knowledge may resemble ours more closely than we suppose, or they may be exceedingly dissimilar. Yet in either supposition, close or far, PRS may be satisfied in such instances as these; and it may therefore be true to say that there is life on other planets, that the bee has an image, that it sees the flower, that God is loving or knowing.

Nonetheless, the virtues of PRS analogy should not be exaggerated. Assuring meaning, the Principle of Relative Similarity does not thereby guarantee truth. Indeed, it does not even assure possibility. In simple illustration, the fact that it is meaningful to surmise that bees form mental images does not establish the possibility of their doing so. Intimate acquaintance with their physiology and deeper understanding than we currently possess of the nature and formation of mental images might reveal the impossibility of bees, actual or imaginable, forming mental images. This important distinction, between making sense and being possible, merits a chapter to itself.

For Further Reflection

1. "Whereas our knowledge of the objects of this world begins by placing them in a general category and then makes that category more specific by adding successively narrower differences, we can distinguish God from all other beings only by successive negations, since God belongs to no category whatsoever"[10] (Gregory Rocca, on Aquinas).

2. "Creator and creature are to be perfect, each in his own way, because between them no similarity can be found so

great but that the dissimilarity is even greater"[11] (Fourth Lateran Council).

3. "Only when this point has been reached, at which God or the gods no longer manifest themselves in the world by becoming directly perceptible, but instead only intimate their reality indirectly through the existence of everything that makes up the world, does the problem arise with which the doctrine of analogy is concerned, and in which doxology is also involved: if the divine reality is not directly experienceable, then it can be spoken of only in an indirect manner, viz., by speaking about whatever worldly being it is through which the reality of God manifests itself. Thus, one speaks of God by speaking about something else, but in such a way that this other being is viewed in its relation to the reality of God"[12] (Wolfhart Pannenberg).

4. "But the risk is always there, on the one hand of treating our religious affirmations about, for example, acts of God, so simplistically that they are patently false, or on the other of giving them so sophisticated a meaning that it makes no difference whether we say that God acts or that he does not act"[13] (Maurice Wiles).

5. "Unless our metaphors and analogies have a univocal backing and are translatable into literal statements about God, they will always be ambiguous or vague. Thus, from a logical point of view the theory of analogical predication can be judged as inadequate. Practically speaking, the consequences are once again unfortunate, for without a clear understanding of who or what God is and that he is and an understanding of his relations to us we have no way of judging the appropriateness or inappropriateness of our emotional or our volitional responses to him"[14] (William Power).

6. " 'Wise' is used in the same sense in 'God is wise' as in 'Socrates is wise.' There are the same synonyms—'knows many things,' 'understands many things,' same antonyms—'foolish,' same determinates and determinables. And there are the same standard examples of wise things—paradigm cases of wise human beings—by which the term may be given its meaning; and, I suggest, the examples play the same role in designating the property. In both cases,

something is wise if it resembles paradigm wise things in the respect that they resemble each other more than it resembles other paradigm non-wise things."[15] (Richard Swinburne).

Chapter 8

Sense versus Possibility

Whereas Kai Nielsen and others have drawn the limits of sense too tightly, the Principle of Relative Similarity draws them more loosely. But does it draw them *too* loosely—or at least so loosely as to admit all sorts of impossibilities among the things that "make sense"? Does PRS-meaningfulness assure real-world possibility? Such is the basic question, of special interest for theology, that this chapter will now address.

To illustrate the distinction between sense and possibility, and its relevance, consider these words of Nielsen about the subatomic particles called mesons:

> Mackie gives us no evidence that there is a *logical ban* on observing mesons. Technically and even physically, it is impossible to observe them, but Mackie gives no evidence that the acceptance of the physical theory in which "meson" plays a functional part commits us to the claim that it would be *contradictory* to say that even an infinitely observant observer, with very different sense organs and in a very different situation, could observe them.[1]

Nielsen does not spell out this closing suggestion. He does not specify in what respects the putative "observer," "situation," "sense organs," or "observations" would be similar to the things customarily called observers, situations, sense organs, or observations, and in what respects dissimilar. He does not need to. For his surmise to make sense, it suffices that he should mean that there might conceivably exist a being sufficiently similar to us to merit the name "observer," endowed with perceptual equipment sufficiently similar to ours to merit the name "sense organs," related to mesons in a fashion sufficiently similar to what we call "observing" to merit the same appellation. Each time, we can suggest on Nielsen's behalf, the test of sufficient similarity would be PRS, or some variant thereof. Without some such explanation, it is difficult to see how his supposition would be intelligible. For as he himself notes, "We have no idea of what it would be like to observe a meson."

In the same sense, we "have no idea"—or, as Nielsen puts it, "have no understanding"—of what it would be like, say, for God to love us or to act on our behalf. However, the same principle that saves his supposition applies to these too, and assures them meaning. If the divine reality resembles more closely human acting or doing than it does human resting, receiving, enduring, suffering, or the like, God may be said to act. If the action in our regard resembles more closely human acting on another's behalf than it does acting against them, acting without regard for their welfare, or the like, then God may be said to act on our behalf. If the disposition thus revealed resembles human loving more closely than it does human hatred, dislike, disinterest, or even mere liking, then God may truly be said to love us. And if this is what is meant, then, regardless of whether it is true, the belief is meaningful. It has determinate truth-conditions.

However, the question raised by Nielsen's account is this: Does a meaningful statement or hypothesis automatically state a genuine possibility? Nielsen might reply that even if observing mesons is not technically or physically possible for us humans, either now or perhaps forever, it is at least a *logical* possibility. And he might explain that a logical possibility is one for which truth-conditions can be stated. And he might go on and explain that truth-conditions can, in fact, be stated for his hypothesis, thanks to some such principle as PRS. So let us restate our original question and ask: Does the statement of truth-conditions for a hypothesis guarantee that the hypothesis is a genuine possibility? The answer seems clearly negative. For all that PRS guarantees is that *if* something verified those conditions, that would establish the existence, hence the possibility, of the state of affairs expressed. Thus, *if*, in our example, something satisfied the phrase "observing mesons," that would establish the possibility of observing mesons. But *that* anything does or can satisfy the stated truth-conditions, the mere stating of the conditions does not assure.

Consider, for example, the statement, "One day someone will trisect an angle using only ruler and compass." Many people, seeing no contradiction in this prediction, have tried to be the first to verify it. Now, however, it has been shown, a priori and not just empirically, that no such thing is possible. Outside of mathematics, the like may hold, for example, regarding the harnessing of nuclear fusion. Despite the meaningfulness of the proposal and its lack of evident contradiction, it may not be a genuine possibility, for us or for anyone. Now, a fortiori, the like may hold in theology, regarding more transcendent mysteries.

To illustrate the theological significance of this distinction between making sense and stating a genuine possibility, consider the problem of evil. It is commonly supposed that, to deal with this problem, we need to know how matters might be as well as how they are, and that to know how they might be we need merely know logic. For an omnipotent agent is not restricted by the actual laws or constitution of the universe but can realize any state of affairs that can be expressed without contradiction. It seems, then, that we can freely hypothesize improvements on the universe, note that they are not realized, and infer that a good and omnipotent God does not exist. Thus, to cite an important instance, reasoning may proceed as follows: "The arguments of Mackie and Flew rest on the contention that it is logically possible that humans be created with or have such a nature or character that they always freely choose the good. Since God is omnipotent, he can do anything that is logically possible, and since a world in which people only do good is clearly a superior world to one in which people do evil as well as (or instead of) good, we would expect that God would have created a world populated only with people who always and only do the good."[2]

This is hypothesizing made easy: to know that a conjecture states a genuine possibility, we need merely state the conjecture in a way that reveals no evident contradiction. If we don't see the impossibility of an hypothesis, it must be possible. If, for instance, we don't see the impossibility of trisecting an angle with just ruler and compass, it must be possible. If we don't see the impossibility of harnessing nuclear fusion, it must be possible—at least "logically." Possibilities can be multiplied at will. But if all "logically" here means is that the hypothesis makes sense, and if all its making sense requires is stating truth-conditions for it, and if these are spelled out in terms of PRS, there is no guarantee that anything ever has or could satisfy the stated conditions, physically, metaphysically, or otherwise.

The contrary assumption, unspoken and generally unexamined, pervades much philosophy and theology. But it seldom surfaces as explicitly as in the preceding quotation on freedom and divine omnipotence or, for instance, in the following passage from Durandus concerning the Eucharist:

> It is not to be denied, that another mode is possible to God, viz. that God could effect that the Body of Christ should be in the Sacrament, the substance of bread remaining. For all

hold that God can do whatever does not imply a contradiction. But, that the Body of Christ should be in this Sacrament, without conversion of the substance of the bread into Itself, no more implies a contradiction, than that it should be in the Sacrament, the conversion having taken place. As then one is possible, so is the other.[3]

Here, for his different purposes, Durandus makes the same supposition as did Nielsen, Mackie, and Flew: whatever can be stated without evident contradiction is a genuine possibility. Even on matters that far transcend our understanding, if we manage to put words together that conceivably might state a possibility, that suffices: it is a possibility.

It is easy to see how this impression might arise. We have had the experience of envisaging things—submarines, flying machines, hydrogen bombs, etc.—without seeing whether or how they are possible, and then discovering both that they are possible and how they are possible. However, outside of mathematical examples such as that of trisecting an angle with just ruler and compass, there are no equally well-known examples of our having envisaged things, then finding that they are *not* possible. Neither, to be sure, have we ever had the experience of envisaging something, without evident contradiction, then finding it to be not just physically but metaphysically impossible—impossible even for an omniscient, omnipotent God. Consequently, when asked for some illustration of what it would be like for a nonmathematical hypothesis that made sense to nonetheless state such an impossibility, we can offer no example. The hypothesis of such a meaningful impossibility may therefore seem vacuous. What would it be like?! The answer: it would, necessarily, be like nothing we can envision. But to suppose that where we see no impossibility there must be possibility is a potent, plausible, but nonetheless unfounded form of rationalism.

A Methodological Necessity?

Though Richard Swinburne does not endorse this assumption of human omniscience concerning possibilities, he holds that we should accept it as at least a default setting in our thinking. Thus, discussing various forms of afterlife, he writes: "The fact that there seems (and to so many people) to be no contradiction hidden in these stories is good reason for supposing that there is no contradiction hidden in them—until a contradiction is revealed. If this were not a good reason for believing there to be no contradiction, we would have no good reason for believing any sentence at all to be free of hidden contradiction."[4] Unbeknown to us, "The milk is sour," "The jury was rigged," or "Easter is early this year" might state impossibilities!

Swinburne's all-or-nothing argument invites comparison with this one: "The fact that people see no snakes in high grass is a good reason for supposing that there are none hiding there. If we started to suspect their presence in high grass, we would have to suspect their presence everywhere—in the house, on the patio, and on the well-manicured lawn." Presented with such an argument, we could distinguish between seeing no snakes in the grass and seeing that there are no snakes in the grass; and we could then note that whereas we can see that there are no snakes on the patio and the lawn, we do not see that there are none in the high grass. Philosophical and theological discourse is high grass. Theological inquiry about Trinitarian processions, the self-emptying of the Word, transubstantiation, and the like, is very high grass indeed. There, many a contradiction—many a real-world impossibility—may lurk without our spotting it, or our being able to detect it if we tried.

It may therefore seem important to accept Swinburne's permissive principle, at least in theology, and to give theological utterances the benefit of the doubt. For, if theological discourse is all high grass and we can never be sure that any of our theological utterances state genuine possibilities, the consequences for theology may appear dire. From the frying pan we might seem to have landed in the fire: PRS may salvage the meaningfulness of theological statements but now, by extending sense far beyond our ken, it lands us in this new problem. Or so, as I say, it may seem. Yet, somehow, this impression does not appear realistic. Perusal of theological literature does not seem to back such a pessimistic assessment. Why is that? If the issue of genuine possibility does not appear all-pervasive in theology, no doubt one reason is that, as already indicated, the issue is so well hidden. However, reflection suggests that the issue does not surface for two further reasons: for much theologizing the issue is not directly relevant, and for much it is not directly problematic.

First, in many areas and types of theology—biblical, historical, liturgical, ascetical, mystical, pastoral, and other—the issue of possibility may seldom arise because attention is not focused directly on transcendent mysteries but, for example, on "the story of the great deeds of God in salvation history," on "the sum total of the problems posed by progress in the spiritual life,"[5] or on "the study of specific social structures and individual initiatives within which God's continuing work of renewal and restitution becomes manifest."[6] That is, the question of genuine possibility may not arise because, for various reasons, on various occasions, theologians have not chosen to explore the really high grass—God, Trinity, incarnation, redemption, revelation, etc.—so have not made or assessed assertions about the most transcendent realities.

Often, of course, they do. But then they generally have reasons for their assertions, and if their reasons are good ones they need not trouble about the assertions' stating possibilities. For truth implies possibility. If it is true that creatures elsewhere in the universe have observed mesons, then it is possible to observe mesons. If it is true that creatures elsewhere in the universe have harnessed nuclear fusion, then it is possible to harness nuclear fusion. Likewise, if it is true, for example, that Jesus is present in the Eucharist along with the bread and wine, or is present in the Eucharist without bread and wine, these, too, are possibilities. The question now, however, is what reason we have to suppose that these or similar hypotheses are true. So we come to the question of *inference*, which the next chapters will consider from a linguistic perspective. How does the fact that theological reflection is linguistic affect our ability to reach true conclusions in theology?

For Further Reflection

1. "Since God is omnipotent, so long as something is not proved repugnant from that very omnipotence of God, it is likely that it can be done by God"[7] (Francisco Suárez).

2. "Biel stood in a well-established tradition which included William of Ockham and Duns Scotus. Characteristic of this tradition was the well-known distinction between God's absolute power and His ordained power. By his absolute power God could do anything which does not violate the law of contradiction. He could have, for example, become incarnate in a rat or even a stone . . ."[8] (Timothy George).

3. "Would you create a world such as this one if you had the power and knowhow to create any logically possible world? If your answer is 'no,' as it seems it must be, then you should begin to understand why the evil of suffering and pain in this world is such a problem for anyone who thinks God created this world"[9] (James Cornman and Keith Lehrer).

4. "The general point I wish to make against restrictive theories of what is thinkable is this. Every concept that we

have contains potentially the idea of its own complement—the idea of what the concept doesn't apply to. Unless it has been shown positively that there cannot be such things—that the idea involves some kind of contradiction (like the idea of things that are not self-identical)—we are entitled to assume that it makes sense even if we can say nothing more about the members of the class, and have never met one"[10] (Thomas Nagel).

5. "So, if a statement is not a contradiction, then the situation it describes is at least logically possible and hence is such as can be brought about by God. But a moral statement such as 'theft is permissible' is not contradictory—even if it is false. Accordingly, if God is omnipotent then it must be possible for him to make it the case that theft is permissible without this being achieved by changing any other logically independent fact of the matter"[11] (John Haldane, on Ockham).

Chapter 9

Inference and Analogy

In the history of Western thought, emphasis long fell on deductive demonstration, which, as in mathematics, does not rely on experience. Given the premises, the conclusion follows ineluctably. With recognition of the limited value of such reasoning, emphasis shifted to inductive reasoning, which, as in the physical sciences, takes repeated experiences as its clue. However, important kinds of inference, generally accepted as sound, do not conform to either of these paradigmatic varieties, deductive or inductive. Thus, Newman memorably remarked:

> Let a person only call to mind the clear impression he has about matters of every day's occurrence, that this man is bent on a certain object, or that man was displeased, or another suspicious; or that that one is happy, and another unhappy; and how much depends in such impressions on manner, voice, accent, words uttered, silence instead of words, and all the many subtle symptoms which are felt by the mind, but cannot be contemplated; and let him consider how very poor an account he is able to give of his impression, if he avows it, and is called upon to justify it. This, indeed, is meant by what is called moral proof, in opposition to legal.[1]

At a more fundamental level, our belief in the past, say, or in physical bodies suggested by our senses, or in the existence of conscious minds other than our own is not grounded in either the mathematically deductive or the scientifically inductive manner.

In theology, inference of this third kind—neither strictly deductive nor scientifically inductive but too varied to be given any single name—is of primary significance. Of the two alternative possibilities, scientific induction, based on constant recurrences, clearly holds slight relevance. Christians do not base their belief in the Incarnation on past incarnations, in the Trinity on previous trinities, in salvation history on other such histories elsewhere in the universe, or the like. Thus, as Paul Avis notes,

> the analogy between physical science and theology breaks down when we consider the particular and indeed unique reference of theological statements. In theology we are concerned above all with a series of particular, unique and unrepeatable phenomena in which God reveals himself, the great symbols of "salvation history": creation, election, exodus; prophecy, priesthood and kingship; the Incarnation, ministry, passion and resurrection of Christ; the coming of the Holy Spirit, the mission of the church and—proleptically—the consummation of all things in Christ. Every doctrine of Christianity is tainted with "the scandal of particularity."[2]

Less obviously, so more importantly, deductive inference, too, has slight relevance in theology—certainly less than has often been supposed. The present chapter will consider language-related problems of a kind long recognized for such inference, and other kinds will appear in following chapters.

Problems from Analogy

Humphrey Palmer voices a traditional concern when he writes: "As arguments become doubtful if ambiguous it is necessary to limit each term in them to a single sense: which is done by listing, in a definition, those features that are necessary and sufficient for correct application of the term."[3] Since analogical uses of terms do not abide by this rule of strict univocity, or singleness of sense, Palmer concludes that analogy spoils inference. And since analogy pervades theology, the spoiling there is correspondingly pervasive. Indeed, Palmer concludes that "if properly thought through, the theory of analogy must be agnostic in effect. The result must be to abolish serious argumentative theology."[4]

To assess this challenge, we must distinguish between two ways in which "sameness of sense" might be required for valid argumentation. It might be necessary, either that terms retain the same sense—however vague, fluid, and heterogeneous—each time they occur in an argument, or it might be necessary that, in addition, the terms' sense be sharply delimited in the essentialistic way (stating "necessary and sufficient for correct application of the term") that Palmer's prescription suggests. Once this distinction is made, it becomes evident that the first requirement holds but the second does not. A simple argument, using Wittgenstein's sample term *game*, can illustrate this verdict.

> All games are activities.
> Poker is a game.
> Therefore poker is an activity.

This is a perfectly valid argument. The premises are true, and they connect rigorously with the conclusion, thanks to the term *game*, which, despite its fluid indefiniteness, retains the same sense in both premises. If everything, however varied, that can rightly be called a game is an activity, then, if poker qualifies as a game, it too is an activity.

How, then, does analogy threaten deductive inference in theology? A common misgiving goes like this. Words such as "love," "will," "know," "act," and "make," it is thought, have one sense when applied to humans and another, analogous sense when applied to God. For divine loving, willing, knowing, acting, making, and the like differ greatly from our own. Hence an argument that had one of these senses in one premise and the other in another premise would be invalid. Premise would not link with premise in the way required to warrant the conclusion. In possible illustration, consider this syllogism derived from Aquinas:

> Whatever can will, can love;
> But God can will;
> Therefore God can love.[5]

If "will" had a human sense in the first premise and a divine sense in the second, the argument would be invalid. However, it is therefore natural to suppose, as the principle of charity enjoins and the wording suggests, that the first premise has an inclusive sense, covering both human and divine willing, and that the second premise retains the same broad sense. So read, the argument is valid. Now, however, the first premise becomes more problematic than it already was. For, although it might perhaps be possible to infer the power to love in a human way from the power to will in a human way, how can it be known that any agent capable of willing even in some mysterious, nonhuman fashion can also love in some perhaps equally mysterious, nonhuman fashion? The problem that analogy here creates is for the truth of the premise, not for the connection between the premises and the conclusion.

The difficulty thus illustrated is not peculiar to theology. How could it be known that *every* being—God, angel, human, hominid, or fantastic inhabitant of some distant galaxy—capable of any sort of willing, is capable of some sort of loving? For reasons the next chapter will suggest, universal premises that are both informative and exceptionless are difficult to come by. Furthermore, once the universal premise in an argument like the one above is known, typically so too is the conclusion, without any need of the argument. The argument neither gives new knowledge nor formulates an inference by which knowledge of the conclusion was originally acquired. Rather than suggest the complex reasons for this general verdict, I will just note that this type of critique differs from the kind urged by Palmer (in terms of valid inference rather than premise truth) as by other critics of deductive reasoning in theology.

Within a PRS perspective, the problem for such reasoning looks different. Figuratively put, in the traditional viewpoint, univocity was the default setting for terms, with analogy the exception and no continuum of cases connecting univocal senses and analogous. For univocity was conceived in the essentialistic way Palmer's wording suggests. In a PRS perspective, diversity, not univocity, is the default setting—diversity so multiple and continuous that the distinction between univocal and analogous, literal and figurative, largely breaks down. The word *bank*, say, may have a "different sense" when applied to the bank of a river than when applied to the Bank of America, but does "game" have a different sense when applied to different members of the "family" Wittgenstein described: some with competition and some without, some with rules and some without, some with winning and some without, some with skill and some without, some with one player some with many, etc.? Does "chess" have a different sense when applied to people playing with a board and pieces, to people playing without board or pieces, to a human playing against a computer, to a computer competing with another computer? Where does one sense leave off and another begin? And why bother counting senses, when PRS allows a continuum of cases? With this shift to greater diversity and complexity, the problems for deductive inference become both more pervasive and more insidious. A fairly fully developed example can illustrate both consequences.[6]

A Paradigm: Eucharistic Inferences

"This is my body," says Jesus, "this is my blood." These words—pregnant, mysterious—sound as though they might identify one thing with another. And so they do in certain readings, but not in what became two chief understandings of the utterances, claiming between them a majority of Christian believers. According to the Catholic doctrine of transubstantiation as traditionally understood, the bread and wine cease to exist; so they are not identified with the body and blood of Christ. Neither are the appearances of bread and wine (which, in this view, are all that remains of the consecrated elements) identified with Christ's body and blood. The words' import, therefore, is this: "This bread and this wine which I hold in my hands cease to exist as I speak and become instead my body and blood." In what appears to be the foremost Protestant perception, the bread and wine do not cease to exist, but the "is" that might identify them with Jesus' body and blood should, for instance, be read: "This bread *represents* my body, this wine *represents* my blood." In neither position, then—the Catholic or the Protestant—is there any identification of one thing with another. Without passing judgment on either view in this dichotomy, it is instructive to consider the kind of reasoning that played a major role in creating the split between them.

Chapter 3 spoke of a simplifying conception of "is," or variants, and of the conception's profound effect on theme after theme of Christian theology. Time and again it is assumed, when not explicitly declared, that there is just one kind of identity, namely strict sameness: whatever holds for one term of an identity statement must hold for the other term; there can be no difference between them. In this assumption, an utterance that appears to state an identity either states a strict identity, of indiscernibility, or it states no identity at all but is merely figurative or metaphorical. When necessary, this default setting may be overridden, but with regard to the Eucharist, as with regard, say, to the Incarnation (see chapter 3), it has functioned powerfully through the centuries. Applied to Jesus' words at the Last Supper, it has yielded the split verdict just noted. For it is hardly conceivable that bread and wine might be strictly, indiscernibly identical with Jesus' body and blood, or vice versa; that possibility has typically (and rightly) been dismissed out of hand. But if the identity is not strict, then—given the supposition that true identity is always strict—the two terms of the relation are not identical at all. Hence, only two interpretive possibilities remain. Either one of the terms must be eliminated, leaving only the other, or the words must be taken as purely figurative. Transubstantiation exemplifies the first option (the bread and wine cease to exist and are replaced by Jesus' body and blood), whereas the popular Protestant position exemplifies the second.

On the Catholic side, in the ninth century, then especially the eleventh, and continuing strong through the Council of Trent and beyond, we encounter the sort of reasoning reflected in Karl Rahner's comment: "[I]f the words of consecration are to be taken in their strict and literal sense, and if they bring about the event of the presence of the body of Christ, then what Christ offers his Apostles is not bread, but his body. This statement, as it stands, must be accepted by all who refuse to give a vague, figurative meaning to the words of Christ."[7] Rahner would not write this way about the Incarnation. He would not speak of a "strict, literal" sense in which Jesus is divine or draw from it the conclusion that either Jesus' divinity precludes his humanity or his divinity is merely "figurative." But here, with regard to the Eucharist, he can and does argue in this "either-or fashion"—the one that a strict reading of "is" demands.

On the Protestant side, Zwingli's early view is representative. Zwingli, too, saw only two alternatives: either a "literal" reading of Jesus' words or a figurative one.[8] But the former option seemed clearly excluded. If the bread was "literally" Jesus' body, then the priest would not be able to lift it.[9] If the bread was "literally" Jesus' body, we could see his body—face, limbs, and all.[10] If the bread was "literally" Jesus' body, the priest would break that body, and communicants would chew it and tear it apart when they masticated the host.[11] Horrendous! Absurd! "All believers know very well that they do not eat the body of Christ in that way. Hence the very nature and truth of the matter will not allow us to take the words literally."[12] Thus, for Zwingli, a figurative reading follows inescapably, "for there is no alternative way of avoiding a figurative interpretation."[13] Such an alternative is ruled out by the underlying assumption that governed Zwingli's dialectic. What repeatedly created the impression of absurdity, we can discern, was his unquestioning assumption that the identity had to be strict. He left no room for analogy.

Luther did allow for analogy, as have others. And the slightest perusal of Jewish, Christian, and other theological discourse through the centuries—indeed of everyday discourse—suggests how baseless is the supposition that linking expressions such as "is," if not merely figurative, must be understood in terms of strict, indistinguishable identity. Musicians, for instance, play the "same" notes as composers hear in their minds and as they write with pen and ink in their scores. The notes the musicians play on pianos are the "same" as they play on violins, clarinets, harps, and other very different-sounding instruments. In no such instance (and there are many others) is the identity strict: the written notes are not indiscernibly identical with the imagined notes, or the played notes with the written notes, or the notes played on one instrument with those played on others. Yet the identity from note to note is not merely "figurative."

Now, how does all this illustrate the original suggestion that with the shift to a PRS perspective, of greater diversity and complexity, the problems for deductive inference become both more pervasive and more insidious than in the traditional perspective? Notice, first, that the reasoning critiqued is, in fact, deductive. On both sides of the Eucharistic debate, we find thinking of this form:

> If one thing is another (e.g., if Shakespeare is the author of *Macbeth*), they are indistinguishably alike.
> But the Eucharistic bread and wine and Jesus' body and blood are not indistinguishably alike.
> So the bread and wine are not the body and blood, as Jesus' words might suggest.

This denial of any identity requires either denying the continued presence of the bread and wine, as in the Catholic position, or denying the presence of the body and blood, as in the figurative Protestant position.

Essentialism of the kind expressed by the first premise of the argument ("If one thing is another, they are indistinguishably alike") is more strongly, widely challenged by PRS than by traditional discussions of analogy and inference. Whereas those discussions focused on a limited selection of analogous terms (e.g., *know, will, love, wise, good, power*, and the like), PRS covers the great majority of expressions, including the little word *is*. All can be extended, meaningfully and truly, according to the rule of relative similarity. Again, whereas the traditional discussions envisaged discrete senses of terms (often, just one literal sense and one analogous), PRS acknowledges far more varied, continuous, and numerous extensions of expressions, as in the case of *is*. A paragraph of theological samples in chapter 3 gave some slight indication of how variously this and similar expressions have been employed.

As our present example illustrates, the pervasiveness and complexity of PRS analogy also make it more insidious. It is easier to spot analogy for a few familiar types of expression than for all those to which PRS extends—especially if, as is usually the case, we are unaware of any PRS-type analysis of analogy or truth. Furthermore, it is easier to spot and take account of just a couple of discrete senses than of a PRS inkblot of applications—again, especially if we are unaware of PRS. Thus, for example, if *will* means one thing when applied to us and something significantly different when applied to God, then it is relatively clear that the term may not be given the first sense in one premise of an argument and the second sense in another premise. When, however, the legitimate applications of an expression, backed by PRS, are both more numerous and less discrete, we may less readily be aware of them and take them into account. Thus, when, for example, we read the words "This is my body," no simple set of alternative senses comes to mind, to warn us against a too simplistic reading of the text. We may therefore proceed as in the arguments cited and draw unwarranted conclusions, deductively.

Naturally, this is not the place to argue for or against any of the contending positions cited—pure symbolism at one extreme, transubstantiation at the other, or real presence without transubstantiation in between. In the present discussion, with its methodological focus, this Eucharistic example has served to illustrate the difficulty of deductive inference in theology and to indicate that the difficulty does in fact arise, importantly. The next two chapters will complement and confirm this initial critique. Further linguistic reasons will appear for the judgment that deductive inference has slight applicability in theology.

If I do not give equal time to the more important kinds of theological inference, that are neither deductive nor inductive, it is because I do not spot equally significant linguistic issues in their regard. Consider, for example, the "retroductive" arguments, neither deductive nor inductive, of which Francis Fiorenza writes: "Explanation and proof are often considered as distinct. However, 'in retroduction, the two are indissoluble. The hypothesis is confirmed or justified precisely to the extent that it is shown to have explanatory power.' "[14] In illustration, I recall some lectures attended long ago concerning the presence of Saint Peter in Rome, in which the professor cited more evidence for that supposition than I can now remember: a long tradition; passages from Revelation and Peter 1; the tomb, bones, and graffiti discovered under St. Peter's Basilica; the construction of the original basilica by Constantine; its location; the absence of any rival city claiming Peter as its own; and so forth. Each bit of evidence for Peter's presence in Rome was something his presence in Rome could explain. The hypothesis was confirmed precisely to the extent that it was shown to have explanatory power. Now, in this demonstration I spot no linguistic problems. Neither do I sense that special linguistic difficulties would surface in theological arguments of a similarly retroductive variety. Indeed, I suggest that a principle such as PRS lends support to certain forms of nondeductive inference, as follows.

Other things being equal, the more specific an argument's conclusion is, the less likely it is to be true, whereas the more broadly disjunctive and indefinite it is, the more likely it is to be true. Suppose, for example, that I infer from the amazing performance of an autistic savant that he is calculating. If by "calculating" I mean something just like what I do when I calculate, my conclusion has less likelihood of being true. If, instead, I allow for notable variations within PRS's range, my conclusion has more likelihood of being true. Having cast my net more broadly, I may have cast it widely enough. Similarly, if I infer from answers to prayers that God has experiences closely similar to the experiences I have when I hear and respond to others' requests, the conclusion has less likelihood of being true than if I allow for some transcendent analog within PRS's ample reach.

In comparison with strict deductive inference, it is less evident how, why, and to what extent such nondeductive inference is valid. And in the next chapters, additional language-related evidence will further support Bernard Lonergan's methodological observation: "Where before the step from premises to conclusions was brief, simple, and certain, today the steps from data to interpretation are long, arduous and, at best, probable."[15]

For Further Reflection

1. "Here it is necessary to repeat the conviction of the early Fathers of the Church: either Jesus is the Son of God in the strongest sense or he is only a creature. In such a domain there is no middle ground"[16] (Bernard Sesboüé).

2. "I designate that concept univocal which possesses sufficient unity in itself, so that to affirm and deny it of one and the same thing would be a contradiction. It also has sufficient unity to serve as the middle term of a syllogism, so that wherever two extremes are united by a middle term that is one in this way, we may conclude to the union of the two extremes among themselves"[17] (Duns Scotus).

3. "The statement 'God is always with his children,' for example, when interpreted in context, entails the factual claim that 'An invisible, eternal, omnipresent, omniscient spirit exists and somehow communes with and guides those who place their trust in him"[18] (Michael Peterson and others).

4. "Although it seems illogical to attribute birth to God, who according to most theological definitions has no beginning and cannot experience any process of becoming, if Jesus

is fully God, then when Jesus is born, logic requires us to say that God is born and to be willing to call Mary, his mother, the 'God-bearing one' "[19] (Harold Brown).

5. "Finally, there are trains of reasoning whose object is to discover, by a process of deduction and, in principle, of demonstration, a middle term for the better understanding of the revealed datum. This may start from a definition and lead to a necessary property (for example, the Eucharist is a sacrament, therefore it must include a perceptible matter) or it may arrive at a definition by starting from an article of faith (for example, at a definition of 'person' which, by modifying the philosopher's definition, would satisfy our faith in the Father, the Son and the Holy Ghost)"[20] (M. D. Chenu).

6. "Traditionally, it has been held that Christ's humanity, the humanity of the incarnate Son of God, was like ours in all respects save that of sin. Christ was certainly subject to temptation. But, being who he was, he could not possibly have succumbed. For God is necessarily good and if Christ was God incarnate, then it follows not only that he did not sin, but that he could not have sinned. Sinlessness was, and is, a necessary property of the incarnate one"[21] (Brian Hebblethwaite).

Chapter 10

Universal Claims (Factual)

"What then is truth?" asked Friedrich Nietzsche. "A mobile army of metaphors, metonyms, and anthropomorphisms," he replied, "—in short, a sum of human relations, which have been enhanced, transposed, and embellished poetically and rhetorically, and which after long use seem firm, canonical, and obligatory to a people."[1] One may wonder at such a sweeping claim. Are none of the items in the morning paper veridical? Are none of Nietzsche's own statements true? What about the one just quoted? Doubtless Nietzsche would have dismissed such cavils: large truths should be stated boldly. Or perhaps, more radically: the false god of truth should no longer hold sway. But in that case, what new deity should replace it?

In this study, I have assumed an interest in truth. Although not all theologians share that commitment, I think most still do, and should. When rightly understood, truth can be recognized as irreplaceable, indispensable. The present chapter will therefore focus on the less radical issue: granted an interest in truth, should theologians indulge, as they frequently do, in bold statements similar to Nietzsche's? Repeatedly, the Principle of Relative Similarity would declare such statements false, and repeatedly one has the impression that no such principle has been consulted but should have been, for effective communication. Yet, surely, on occasion there is place for the bold statement, the sweeping generalization—precisely for the sake of more effective communication? This I grant, with reservations, but theologians' universal claims are often motivated by something other than a desire for successful communication.

The Appeal of Universality

By "universal" claims I mean broad, definite assertions excluding all exceptions. Statements employing "all," "always," "every," and the like qualify, as do those employing "no," "none," "never," and the like. The term *only* may also be included since, although it makes no claim about every member of the indicated class, excluding or including it, it does exclude all nonmembers. Thus, the Council of Florence, for example, might have asserted, equivalently, that *only* those inside the church could be saved instead of declaring, as it did, that *no one* outside the church could be saved.

As one attraction of such assertions the last chapter suggested their role as universal premises permitting valid deductive inference. From "*Some* people are sinners" it is not possible to infer "*I* am a sinner." From "*Most* people are offered forgiveness" it is not possible to infer "*Judas* was offered forgiveness." "All," "none," "never," "only," "always"—such are the words that valid deduction typically has need of; "some," "most," "usually," "typically," "seldom," or the like do not suffice.

Universal claims also enjoy greater prestige than limited, particular assertions. "All" or "only" statements may rate as "theses" or "theories," whereas mere assertions of what is "usually," "often," or "seldom" the case do not merit such recognition. Galileo did not say that the Earth *usually* revolves around the sun. Newton did not claim that *most* bodies attract one another. Chemists have not maintained that water *typically* is H_2O. I cite scientific examples because in our time scientific thinking powerfully affects that in other areas, including theology to some extent (recall quotations in chapter 1 concerning the "scientific" conduct of theology).

However, more than the deductive utility or theoretical prestige of universal assertions accounts for their appeal. The great attraction of such claims is precisely their universality. "Most" and "usually" have considerable breadth, but "all" and "always" have more. "Most" and "usually" introduce some order into the chaos of varied individual cases, but "all" and "always" introduce more. They and their kin ("none," "never," "only," etc.) are, in addition, more definite and precise. They include all or exclude all, whereas "most," "usually," "often," and the like leave indefinite the status of any individual member of the class named. And natural science has no monopoly on the desire for such precision and such comprehensive grasp. Both are values. Both attract theologians as well as philosophers, scientists, and others.

Language has played a subtle but powerful role in making universal claims look feasible as well as attractive. In ways chapter 3 noted, general terms for a class of things suggest essences shared by all and only members of that class. Thus, general terms being basic components of language, the essences which they suggest seem basic components of reality. Life is one thing, humanity is one thing, truth is one thing, faith is one thing, and so forth. Since each is a single, invariant reality, it appears that it should be possible to make universal assertions about it. If, for instance, rational animality is the essence of human nature, then *all* humans share that essence, *every* human shares it, *only* humans share it, *no* nonhumans share it, and so forth. Recognition that, on the contrary, reality does not so neatly parallel language, term by single term,[2] makes the terms' use in accurate universal claims look less feasible. However, such recognition, regarding general terms and their referents, is still far from universal.

These varied observations help to explain why the urge to universalize, being widespread, frequently challenges language's claims as a co-determinant of truth and why, being strong, the universalizing tendency so often prevails. It will be helpful, now, to become more specific and to illustrate how, why, and with what consequences universal claims repeatedly clash with the authority of language. Since the conflict looks different for factual and for moral assertions, we will consider the two kinds separately—the factual here and the moral in the next chapter.

Factual Claims

"It must be remembered," observed Samuel Johnson in one edition of his famed *Dictionary of the English Language*, "that while our language is yet living, and variable by the caprice of everyone that speaks it . . . words are hourly shifting their relations, and can no more be ascertained in a dictionary than a grove, in the agitation of a storm, can be accurately delineated from its picture in the water."[3] Living, shifting, variable—if such is the "established use" of words, and if true utterances must typically take such use into account, then trenchant generalizations of the kind philosophers and theologians often indulge in face problems—problems of validity and utility, problems of the kind that prompted Wittgenstein to remark: "If one tried to advance *theses* in philosophy, it would never be possible to debate them, because everyone would agree to them."[4]

This assertion itself sounds like a thesis. What, then, did Wittgenstein have in mind? In simple illustration, consider games. If, as previously noted, the familiar use of the word *game* reveals no essence, and if, as in chapter 4, the pertinence of usage for truth is recognized, one will advance no thesis asserting an essence of games. Blocked in this direction, one may attempt to state at least sufficient or necessary conditions for something's being a game. Sufficient conditions look easy: to qualify as a game it suffices, for example, that an activity be poker or football. Whatever is poker or football is ipso facto a game. No one will disagree with that; neither, however, will anyone think it worthwhile to propose such an obvious "thesis." What, then, of necessary conditions? To be a game, one might suggest, an activity must have competition, or winning and losing. But then Wittgenstein cites patience (solitaire), that has neither winning nor losing and which, nonetheless, we call a game. Such is usage. So one resorts, perhaps, to "conducted by people" as a necessary feature of games—only to recall the "games" played by otters or computers. Again, such is usage. Well, then, mustn't games at least be *activities*? To be sure, but once all doubt disappears and everyone agrees, what is the point of advancing such a "thesis"?

This jejune example illustrates the following general situation. The borders traced by linguistic usage for any class of things concerning which philosophers or theologians might wish to generalize are as fuzzy, vague, and irregular as clouds in the sky. The only way, therefore, to make safe "all" or "only" claims about such classes while taking usage into account is to stay well inside or outside those borders. (All games, for example, fall safely well within the border of "activities," all thermometers fall safely well outside them.) But the very sureness of such claims deprives them of interest. (Everyone knows that games are activities and that thermometers are not.) A dilemma therefore results: on the one hand, the more interesting abstract generalizations are, the less likely they are to satisfy the linguistic test of truth; on the other hand, the more surely they satisfy that test, the less likely they are to hold theoretical interest.

Thus, for inclusive terms such as "all," "always," and "every," consider the last chapter's Eucharistic example. The inference from "This is my body" to "The bread no longer exists" would require some such premise as, "The relationship expressed in English by 'is' and in other languages by equivalent expressions is *always* one of strict identity." Though impressive, this thesis would clearly be false. The three different uses of "is" that Wittgenstein cited are a mere sampling of the term's diversity. On the other hand, "The relationship expressed in English by 'is' and in other languages by equivalent expressions is *sometimes* one of strict identity," though safely true, would be a mere commonplace, known to everyone, and would have no evident theoretical interest. It could not serve, for instance, as a premise in arguments such as we have seen, either for transubstantiation, on the one hand, or for a purely figurative reading of Jesus' Eucharistic words, on the other.

With regard to restrictive terms ("only," "never," "none," etc.), consider Ebeling's claim in chapter 6: "The one thing that is true is love." This, too, sounds impressive, yet it fails the test of established word use still more evidently. Statements, propositions, theories, theses, beliefs, and so forth may all be true. And although, among its varied applications, the word *true* is sometimes applied to love (as in "true love"), this use holds only slight philosophical or theological interest and surely did not motivate Ebeling's pronouncement.

This quick critique may elicit misgivings. Readers may wonder whether Ebeling, despite his apparent disregard for established linguistic usage, was not saying something important and worthy of more careful consideration. Perhaps, for all its literal falsity, his assertion expressed some hidden truth. If so, PRS might not be an entirely reliable guide to acceptable predication. So let us consider what valid message Ebeling might convey by saying that the only thing true is love. Would he be denying that statements, propositions, beliefs, doctrines, teachings, and the like are true? Probably not. But in some deeper sense, he might suggest, only love is true. In what sense, then? If he means that love is, for instance, more precious or important than any of the things customarily called true, why not say that, more intelligibly? If he means something else, what is it? The Principle of Relative Similarity is for successful communication, and by ignoring it Ebeling failed to communicate.

This example, though extreme, illustrates a general fact about theological discourse. In theology more often than in less speculative disciplines, the problem for universal claims lies with language, rather than with the reality described. Thus if, for example, someone asserts that all swans are white, doubtless her knowledge of swans is at fault (she doesn't know about the black swans in Tasmania), not her command or use of the English language. If, in 1898, someone claims that there are only ninety-three chemical elements, language is not his problem; he just needs to wait a few months for the discovery of radium. It is not so, however, for most faulty theological generalizations. Ebeling, for example, was not unaware of the things we call true—weather reports, scientific theories, theological explanations, etc.—when he asserted that only love is true. His problem, it appears, was his lack of interest in language and its authority. The very idea that language possesses any "authority" might have mystified him. He was, after all, a theologian, not a lexicographer.

In conclusion, reflect now on the preceding paragraph. It speaks of a "general fact about theological discourse." "In theology," it says, "more often than in less speculative disciplines, the problem for universal claims lies with language rather than with the reality described." Thus, it makes a general, though not universal, claim and thereby suggests the possible validity and utility of such broad assertions. Chapter 2's still stronger thesis, concerning the nonequivalence of nonlinguistic thoughts with linguistic, suggests that, as in this instance, significant generalizations may admit so few exceptions as to make little difference. The present comments, then, are not meant to veto attempts at factual generalization. They are intended to improve the ratio of successful generalization to unsuccessful by calling attention to the linguistic conditions of success. The like holds for the next chapter's remarks about moral generalizations.

For Further Reflection

1. "We must insist that no matter how environments differ human nature is, always has been, and always will be the same everywhere"[5] (Robert Hutchins).

2. "What then is the specific nature of the religious phenomenon? All religion is based on the recognition of a superhuman Reality of which man is somehow conscious and towards which he must in some way orientate his life. The existence of the tremendous transcendent reality that we name GOD is the foundation of all religion in all ages and among all peoples"[6] (Christopher Dawson).

3. "There is so much talk today about temporary commitment. There is no such thing. Long-term commitment is the only kind of commitment that is possible. I think it is nice that people make a pledge to work with things like the Jesuit Volunteer Corps for a year, but I wouldn't call that commitment. To me a commitment is like marriage. A man doesn't commit himself to a woman for the next three months or two years. A marriage commitment has to be total and permanent"[7] (Charles Gallagher).

4. "[W]e have already charged that all, both Jews and Greeks, are under the power of sin, as it is written:

    'There is no one who is righteous, not even one;
    there is no one who has understanding,
    there is no one who seeks God.
    All have turned aside, together they have become
       worthless;
    there is no one who shows kindness,
    there is not even one'" (Rom. 3:9–12).

Chapter 11

Universal Claims (Moral)

Language, the last chapter suggested, has played a subtle but powerful role in making universal claims look feasible as well as attractive. The relative uniformity, in sound or shape, of individual words in their repeated occurrences ("blue" resembling "blue," "game" resembling "game," etc.) suggests similar uniformity in what the words represent. There thus arises the conception Wittgenstein referred to: "proposition, language, thought, world, stand in line one behind the other, each equivalent to each."[1] Therewith, universal claims, marching in parallel with reality, appear both more feasible and more significant than they otherwise would. Now, what holds for descriptive terms ("blue," "game," "language," etc.) holds also for moral expressions ("right," "wrong," "just," etc.)—with, however, this difference, that reflection on these expressions reveals extra dimensions of diversity and complexity hiding beneath the relative uniformity and simplicity of the written or spoken words.

Discussion of moral meanings has taken a dialectical path. Ethicists long tended to view moral assertions as statements much like those in other areas, but just differing in their content. As there are historical statements, scientific statements, philosophical statements, theological statements, so there are ethical statements. They too are factual, they too are descriptive. All are on a par. Reacting to this assimilation, with its one-sided emphasis on the cognitive aspect of ethical utterances, thinkers such as A. J. Ayer and Rudolf Carnap swung to the opposite extreme: moral statements, they maintained, are veiled cheers or jeers (mere expressions of favorable or unfavorable feeling) or camouflaged commands. Subsequently, philosophical opinion has shifted back toward fuller recognition of the descriptive aspect, while retaining the element of truth in these noncognitive accounts. Moral expressions may not be purely emotive or act-inducing, but they are that too. More typically than "red" or "rough" or "perpendicular," words such as "right" and "wrong" express the feelings and attitudes of those who utter them. More characteristically than such descriptive terms, they serve to evoke kindred sentiments in those addressed. More frequently, again, they function to elicit or curb behavior (either having that effect, or being intended to, or both). Their meanings, we might say, are multidimensional: not just descriptive or cognitive but emotive and dynamic as well.

Even the cognitive aspect of moral expressions is more varied and complex than that of strictly descriptive expressions. Whereas there is relatively little disagreement about what features warrant describing an action as "walking" or "talking," there is far greater disagreement about what features warrant describing an action as "right" or "wrong." Theory vies with theory and popular conception with popular conception. Thus, applying to moral utterances the PRS test of agreement with "established word uses," were we to equate these uses with standard, language-wide descriptive criteria, we might conclude that such utterances are neither true nor false. The standards of rationality that govern moral discourse lie at a deeper, less readily accessible level.[2] It is understandable, therefore, why the impression should arise that "nothing is right or wrong but thinking makes it so."

This quick thumbnail sketch suggests why universal moral claims, differing so importantly from factual, need to be considered separately, and why, given this added complexity, attention to the linguistic aspect of such claims is, if anything, still more necessary.

Moral Claims

Like their factual counterparts, universal moral claims enjoy greater prestige than limited, particular moral assertions. They cover more cases. However, there is more than this to their appeal. To declare, for example, that lying is invariably wrong conveys an impression of uncompromising moral integrity. No hedging, dodging, or compromising: lying is wrong! To suggest, on the contrary, that lying may sometimes be permissible—indeed, that the lie one is contemplating may be legitimate—may easily convey the opposite impression, of rationalization, accommodation, or moral laxity. Valid or invalid, there is no mystery about the source of this impression. Even on the supposition that lying is not always wrong, if "lying" is the name for a class of actions the great majority of which are wrong, it is natural that approval of such an action—a "lie"—should appear suspect. With subtle power, the general norm suggests an absolute, exceptionless norm. We shall return to this point in a moment.

Again like their factual counterparts, universal moral claims look attractive for their role in deductive reasoning. Such claims can serve as premises in practical inferences: if actions of a given description are always right and a specified action fits the description, the action is right; if actions of a given description are always wrong and a specified action fits the description, the action is wrong. Our duty is clear. However, given the complexity of moral expressions, we may here be duped. To assess the merits of such ethical inferences it is frequently necessary to take a closer look and ascertain whether the descriptive expression in the universal premise is morally committed or morally neutral. Murder, for instance, is wrong by definition, whereas killing a human being is not.

This distinction between morally committed and morally neutral expressions has both epistemological and practical importance. Epistemologically, with respect to assessment of a statement's truth, there is no point in trying to spot exceptions to the claim "Murder is always wrong," whereas it makes good sense to consider whether there are exceptions to the claim "Intentionally killing a human being is always wrong." In the former assertion, the term *murder* already conveys a moral verdict; in the latter, the phrase "intentionally killing a human being" does not. Practically, for moral guidance, from the claim "Murder is always wrong," no inference can be drawn to the wrongness of any specific act of killing (in order to qualify as murder, the act's wrongness would already have to be known), whereas from "Intentionally killing a human being is always wrong" an inference can be made to the wrongness of any action (e.g., in war or self-defense) that satisfies that description. Though problems now arise for the truth of the premise, the inference is valid. The conclusion follows from the premises.

I imagine that the difference between "murder" and "intentionally killing a human being" is sufficiently clear. The latter characterization is morally neutral, the former is not. Often, however, the difference is not so evident, and epistemological and practical confusion may therefore result. A treatment of organ transplants can illustrate the danger. "Are these transplantings permitted by the moral law?" asked the 1962 *Dictionary of Moral Theology*, then replied: "The larger number of moral theologians hold a negative opinion. According to them, the removal of organs or parts of organs from a healthy man is unlawful, because it would involve mutilation (*q.v.*) of a living individual, which is unlawful."[3] Consulting the *q.v.* cross-reference, we find: "An action by which one deprives himself or another of a bodily organ or its use is called mutilation."[4] Though the word *deprives* has a negative sound (as indeed it should, since such a loss is unfortunate), this definition seems morally neutral; for it applies to many a surgical intervention that the dictionary's authors would doubtless accept as legitimate. How, then, do they pass from the morally neutral premise that organ transplants are mutilation to the conclusion that they are illicit? They may not have noticed that the term *deprive*, though negative, warrants no moral verdict by itself; or they may not have noticed that the term *mutilation* typically does express such a verdict and therefore may require a stronger, less ambiguous definition than the one just cited. The term is not applied to the removal of diseased organs for the health of patients but, for instance, to genital cutting, the punishment of Saudi Arabian thieves by cutting off their hands, Van Gogh's slicing off his ear, and the like. Thus, though it may be permissible to remove a diseased lung or gall bladder, surely you should never *mutilate* yourself or another!

For a clearer view of this and other examples, we can consider the cluster of terms to which "mutilation" belongs. Words such as "mutilate," "cheat," "lie," "robbery," "theft," and "adultery" exemplify the following treacherous configuration:

1. The term is a handier label than a full, neutral expression. It is easier, for example, to call a given action a lie than to call it an intentional telling of an untruth.

2. Most actions so labeled—for instance, most lies—are considered wrong.

3. To apply the label to an action therefore suggests that the action is wrong. The word acquires this moral connotation.

4. This being a characteristic feature of the word's use, its semantic status is unclear: is the negative verdict merely "connotation" or part of the word's meaning? How much is "meaning" and how much is mere "connotation"?

5. It is therefore unclear whether a universal statement such as "Lying is always wrong" is true by definition or whether, if true, it is so for some substantive, nonverbal reason.

6. This unclarity is not readily resolved. It may be clear, for example, that a word such as "murder" is not neutral. But "lie," "cheat," "rob," and the like are trickier; there is no general agreement about what belongs to the meaning of the word and what does not.

7. If not resolved, this semantic unclarity can muddy the moral waters. The negative-sounding label attached to an action—for instance, "lying"—may suggest not only that the action so labeled is always wrong, but that it is wrong regardless of the consequences and so must be "intrinsically evil."

8. Those who, focusing on substantive moral issues, attend little to words may not notice the problem occasioned by the loaded term, much less deal with it effectively (e.g., by avoiding that word, replacing it with a purely descriptive expression, or giving it an explicitly neutral or non-neutral definition).

The pertinence of these remarks can be sensed from a passage such as the following from the papal encyclical *Veritatis splendor*: "In teaching the existence of intrinsically evil acts, the Church accepts the teaching of Sacred Scripture. The Apostle Paul emphatically states: 'Do not be deceived: neither the immoral, nor idolaters, nor adulterers, nor sexual perverts, nor thieves, nor the greedy, nor drunkards, nor revilers, nor robbers will inherit the Kingdom of God' (1 Cor 6:9–10)."[5] In this catalog of wrongdoers, the "immoral" are bad by definition. So too, no doubt, are the "greedy." Thus, it is safe to assert, "One should never be immoral," and, "One should never be greedy." However, neither "immorality" nor "greed" being the name of an action, these prohibitions pinpoint no specific form of immoral behavior. The terms *thief* and *robber*, like their Greek counterparts in 1 Corinthians, are more action-specific; but are they purely descriptive or are they value-loaded? Can one reason from the epistle's condemnation of robbers and thieves to the condemnation of every action depriving others of their lawful property? Aquinas, for one, thought not. The father in desperate need of food for his family may lift a loaf or two. In general, it seems risky to pass from any one of Paul's negative characterizations of persons to a neutral description of a specific action and to conclude, on the strength of his censure, that every such action is wrong without exception, regardless of consequences or circumstances, and therefore qualifies as intrinsically evil.

Such an inference would require close attention not only to the Apostle's words but also to the problematic expression "intrinsically evil."[6] This characterization of an action may arise in significantly different ways, that deserve consideration here, since all of them can beget universal moral claims. An action might be characterized as intrinsically evil:

1. because the term used to name the action (e.g., "murder") makes it wrong by definition;
2. because, in addition to the type of behavior, the term indicates the subjective attitude or intention of the agent (e.g., a "blasphemer" does not simply say certain words, an "idolater" does not simply perform certain actions);
3. because the action is so named or identified that it takes in consequences that make it "intrinsically" evil (e.g., though it may not be wrong to pull a trigger, fire a pistol, or hit one's target, it may be wrong to shoot a human being);
4. because, though the action is so identified as to take in consequences, something besides the consequences accounts for the action's condemnation (e.g., killing an *innocent* human being);
5. because the consequence included in the characterization of the action (e.g., the pain or mental anguish inflicted by torture) is taken to exclude any justifying circumstances or consequences;
6. because the action, being wrong, is not justified by any good consequences or intentions. Thus Augustine writes: "Those things which are clearly sins ought not to be done under any pretext of a good reason, for any possible good end, with any seemingly good intention."[7] This holds, of course, for all wrong actions—including those made wrong precisely by their consequences. Calling them all "intrinsically evil" would obscure this possibility.

The complexity of this listing highlights its necessity. It is easy to lose one's way in this maze and to draw unwarranted conclusions about what actions are wrong, or are always wrong, or conflict with Christian tradition, and, accordingly, about what moral theories are faithful to that tradition.

For Further Reflection

1. "There are actions which are right or wrong intrinsically and of their nature, so independently of any external precept. . . . Such, for example, are all acts which help a

man toward his final end, as the love of God, or which withdraw him from it, as hatred, contempt of God, blasphemy, etc."[8] (Viktor Cathrein).

2. "It is the express command of God that we take no human life. On this point his command is quite explicit. Nor do either wording or context of 'Though shall not kill!' allow of exceptions. Euthanasia, however, is the deliberate killing of a human being. Consequently, it is a deliberate transgression of an explicit command by God"[9] (Eike-Henner Kluge; not Kluge's own position).

3. "No discussion of this question however incomplete can neglect the argument that the atomic bombs were used to bring about a quicker surrender of the Japs and thereby in the end save lives. The plea is specious but unethical. The end does not justify the means. It is not permissible to do evil that good may come" (Editorial Comment, *The Catholic World*, Sept. 1945, 451).

4. "For it has been characteristic of that [Hebrew-Christian] ethic to teach that there are certain things forbidden whatever *consequences* threaten, such as: choosing to kill the innocent for any purpose, however good; vicarious punishment; treachery (by which I mean obtaining a man's confidence in a grave matter by promises of trustworthy friendship and then betraying him to his enemies); idolatry; sodomy; adultery; making a false profession of faith. The prohibition of certain things simply in virtue of their description as such-and-such identifiable kinds of action, regardless of any further consequences, is certainly not the whole of the Hebrew-Christian ethic; but it is a noteworthy feature of it."[10] (G. E. M. Anscombe).

Chapter 12

Privileged Senses

With his characteristic wit, style, and good humor, plus a slight edge, the philosopher Peter Geach recounts:

> After a lecture I gave to first-year students at Leeds, an overseas student gravely rebuked me: "Professor, in your lecture you spoke of perfect circles. That was very wrong: only God is perfect." I could not help remembering, though I was too kind to say, that in English (and in several other European languages) the adjective for "perfect" is often attached to the noun for "imbecile" or "idiot."[1]

One senses that Geach was right to take lightly this innocent bit of essentialistic dogmatism. It reveals kinship, though, with solemn pronouncements of eminent theologians. In similar fashion Karl Barth, for example, declared: "God is known by God and by God alone."[2] Still more trenchantly he insisted: "At this very point the truth breaks imperiously and decisively before us: God is known only by God; God can be known only by God."[3] Not by humans, hominoids, or angels. By God alone. Yet elsewhere Barth wrote, for instance: "We are now speaking of the revelation of this event on high and therefore of our participation in it. We are speaking of the human knowledge of God on the basis of this revelation and therefore of an event which formally and technically cannot be distinguished from what we call knowledge in other connexions, from human cognition."[4] Only God knows God, yet we too "have knowledge of God." If this apparent contradiction were brought to Barth's attention, he might reply that he was speaking of what we can know about God on our own. Or perhaps he would explain that in one place he was speaking strictly and properly, in the other place loosely and improperly. Strictly speaking, only God knows God. Or, as Hick (speaking of the Scholastic tradition) has put it, "only God knows, loves, and is righteous and wise in the full and proper sense."[5]

This exegetical surmise is made plausible by the frequency with which theologians, in particular, speak this way. Expressions such as "strict," "proper," "primary," "true," "authentic," "genuine," "essential," and "literal" sprinkle theological discourse, privileging certain applications of terms over others. In the "strict," "literal," "proper," "primary" sense of the word, faith is only this, revelation is only that, grace is only this other, and so forth. With advertising techniques in mind, one might suggest that theologians often indulge in theological "puffery." If they said simply that in one sense of the term, or in one of its varied applications, faith is this, revelation is that, and the like, it would sound much less impressive. Although this unflattering surmise may contain a grain of truth, there is more to this widespread feature of theological linguistic practice than shady salesmanship.

It can be viewed, for example, as a more circumspect version of the generalizing tendency examined in the last two chapters. There Ebeling, for example, touting his privileged paradigm, declared: "The one thing that is true is love." To this we might object, "What about true beliefs, statements, or propositions?" In reply, rather than simply deny that these, too, may be true (which would be a hard saying), Ebeling might explain that in the original, primary, strict, proper, fundamental, or most profound sense of the term *true*, only love is true. And this he might suggest for reasons similar to those that motivated his actual, less qualified assertion. He might, for instance, aspire to a certain theoretical profundity, or to unity and clarity amid all the heterogeneous multiplicity of things called "true." More surely, one can sense that he wished thus to honor his favorite, that very special thing, love. Repeatedly, as here in Ebeling's assertion, in Barth's, and in that of Geach's student, we can spot an underlying value motivation. The Principle of Relative Similarity would suggest that other things besides God (e.g., "the precepts of the Lord") may be perfect in some way, that others besides God may have at least some minimal knowledge of God, and that other things besides love (e.g., beliefs or propositions) are true. But time and again, the desire to laud and glorify overrides PRS: only God is perfect, only God knows God, only love is true, and so forth.

This style of predication is so common in theology, and so linguistically problematic, that it merits attention in a work such as this, on language and method in theology. The sampling below can suggest the frequency of such talk and the variety of honorific labels employed in this manner. One way or another, to a greater or lesser degree, all the quoted sayings privilege certain paradigms over others. Readers familiar with theological literature may not have noticed how abundant and characteristic is this feature, but specimens such as the following should bring instant recognition:

> "primary" ("The primary referent of faith, then, is not some realm beyond the stars but is man's existence in the world")[6]
>
> "primarily" ("all agreed that revelation is primarily a personal dialogue or encounter rather than the communication of a body of truths")[7]
>
> "proper" ("The actual reality which occurs in Christian revelation is nothing and no other than Christ himself. He is revelation in the proper sense")[8]
>
> "real" ("The 'real symbol,' the full correct meaning of 'symbol,' is therefore a form that can be experienced by the senses and through which a higher transcendent reality announces itself as present and active")[9]
>
> "really" ("If God is triune in his nature, then really to know God means that we must know him in accordance with his triune nature from the start")[10]
>
> "true" ("It is only a pseudo-mysticism that is individualistic and introverted. The true mystic is the ecstatic, the person who has gone out from himself")[11]
>
> "truly" ("Only God is truly personal, truly free and responsible, whereas human beings are personal only by way of analogy to God's personhood")[12]
>
> "full" ("if we are to understand the healing mission of the physician, then we must see that mission in the light of the full and true notion of Healing as evidenced in the New Testament healing stories")[13]
>
> "strictly" ("Strictly speaking, it is not *sentences* that mean at all; we speak as if this were so, but this way of speaking is an ellipsis; actually it is *we* who mean various things by our sentences")[14]
>
> "authentic" ("It is enough simply to observe that a philosophy of religion that does not intend to be a mere description of the cultural phenomenon of religion, but that inquires about the truth and the nature of authentic religion as a whole, must at any rate come to the knowledge of the transcendent, absolute and personal God")[15]
>
> "as such" ("we might discuss in detail the meaning of 'truth' and 'falsity,' argue that as such truth belongs to the act of judgment [and not to propositional formulations], and

go on to elaborate the reasons and criteria for calling judgments true or false")[16]
- "ultimately" ("The only linkage of facts that is ultimately and intrinsically intelligible is one which is interpretable in terms of value")[17]
- "essentially" ("Religious faith, then, is not essentially a matter of belief, a claim regarding cognitive truth")[18]
- "par excellence" ("The mystery par excellence is not so much God in his essential nature, or the counsels of the divine mind, but rather God's plan of salvation as it comes to concrete realization in the person of Jesus Christ")[19]

Other expressions could be added to this list, and countless other quotations of this kind, privileging some preferred paradigm and doing so for reasons of interest, importance, significance, value, or the like. Besides this shared function and motivation, such examples typically have something else in common: in one way or another, to a greater or lesser degree, they are problematic.

Often, sayings such as those cited tend to denigrate alternative applications of terms which PRS would find acceptable. Thus, as in our sampling, instead of stating outright that only Jesus is revelation, they say that only he is revelation "in the proper sense." Instead of stating explicitly that only God is personal, they say that only God is "truly" personal. Instead of denying outright that statements or other utterances have meaning, they suggest that "strictly speaking" they do not. Yet there is nothing linguistically loose, second-rate, or reprehensible in saying, for example, that an utterance (and not just the speaker) meant this or that; that human beings (and not just God) are persons; that revelation occurred already in the Old Testament (and not just in Jesus); and the like. All this is briefly stated, and may sound dogmatic. So, for surer understanding of this widespread phenomenon, let us linger on a single sample, and experience something of its real-life complexity.

A Closer Look

In "The Concept of Mystery in Catholic Theology," Karl Rahner writes:

> [T]he Whither of an absolute transcendence of freedom, the nameless being which is at the disposal of none and disposes of all, which rules over transcendence by being loving freedom,

is uniquely and precisely that which we call 'holy' [*heilig*] in the strict and original sense [*im ursprünglichen und strengen Sinn*]. For how should one name the nameless, sovereign beloved, which relegates us to our finitude, except as "holy," and what could we call holy if not this? Or to what does the name "Holy" belong more primordially than to the infinite Whither of receptive love which before this incomprehensible and inexpressible being becomes trembling adoration?[20]

There is no mistaking the motivation of this passage. The name *holy* is drawn to the one supreme being as to a magnet. Honor where honor is due! But what, we may ask, does Rahner mean by asserting that the word applies to God "in the strict and original sense"? And what is the significance—in particular, what are the methodological implications—of this double assertion, of strictness and originality?

Let us start with the latter, originality. One sense of a word might precede another temporally: first the word has one sense, then, later on, it has the other. Or one sense might not only precede another in time but might originate the other; the second sense might derive from the first. Or one sense might not only derive from the other, historically, but might depend on the other in its current use. (For example, in order to know what makes a *letter* "friendly" you must know what makes a *person* "friendly.") This third sort of priority would have greater methodological significance than the first two (the temporal and the causal) and might be worth mentioning. However, it is far from evident that application of the word *holy* to places, rites, people, scriptures, and the rest does depend in this way on our understanding what the word means when applied to God, still less that the latter application precedes the others temporally or causally. Nor does Rahner suggest such a connection—temporal, causal, or conceptual. Indeed, he does not clarify for his readers what he means by saying that God is holy in the "original" sense of the word. So let us turn to his other privileging expression. In what sense does the word *holy* apply "*strictly*" only to God?

In this connection, think of circles. In the strict sense, it might be said, a circle is a plane curve everywhere equidistant from a given fixed point. Calling this the strict sense of the word might mean merely that it is a very restricted sense, excluding a great many things we call "circles," not that it is in any way superior to a looser, ampler sense of the term. The like might hold for Rahner's allusion to the strict sense of the word *holy*, for this sense, too, is very restricted, excluding the majority of the things we call holy (people, places, names, seasons, rites, etc.). However, there would be little point in indicating this obvious fact, which in no way privileges the narrower sense of the term or confers any distinction upon it. (One sense covers less, others cover more: so . . . ?) And such is clearly not Rahner's style of thinking, the style revealed for instance in his kindred remarks about the "true and perfect" sense of the word *mystery*.

Here, particularly suggestive are his comments on experiencing the divine mystery. In such experience, writes Rahner,

> the concept of mystery receives a new content, which does not contradict the standard notion but becomes for the first time authentic and primordial. It is no longer the limitation of a knowledge which should by right be perspicuous. It is an intrinsic constituent of the very notion of knowledge, and the old, traditional criterion of mystery is basically reduced to a defective mode of a knowledge which is essentially orientated to the mystery as such.[21]

Notice the parallel between Rahner's characterization of one concept of mystery as "authentic and primordial" and his characterization of one sense of the word *holy* as "strict and original." And notice how similarly Karl Barth expresses himself on another topic. "What," asks Barth, "does temptation originally and properly mean? Not something that we can know and experience in ourselves, and can therefore fashion for ourselves."[22] The parallelism starts to look intriguing: Rahner speaks of the "strict and original" sense of the word *holy* and of the "authentic and primordial" concept of mystery, while Barth speaks of what temptation "originally and properly" means. In this sampling "strict," "authentic," and "properly" go together, suggesting some kind of normativity, while "original," "primordial," and "originally" go together, suggesting some kind of priority. This repeated linking of the normative and the prior makes one wonder: In these authors' view, is an "original," "primordial" sense or concept, as here understood, automatically a preferable, superior one?

This query might lead us into still murkier depths; for far in the background there looms the figure of Immanuel Kant, whose similar, perhaps influential claims pose similar problems of interpretation. In a methodologically crucial but little-studied section of his *Critique of Pure Reason*, Kant wrote:

> Yet, before closing these introductory remarks, I beseech those who have the interests of philosophy at heart (which is more than is the case with most people) that, if they find

themselves convinced by these and the following considerations, they be careful to preserve the expression "idea" in its original meaning, that it may not become one of those expressions which are commonly used to indicate any and every species of representation, in a happy-go-lucky confusion, to the consequent detriment of science.[23]

Here Kant, too, links conceptual normativity with conceptual priority, but his reasons are too unclear to cast any light on similar assertions by later thinkers such as Barth and Rahner. Scrutinizing this passage, this section of Kant's *Critique*, and related passages elsewhere in Kant's writings, I have not been able to discern a coherent interpretation of his remarks. Neither have I discovered any Kantian commentary that clarifies them. This is important for our linguistic, methodological concerns. In Kant's thought, as in that of like-minded theologians, the "original" senses of expressions vie with their currently established uses and override them; such a principle as PRS carries little weight. Without fuller light on the alleged originality and its claims, this challenge to PRS fails. Other things *are* holy, other things *are* mysteries, other things *are* temptation, other things *are* ideas—and not in some second-rate, unfortunate sense of the words *holy, mystery, temptation,* or *idea*.

Rahner, Barth, Kant—these are weighty names. So, before I continue, let me make a general observation about the many worthy thinkers whose thoughts I cite, often critically, in the course of this study. Of Wittgenstein, a friend wrote: "He revered the writings of St. Augustine. He told me he decided to begin his *Investigations* with a quotation from the latter's *Confessions,* not because he could not find the conception expressed in that quotation stated as well by other philosophers, but because the conception *must* be important if so great a mind held it."[24] So it is here. The stature of many whose thinking I question attests the importance of such thinking and the problems it exemplifies.

Guidelines

Emerging from the preceding discussion, readers may feel that I owe them an apology. What a morass! However, as noted, I wished to intimate at least something of the real-life complexity of an actual sampling. Many of the examples in the long listing above, I can now suggest, are similarly problematic, not only at first glance but on closer scrutiny; and they represent countless others. This abundance of examples and their difficulties explain the inclusion of the present chapter, on its seldom-treated topic. It should not be supposed, however, that the use of what I have termed privileging expressions ("strict," "proper," "genuine," "primary," etc.) is uniformly problematic or unfortunate.

It can be important, for example, to distinguish between the "primary" and "secondary" senses of an expression and to make clear what kind of primacy is intended: temporal, causal, statistical, conceptual, functional, or evaluative. One may note, for example, that the application of "true" to beliefs, opinions, and the like is parasitic on the term's application to statements, utterances, and the like. The linguistic use, I have argued fully elsewhere, is conceptually primary; the mental is secondary.[25] However, this does not entail that there is anything second-rate about mental truth, or that beliefs, opinions, and the rest are not "really" true. Indeed, the conceptual primacy of linguistic truth is perfectly compatible with the evaluative primacy of mental truth: it may be more important to believe what is true than to say it.

In theological discourse, occasionally some such clarification of a privileging term is offered, and occasionally no explicit clarification is needed. A passage from Avery Dulles illustrates the first possibility. "There is something of a consensus today," writes Dulles in *Models of the Church*, "that the innermost reality of the Church—the most important constituent of its being—is the divine self-gift."[26] Had Dulles spoken only of the Church's "innermost" reality, I might have added this term and this passage to my initial sampling. Without Dulles's elucidation, in terms of importance, "innermost" would not have clearly signaled that sense, any more than "proper," "true," "full," "authentic," and the like do in the sampling. With his added clarification, there is no problem, or at most a slight stylistic one. As with respect to other, similarly unperspicuous expressions used to privilege favored paradigms, one might question the need for the ambiguous term *innermost*, but, thanks to Dulles's addendum, the reader does know what he is saying. He is speaking, straightforwardly, about a claim of relative importance.

Often there is no need of such clarification, even of the brief kind Dulles provided. Thus, the following passage, for example, from O'Collins and Kendall's *The Bible for Theology*, seems sufficiently clear as it stands:

> Philosophy comes into play as well when reflecting on causal conditions and difficulties about the particular way the incarnation took place: through the virginal conception. Is it true that this belief is incompatible with a genuine incarnation: that is, with the assumption of a genuine humanity? Since human beings uniformly come into existence through the

agency of two human parents, a virginal conception would throw grave doubt on Christ's being truly human.[27]

"Genuine incarnation," "genuine humanity," "truly human"—these expressions sound familiar. However, there is no puffery here, no veiled expression of value preferences, no verbal sleight of hand. The words *authentic* and *truly* do not implicitly or surreptitiously contrast a better incarnation with an inferior kind or a superior humanity with a lesser variety. Rather, they contrast an incarnation with something that is not and a humanity with something that is not. The term *incarnation* is rightly applied to one, the term *humanity* to the other. Both applications result in true statements. Such, it seems, is the unproblematic thrust of the quoted passage. Here, too, we have a good idea what is being said.

Such examples make clear that a veto on words such as "genuine," "true," "strict," "proper," "primary," and "authentic" is not called for. The words' sense just needs to be made clearer than it often is. More fully, this chapter's illustrations suggest the following guidelines:

1. Be slow to use such privileging expressions. Be sure you know what you mean by them, and why, if that is what you mean, it needs saying.

2. If the expressions serve simply to praise or honor preferred paradigms, replace them with more clearly evaluative expressions—if there still seems any need to do so. (It may be clear enough already, for example, both to you and to your audience, that God is superior to other realities rightly called "holy" or called "mysteries.")

3. If you do use privileging expressions and understand what you mean by them, make sure that your audience does also. (Spare them our problems here!)

4. Do not suppose that a word applied to something superior is applied in a superior way—that the sense the word then has is better than the sense it has in other applications. That would be to confuse word and thing, language and its referents.

5. Still less, suppose that the paradigm so honored is the only one to which the expression can rightly be applied. Talk of "strict," "proper," "authentic" senses of terms suggests that the alternative senses are inferior or improper. They

are not. They, too, are a standard by which the propriety of individual utterances is and may be judged. Thus, (*pace* the claims we have seen) people do have perfect pitch, statements do have meaning, doctors do heal patients, revelation can take propositional form, and so forth. Denials of such statements are more problematic than the statements denied; for the targeted statements have the backing of standard, established uses of terms, as PRS's norm enjoins, whereas the denials do not.

The passages below, with the sampling above, suggest how pertinent these guidelines are for theological discourse.

For Further Reflection

1. "Jesus said to him, 'Why do you call me good? No one is good but God alone' " (Mk. 10:18).

2. "What is not comprehended by the eyes but is seen by the mind and the soul is seen in a truer and deeper sense"[28] (St. Ambrose).

3. "The titles given to the Holy Spirit must surely stir the soul of anyone who hears them, and make him realize that they speak of nothing less than the supreme Being. Is he not called the Spirit of God, the spirit of truth who proceeds from the Father, the steadfast Spirit, the guiding Spirit? But his principal and most personal title is the Holy Spirit"[29] (St. Basil the Great).

4. "A name is applied to that wherein is perfectly contained its whole signification, before it is applied to that which only partially contains it; for the latter bears the name by reason of a kind of similitude to that which answers perfectly to the signification of the name; since all imperfect things are taken from perfect things"[30] (Thomas Aquinas).

5. "Essentially this means that, contrary to the conventional wisdom about these matters, dogmatics does not arrive at a concept like the fatherhood of God anthropomorphically. It is not the concept of human fatherhood that generates the idea of God the Father, but rather the other way around: we learn what it is to be a human father by first knowing

the fatherhood of God. This has important implications for the data and method of theology"[31] (John Carnes).

6. "Human beings have used the word 'love' for a very long time. In the Western World, particularly through the vehicle of the Christian tradition, the word has perhaps been more frequently used or, at least, thought, than in any other culture area—more frequently and in more senses. Yet how many persons in our culture have understood the *true* meaning of this word? The true meaning, what is it? That is the question which this book will attempt to answer. I believe that it is extremely important for the world as a whole that we discover or perhaps rediscover the genuine meaning of love"[32] (Ashley Montagu).

Chapter 13

Defining and Saying What Things Are

Definitions so proliferate in theology that this tour of linguistic methodology must say something about them. Something in praise is in order, because definitions can be useful, even necessary. Also something in warning, because definitions are often overrated and can obscure more than they clarify. The most useful kind focus on words and their meanings, whereas others, though more highly regarded since they focus on nonlinguistic realities rather than mere words, are nonetheless more problematic. It is this contrast, above all, that requires attention—especially since definitions of the problematic kind appear to be more plentiful in theological discourse than the relatively unproblematic variety.

Verbal Definitions

The most useful definitions typically do four things: (1) they state word meanings, (2) they make clear that this is what they are doing, (3) they state the meanings so as to facilitate communication, and (4) they do so insofar as is required for this purpose. To illustrate these points, one by one, we can return to the first chapter's remarks about "language." (The example has the double advantage of already being familiar and of providing a useful reminder of how a key term is employed in the present study, and why.)

1. Definitions can state word meanings in two ways: they can indicate what meanings words have at present, or they can indicate what meanings words will have in a given discussion or work. That is, they can report meanings or they can stipulate meanings. Chapter

1 did both things for the word *language*. First, it distinguished two standard meanings of the word: language as discourse and language as medium of discourse. (Thus, my dictionary characterizes language both as "the use by human beings of voice sounds, and often written symbols representing these sounds, in combinations and patterns to express and communicate thoughts and feelings"[1] and as "a system of words formed from such combinations and patterns, used by the people of a particular country or by a group of people with a shared history or set of traditions.") Having thus indicated what the word *language* does mean in English usage, the chapter then indicated the sense the word would have in the present work: "In the following pages as in the preceding—save for some quotations from other writers—the word *language* will always refer to the medium, the system of signs, and not to the linguistic activity carried on by its means."

2. The chapter made clear that this terminological option was simply that: a choice of senses. It was not a theory or factual claim of any kind, competing with others. The alternative application of the term *language*, for discourse rather than the medium of discourse, is neither mistaken nor unfortunate. It is a standard use cited in dictionaries along with other uses. It just is not the sense the word has had and will continue to have in the present work, by reason of the work's special focus.

3. It was necessary to note these two different senses of the word *language*, because they are so different, because the difference is so important, and because it is easily and often overlooked, with unfortunate results. It was necessary, next, to indicate the sense appropriate for the interests of the present study and to stress that such was the sense the word would have in these pages. It was especially necessary because, as the chapter noted, in theological literature relatively seldom is the term *language* employed with clear reference to just the medium of discourse. Much more frequently, as in sample quotations given there in chapter 1, the word refers to uses made of the medium.

4. Although the dictionary entry above, in terms of "a system of words," is fuller than chapter 1's characterization, some might find even this ampler definition inadequate. What is meant by a "system" and what by "words"? For "word," the same dictionary gives: "A sound or a combination of sounds, or its representation in writing or printing, that symbolizes and communicates a meaning and may consist of a single morpheme or of a combination of morphemes." This, in turn, might appear inadequate: the unrelenting demand for precision might require definitions of "sound," "representation," "meaning," "morpheme," and the rest. This process could continue indefinitely if there were any need, but of course the sharpening can and should stop somewhere—namely,

Defining and Saying What Things Are

when the intended sense is sufficiently clear for the context, the audience, and the aims of the clarification. In chapter 1, all that was needed was a reminder of two familiar senses of the word *language*, so as to permit identification of one rather than the other as the sense intended in subsequent appearances of the word. "Language" would, for example, be the English or Greek language and not, for instance, the Gettysburg Address or the Apostles' Creed.

Aside from its familiarity, from chapter 1, and its relevance for this study, there is nothing special about this chosen illustration. It represents standard defining practice of a relatively unproblematic variety. That is why I could be brief. However, this example shares the name *definition* with theological samples that are very different and that, being both more numerous in theology and more problematic, demand closer scrutiny. These other definitions are credited, not with communicative utility, but with theoretical significance. They do not, it is thought, concern merely words, but somehow the realities that the words indicate.

Theoretical Definitions

In full illustration, notice how notably the "definitions" in the following historical account (from M.-D. Chenu's *Is Theology a Science?*) differ from the sort of definitions just examined:

> The Father, the Son and the Holy Ghost are "persons." This is another non-scriptural term, and its human significance, both in its breadth and its limitations, made St Augustine careful when he used it. We speak of a *person* in God for want of a better word and to avoid remaining silent. But how is this? Is there any believer who does not regard Jesus Christ as a "person"? Maybe not; but the theologian, so soon as he starts to think about the matter, finds himself in the toils of conceptual definition: What is a "person"? What does the fact of being a person add to a nature? How does existential independence enter into this concept? This is the cue for metaphysical analyses, and contradictory ones, to enter upon the scene. Boethius, operating on the borderland of philosophy and faith, had proposed a very fair definition: *Persona est rationalis naturae individua substantia*—"a person is an individual substance of a rational nature." But each of these terms is unintelligible unless it is defined in its turn, and each definition presupposes a theory which can only be

expounded through another series of definitions. The theologians then observed the inadequacy of the Boethian definition when applied to God. This is a philosopher's definition, they said, formulated without benefit of the light of faith. So they sought to substitute another—either on entirely fresh lines or else by profoundly modifying the Boethian one. And so from century to century the theological work goes on, down to the minutest subtleties; yet all this is brought about by the ordinary needs of the rational appetite of faith.[2]

One may wonder whether "all this" really does reflect the genuine needs of a truly rational faith. For one may wonder about the nature, worth, and validity of this whole defining enterprise. Whereas the most useful definitions reveal the four desirable traits cited above, the least useful definitions reveal none of those traits but, instead, manifest the following four undesirable characteristics. Collectively or individually, they: (1) do not clearly distinguish between clarifying word meanings and describing reality, (2) pay little heed to standard, familiar meanings of the specified word, (3) leave unclear the nature and purpose of the defining, and (thanks to 1 and 3) (4) overrate its significance or utility. There are indications of all four traits in the historical account just quoted, which can therefore serve in illustration of typical problems for theoretical definition in theology.

"The theologian," Chenu aptly observes in his account, "as soon as he starts to think about the matter, finds himself in the toils of conceptual definition." Not of mere semantic clarification, notice, as in a dictionary, or of factual description, but of "conceptual definition." What, then, are these "concepts," to be captured in ever more accurate, adequate "definitions"? They are the entities of which we saw Putnam remark: "Concepts and ideas were always thought important; language was thought unimportant, because it was considered to be merely a system of conventional signs for concepts and ideas (considered as mental entities of some kind, and quite independent of the signs used to express them)." This whole viewpoint appears with special clarity, point by point, in remarks of G. E. Moore. For insight into the centuries-long inquiry into the concept "person" and many another like it, we can profitably look again, from this new perspective, at Moore's remarks about the concept "good," where the problems for such "conceptual definition" rise close to the surface.

For Moore, in *Principia Ethica*, the question how "good" is to be defined is the most fundamental question in all of ethics. This question, he says, is not merely verbal, nor is the desired definition of the sort that interests lexicographers. "If I wanted that kind of definition," he explains, "I should have to consider in the first place how people generally used the word 'good'; but my business is not with its proper usage, as established by custom."³ How, then, does Moore conceive his task? Though perplexing, his answer is also revealing. "I should, indeed, be foolish," he explains,

> if I tried to use [the word *good*] for something which it did not usually denote: if, for instance, I were to announce that, whenever I used the word "good," I must be understood to be thinking of that object which is usually denoted by the word "table." I shall, therefore, use the word in the sense in which I think it is ordinarily used; but at the same time I am not anxious to discuss whether I am right in thinking that it is so used. My business is solely with that object or idea, which I hold, rightly or wrongly, that the word is generally used to stand for. What I want to discover is the nature of that object or idea, and about this I am extremely anxious to arrive at an agreement.⁴

As I say, this explanation is puzzling. Moore would like his use of the word *good* to agree with its familiar sense, yet he sees no need to determine whether it does, in fact, do so. Though his concern is with the object that he believes the word is generally used to stand for, he feels free to ignore whether the object he describes is indeed the one which that word denotes. Who knows? Perhaps it is the object usually designated by the word *value* or *fruitfulness* or *satisfaction*; it does not matter. His account will still be an account of good, regardless of how anyone else uses the word *good*. Once we have had our attention called to the object, we can simply forget about the word and concentrate on the object. And yet, if Moore has used the wrong word, how will our attention be called to the intended object? If our attention is directed to some other object, or to no object at all (since, perhaps, the word *good* does not customarily name any object), how can he expect us to accept his account as accurate? If the account has no backing from the language employed in giving it, how can the object described, by itself, establish the truth of the account? Later, Moore himself characterized the pages from which I have quoted as a "mass of confusions."⁵

The attitude made revealingly explicit in Moore's account lies implicit in many a theological inquiry such as the one Chenu traced above. As Moore was interested in the question "What is the good?" so theologians were interested in the question, "What is a person?" As

Moore was not interested in "proper usage, as established by custom," neither were these theologians. They wished to clarify the nature of personhood, not the meaning of some Latin, Greek, German, French, or English word used to tag it. So the same queries arise for them as for Moore. How does the object or idea inquired about connect with the word used to express it? If the definition need not conform with existing usage, why use that word in the definition? If the definition serves as an implicit redefinition of the word, why is that needed, if interest lies elsewhere than in the word? Conceivably, such queries as these might receive satisfactory answers, but that is not likely; for this theological discussion, like many another, reveals no more concern about such methodological issues than did the similar discussion of Moore, the noted twentieth-century analytic philosopher. In any case, the purpose of the present probing is not to reach a verdict on past or present practice but to indicate how problematic that practice has been and to suggest the sorts of concerns to address when one encounters or proposes theoretical definitions in theology.

Typically, such a definition is the shadow cast by a word. Whereas the reality, both linguistic and nonlinguistic, with which the word connects is multiple, varied, and complex, the word is single and is used in the singular to ask, for example: What is a person? (What is faith, revelation, grace, religion, etc.?) So the question begets a simple, single answer (faith is this one thing, grace is that one thing, and so forth). And the resulting definition, being a mere shadow cast by the word, lacks the importance typically attached to it. Thus, with regard to our illustrative concept "person" it is sometimes supposed, for example, that a fuller, richer, more up-to-date definition of personhood, in terms of love and personal relationships, will permit more perfect understanding of the Council of Chalcedon and of the mystery of the Incarnation. But the Council did not use the word *person*. And to the word it did use (*prosopon*) it did not give that modern, up-to-date sense. And if we wish so to understand the Incarnation, we have no need of a specially tailored definition of personhood: anything we might put in the definition we can put in our description of Jesus' personhood. Instead of saying, "The essence of personhood is love," we can say that Jesus was a loving person, or was united by a bond of love with his Father.[6] Any factual issue we wish to consider we can address more clearly by avoiding needless debate about the "nature of personhood."

Many see more than purely theoretical interest in answers to such questions. Thus, Melford Spiro gives strong, explicit expression to a widespread viewpoint when he writes: "It is obvious, then, that while a definition cannot take the place of inquiry, in the absence of definitions there can be no inquiry—for it is the definition, either ostensive or nominal, which designates the phenomenon to be investigated."[7] We have already encountered this viewpoint in chapter 1, where Wolfhart Pannenberg, for instance, urged: "Any rational reform of the theology course must be guided by a decision about what theology in fact is and what knowledge and skills a person must acquire to become competent in theology. The crucial question here is what specific subjects make up the essential area of theological enquiry."[8] This, I noted, sounds reasonable and suitably scientific: how can you teach theology if you don't know what theology is, and how can you teach theology properly if you don't know *precisely* what theology is? The answer, I also suggested, is simple: you can specify as precisely as you wish just what areas or topics, of the kinds commonly termed theological, you desire to study, without formulating any definition of what theology "really is."

Recall the comparison with London. To tour London, you need not define London. To tour London effectively, you need not define London precisely. If you decide for or against visiting some interesting section or suburb, you need not first determine whether it belongs to the essence of London. Similarly, if you decide for or against studying some of the things called theology, you need not first determine whether they belong to the essence of theology. As there is no essence of London, so there is no essence of theology. A search for one would only divert attention from truly practical considerations: what theological areas or topics should be treated, how, why, for the purposes of a given monograph or course, with these readers' or those students' interests or needs in view.

Value-Driven Definitions

Theological definitions are variously motivated. Some seek an essence, others seek guidance, while still others are value-driven. The following nontheological example reveals with special clarity how this third sort of motivation often works, in theology and elsewhere:

> A major study of family in the United States, funded by Massachusetts Mutual Life in 1989, offered respondents three definitions of family and asked them to select the one that best fitted their understanding. The three definitions were: 1) a group of people related by blood, marriage or adoption; 2) a group of people living in one household; 3) a group of people who love and care for one another. The

first definition, used by both the Census Bureau and the U.S. Catholic bishops when they speak of family, was selected by a mere 22 percent of respondents; the second by 3 percent, the third by an overwhelming 74 percent. The traditional definition of family, based on blood and law, has been supplanted for three out of four adult Americans by another definition, based on love and nurture.[9]

How fascinating! For the "traditional definition" is, of course, the one that still guides people's use of the word *family*. They speak of single-parent families, large and small families, dysfunctional families, and the rest, without pausing to correct themselves and distinguish the true, loving families, from the others, that do not merit the name *family*. People who so used the term, restricting it to people who love and care for one another, would not be understood and would spark much idle altercation. So how did the questionnaire elicit this result? It formulated an ideal, and accepting a different, purely descriptive definition might seem a denial of that ideal. A minority resisted this impression and chose a definition closer to the actual use of the word—the one to be found in a dictionary. It is doubtful that this minority disagreed with the ideal; they just took the question differently. As for the majority, it is equally doubtful that, if asked, they would disagree with the semantic reporting of the dictionary. It is far from evident, therefore, that the traditional definition, based on blood and law, has, as claimed, been supplanted by a new one, based on love and nurture.

It appears that in this inquiry the question was badly put and the results were badly interpreted. Clarity would have been served by asking either an explicitly semantic question, about the use of the word in the language, or an explicitly evaluative question, about the ideal family. Once this distinction was made, it might be evident in advance which of the two main answers people would give, one to the semantic question and the other to the evaluative question, and therewith the inquiry might lose whatever point it appeared to have. Similar clarification is still more desirable in theology. For this split in the questionnaire's results reflects no split in the population, provoking debates about what is or is not a family, whereas such disputes are common in theology. Value-driven definition competes with value-driven definition, and, as in the questionnaire, only a minority of the disputants take account of familiar linguistic usage.

Consider a theological example. "What are our criteria for determining *faith*?" asks Neil Ormerod. "What is *faith*? Is it simply an intellectual assent to what is proposed by divine authority? Or does it involve a fully existential commitment, not only of mind but also of heart? How we understand faith will greatly influence how we do our theology."[10] Once the question is posed in this undiscriminating, either-or form, there is little doubt how the majority will answer it. As in the questionnaire, they will opt for the ideal. And in this instance one can surmise still fuller motivation for their choice. "Faith," still more than "family," being such an honorific term, and faith being such a highly prized virtue, surely too many good things cannot be said of it. Would something less estimable still be *faith*? Yes, going by the ordinary use of the term, it might.

To see why attention to usage might be a good idea, we may recall Aquinas's definition of law ("an ordinance of reason for the common good"), according to which unjust laws are not laws.[11] People call them laws. It is handy to have an expression that covers both just and unjust laws. If we restricted the term in the way Aquinas enjoins, we might have to introduce a new term to fill the spot on the conceptual map that "law" presently occupies. Now, the like holds for "faith." Much as we speak of bad or unjust laws, so we speak of this person's "weak faith," that person's "notional faith," and so forth. Not every believer believes in the fully committed way Ormerod describes. Yet, what other term can serve so handily as "faith" to cover the same range of possibilities?

Terms such as "faith" and "law" are more than purely descriptive. Designating good and desirable things, they acquire positive connotation. Possessing such connotation, they become attractive labels for things people esteem—labels that get attached by the sort of rhetorical sleight of hand termed "persuasive definition." Thus, valuing a fuller form of faith, one reserves the term *faith* for that form; valuing laws that promote the common good, one reserves the term *law* for those; and so forth.

In defense of such definitions, Philip Devine has written:

> It is now far too late to complain of persuasive definitions, as if they constituted a species of intellectual sharp practice. A definition of "violence" that includes *ad hominem* arguments along with rape and arson, or a definition of "fanaticism" that includes Kantians as well as Nazis, can be censured for attempting to win cheap and therefore spurious intellectual victories. But no non-persuasive definition of an evaluatively charged expression is possible.[12]

Where, one may wonder, is the problem? Looking in my dictionary under "violence," I find, for example: "abusive or unjust exercise of power." I find nothing about rape, arson, or *ad hominem* arguments. Under "fanaticism," I find "excessive, irrational zeal." I find nothing about either Kantians or Nazis. Of course, these dictionary entries are not theories; they just report familiar word usage. Evidently, then, Devine has something more theoretical in mind. And what purpose this different sort of definition might serve seems unclear. Leaving the term *fanaticism* as it is, available for common use, we can argue for or against the fanaticism (the excessive, irrational zeal) of Kantians or Nazis. Leaving the word *faith* as it is, we can argue the merits of a more or less intellectual faith. Leaving the word *law* as it is, we can argue for or against the justice of some law. If we tuck our debatable verdict into our definition of the term, we may hinder discussion and end in idle verbal altercation. ("A good law? Why, it isn't even a law!") Repeatedly, the problem with persuasive definitions, tugging terms this way and that to accommodate personal values or verdicts, is that they undercut effective communication.

Devine's own definition illustrates the danger. A proper definition of religion, he explains, might state properties possessed by all and only religions, or it might establish a family resemblance among the various phenomena called "religion." However, in his view, "Neither pattern of analysis is altogether satisfactory."[13] For both, he sees problems:

> Anyone who can find a useful set of necessary and sufficient conditions distinguishing Homeric religion and the more austere forms of Buddhism from all non-religious forms of belief and action will have performed a remarkable feat. But merely to list religion-making characteristics is to leave the subject in as much chaos as one found it: unless we can say that the idea of salvation is more central to religion than the existence of sacred objects, little understanding of religion will be possible.[14]

This said, Devine takes "the standard forms of Christianity" as his paradigm from which defining traits can be educed, "rather than Judaism or the movement headed by the Reverend Sun Myung Moon."[15]

A different solution stares from Devine's statement of his problem. If, as he claims, understanding of religion requires us to say that salvation is more central to religion than the existence of sacred objects, we can say precisely that (while explaining both the meaning and the basis of the claim). But we should not conflate such a theory with the analysis or definition of a term. That way lies chaos: the chaos of treating each competing theory as a matter of definition, the chaos of each theoretician meaning something different by the common, shared expression.

Here we meet again the contrast noted at the start of this chapter. The most useful kind of definitions, I suggested, tend to focus on words and their meanings, whereas the more problematic kind focus instead on things the words designate. The latter, problematic variety fall between simple, straightforward indication of word meanings, on the one hand, and simple, straightforward description of reality, or statement of values, on the other. What they can or do achieve in this in-between zone remains obscure. Chenu may have dropped a revealing clue when he cited vying "metaphysical analyses" of personhood. For in the present context Wittgenstein's remark seems both relevant and enlightening: "The essential thing about metaphysics: it obliterates the distinction between factual and conceptual [linguistic] investigations."[16]

For Further Reflection

1. "The best sort of instruction we can expect at all from a doctrine of God is surely precisely that it should tell us what 'God' means, if indeed that can really be learned by instruction"[17] (Gerhard Ebeling).

2. "The final reason behind the apparent necessity of defining 'religion' relates to the need for a theory of religion to show religion's unity. If an explanation of religion as a whole is offered its proponent must be convinced that religion is the kind of thing which can be explained uniformly"[18] (Peter Clarke and Peter Byrne).

3. "How is justice to be defined? The starting point for such a definition is crucial. We may begin with a definition which is either humanistic or reducible to purely human terms. Alternatively, we may begin from the divine perspective of how God Himself is just in His very nature and is thus the basis of justice for human beings. It is God Who defines what justice means for human beings and He sets the standard"[19] (E. David Cook).

4. "Faith is a universal human phenomenon. All people live by some faith. An approach to faith as a common dimension of human existence itself enables one to characterize its most fundamental structure and most salient qualities.

    "The reflections and conclusions which follow are generated by a transcendental analysis. This consists in an appeal to a reflection on common human experience, to a descriptive and critical analysis of the phenomenon of faith in the human subject. Many of the advances in the theology of faith in the modern period have come from a turn to the human subject and a description of faith in its first moment as a human act, response, and attitude"[20] (Roger Haight).

5. "Religion cannot be defined very easily because it thrives both within and outside of boundaries. It crosses and crisscrosses the boundaries that definitions want to set up because, paradoxically, it, too, concerns boundaries. The boundaries of religion, however, are different from the logical boundaries of good definitions. In the end, religion is a feature that encompasses *all* of human life, and therefore it is difficult if not impossible to define it"[21] (Catherine Albanese).

6. "In undertaking to compose a brief history of Christian views of revelation, the author is conscious of a methodological difficulty. Should one presuppose some definite notion of revelation? If this is done, there is a risk that the whole survey will be prejudiced by a view that is partial and to some extent personal. But if no clear notion is presupposed, it would seem impossible to decide what ought to be included in the survey. In practice we shall discuss that which has popularly gone by the name of revelation or has been regarded as such by significant Christian thinkers. Only after the survey is complete will it be possible to take an informed stand on what the true nature of revelation is"[22] (Avery Dulles).

Chapter 14

The Need of Examples

The noted philosopher-theologian Bernard Lonergan once gave a talk at Woodstock College in Maryland. The talk proceeded for some time at a stratospheric level that left his audience gasping for oxygen. Then, to their momentary relief, he proposed considering a concrete example. "Take, for instance," he suggested, "the distinction between essence and existence." One can understand why his hearers found some humor in this suggestion. Yet didn't Lonergan give an example, and wasn't it specific? What did they want, what did they need, and why? Since much theological discourse is similarly abstruse and short on examples, queries such as these have broad relevance. How necessary are examples in such discourse? Do they need to be simple, concrete, and down-to-earth, or does it suffice that they be specific, like Lonergan's metaphysical specimen? And, since examples are not words, why discuss them here in a treatment of language and its methodological implications in theology?

The use of examples might appear to be a stylistic topic, under the heading "How to make things clear." Or it might be viewed as a pedagogical concern, in view of the needs of those less endowed for abstract speculative thought. Or it might find its place in a more psychological perspective. The "intellectualist," suggested William James, is content with generalities, whereas the "pragmatist" wants to know the "particular go" of things. Give him examples! However, preceding chapters reveal a further perspective besides the stylistic, pedagogical, or psychological—a deeper, linguistic perspective that highlights the significance of examples in theological discourse.

Abstract Versus Specific

Recall chapter 2's challenge to the long-dominant conception of the relationship between language, thought, and world. In that classic conception, the world is made intelligible by the essences that pervade it, thought is given unity and clarity by the concepts that mirror these essences, and speech, in turn, is made intelligible by the concepts or mental likenesses that the words express. Right at the start, before words get their meanings, the process of abstraction filters out everything particular and specific, like so much confusing dust and debris, and brings forth the clear, purified concepts. In this perspective it is not evident why Lonergan's hearers should have been gasping for breath. Up there on the heights, he was giving them pure intellectual oxygen. Down below lay the smog of variety, multiplicity, and fuzzy indefiniteness.

In illustration of the viewpoint thus sketched in suggestive caricature, recall chapter 2's example, "blue." The shades of blue are many. No language has names for them all, and most people could not list all the shades for which a language such as English does have names. Neither could they distinguish sharply between one shade and the next or between fringe shades of blue and bordering shades of other hues. The sensible reality is varied, multiple, and indefinite. But amid all this complexity, Moore discerned unity, clarity, and definiteness. All shades of blue, he believed, share a single, common essence, expressed by the single, common word. If, then, somebody says, for example, "Blue is my favorite color," there should be no problem. The speaker need not give illustrative examples, for both speaker and hearer share the same simple, undifferentiated concept. Indeed, examples could be distracting or confusing, since they would add specificity not contained in the essence, abstracted in the concept, and expressed by the word. If, however, there is no essence of blue present in all and only shades of blue, but only a continuum of contiguous shades, it could make sense for the hearer to inquire, for example, which shade, if any single one, is the speaker's favorite color, or whether all are, indiscriminately, or perhaps some shades more than others. The single term, "blue," leaves much indefiniteness. Thus, in this nonessentialistic perspective, greater specificity may bring greater clarity rather than less.

This illustration may seem far removed from theological discourse, where a term such as "blue" rarely occurs. However, the illustration has advantages of the kind Wittgenstein suggested:

> If we want to study the problems of truth and falsehood, of the agreement and disagreement of propositions with reality, of the nature of assertion, assumption, and question, we shall with great advantage look at primitive forms of language in which these forms of thinking appear without the confusing background of highly complicated processes of thought. When we look at such simple forms of language the mental

mist which seems to enshroud our ordinary use of language disappears. We see activities, reactions, which are clear-cut and transparent. On the other hand we recognize in these simple processes forms of language not separated by a break from our more complicated forms.[1]

Theologians may typically employ more abstract terms than "blue," yet the terms they employ raise the same questions as for "blue." Where does clarity lie: in the abstract or the specific? Do theological terms function differently than "blue"? Do they, unlike this relatively simple expression, pick out single, invariant essences?

In one way, a negative answer to this query seems clear. In order for there to be an essence shared by all and only the things covered by any single term, theological or other, the term would have to be employed by the speakers of the language with greater precision and constancy than appears at all likely on their part. "Blue," for example, would have to be used, rigidly and consistently, for some single, invariant shade—that is, very differently than it actually is. But theological terminology fluctuates more, not less, than does the everyday employment of a word such as "blue." People do not get into disputes about whether something is blue, whereas theologians do commonly debate about whether something is faith, grace, revelation, or the like. If, then, examination reveals no essence of blueness, it is still less likely that it will reveal single essences designated by such theological expressions.

In another way, however, the absence of essences is less evident for theological terms than it is for "blue." Whereas our use of color terms is not enshrouded by the mental mist that Wittgenstein mentioned, our use of theological expressions is. We can examine the former "without the confusing background of highly complicated processes of thought," but not the latter. And yet, as Wittgenstein remarked, we recognize in the simple, concrete concepts "forms of language not separated by a break from our complicated forms." To designate invariant essences, theological terms would have to satisfy the same conditions as nontheological expressions, but are still less likely to do so.

By this time, readers may feel some sympathy with Lonergan's audience. How does all this discussion relate to real-life examples? How does it relate—specifically, concretely—to the doing of theology?

An Illustration

From early on, chapter 3 noted, theme after major theme of Christian theology has been profoundly affected by a simplifying conception with regard to "is" similar to Moore's with regard to "blue." Time and again it is assumed, when not explicitly declared (as it sometimes is), that there is just one kind of identity, namely, strict sameness: whatever holds for one term of an identity statement must hold for the other term; there can be no difference between them. This default setting repeatedly appears, for example, in discussions of the Incarnation. There, if the identity expressed by such statements as "Jesus is God" or "Jesus is the Second Person of the Holy Trinity" is strict, admitting no distinction or difference, then there are only three alternatives, each of which has in fact been adopted: it will be necessary either to limit Jesus' humanity or to limit his divinity or to deny the identity. Once we drop this recurring assumption of strict identity, chapter 3 suggested, the solution of Cyril of Alexandria, reflected in the Council of Chalcedon, becomes available. God is fully God and man is fully man, but the nature of the hypostatic union is mysterious.

Thus did that earlier chapter illustrate the significance and enduring power of the strict-identity supposition. Yet that is all the supposition is—an unexamined assumption. So, within the present perspective (the utility of examples), recall now, as an antidote, our earlier example. The "same" note may be thought, written, played, sung, or recorded. It may be thought in various ways, written in various ways, played, sung, or recorded in various ways. Nonetheless, we call it the "same note." It is, for example, a high C. The common name, as well as the talk of sameness, can veil the fact that none of these high C's, differing from one another in these multiple, important respects, is strictly identical with any other. And the like may hold for the identity, or sameness, between Jesus and God or between Jesus and God the Son. Strict sameness is not the only kind of identity.

Here a specific, concrete example—the sameness of notes—is used to clarify a complex theological issue. Now, to bring out its relevance, let us scrutinize the example more closely.

First, as noted, the example's significance is not limited to this single theological issue. The same assumption of strict identity that has powerfully influenced theological treatments of the Incarnation has similarly affected other important themes of Christian theology. In what sense is Jesus identical with God or with the Second Person of the Trinity? In what sense, if any, can each divine Person be identified as God? In what sense is the Eucharist the body and blood of Christ? In what sense is Trent's eucharistic teaching, for example, identical with that of the Apostles? What contemporary church or constellation of churches is identical, in what sense, with the church of the Apostles? How is the risen Christ identical with the crucified Christ, and how, in their turn, are citizens of heaven identical with antecedent citizens of earth? To query after query concerning identity or sameness the strict-identity supposition gives an unnecessary answer, grounded in neither scripture nor tradition, that complicates faith's task of seeking understanding. A simple example such as the sameness of notes can suggest how gratuitous is this underlying assumption. Identities need not be strict.

Second, this problem with regard to identity arises from language and requires attention to language. In many instances, a word such as "is" expresses a strict identity. If, for instance, George is the only son of William and Mary, then whatever is true of George must be true of the only son of William and Mary, and vice versa: same age, same parents, same appearance, same character, and so forth. In many other instances, as in the same-note illustration, a word like "is" does not express a strict identity. However, the former, strict type of identity is simpler than the latter. So, as often happens, the simpler paradigm determines the default setting for the word: if one thing "is" another, the sameness (it is thought) must be strict.

Third, without thorough, in-depth attention to language, this assumption and the problems it creates may not go away. For essentialistic thinkers may not be swayed by the word *blue* or the sameness of notes or any such simple examples. "Granted," they may suggest, "people say, for instance, that a pianist plays the same note that the composer wrote, though clearly the two notes are not strictly identical: the note produced is a sound, the written note is a mark. But that just shows that people are careless or mistaken in their speech. The one note is not really the same as the other." Contemporary philosophers do in fact speak this way, without regard for the authority of language. "Identity," David Lewis, for instance, has declared, "is utterly simple and unproblematic. Everything is identical to itself; nothing is ever identical to anything else except itself. There is never any problem about what makes something identical to itself; nothing can ever fail to be. And there is never any problem about what makes two things identical; two things never can be identical."[2] Popular speech is just sloppy and serious thinkers like philosophers and theologians can ignore it. They know better what identity really, truly is; what authentic, genuine identity consists in; what the word *identical* means when properly, strictly applied—and so forth. Here the relevance of chapter 5, on the authority of language, becomes apparent, as does, more specifically, the pertinence of the next-to-last chapter, on privileged paradigms.

So the same-note example really is relevant for theological discussion, on the Incarnation, the Trinity, the Eucharist, resurrection, and so on. Why, then, are such simple, concrete examples so rare in theology?

Why is Wittgenstein's suggestion so seldom followed? Doubtless lingering essentialism, like Moore's with regard to "blue," is one explanation: essences are clear, whereas inessential details, it is thought, are confusing, distracting, and unnecessary. A concern for appearances may be another explanation: how trifling and superficial a theological discussion might appear if it descended to such trivia as the sameness of musical notes. We can therefore inquire whether less trivial-seeming examples might serve equally well as antidotes, despite their greater complexity.

Consider some possible substitutes with regard to identity. Paul could write: "Now you are the body of Christ and individually members of it" (1 Cor 12:27). Ephesians speaks of the Church "which is his body" (1:23). "Thus," notes Augustine, "if you are the body of Christ and His members, it is your mystery which has been placed on the altar of the Lord; you receive your own mystery."[3] Lucien Cerfaux becomes still more explicit: "In the mystical order, nothing is opposed to a true identification of the Church with the glorious body of Christ. The Church and Christ are the same body in virtue of an equation by means of the (mystical) identity between the Church and the risen body."[4] Now, despite the strength of such assertions, no one has understood them as stating strict identities, requiring perfect sameness between the two terms of the relationship. The difference between Jesus, or his body, and the millions of individuals (men, women, children, young and old, etc.) who have constituted the church is as notable as that between the individual written, played, and recorded notes that we call the "same." Thus, the strict-identity supposition is again revealed as gratuitous. It should not serve as a default setting in theology.

So yes, less jejune examples, challenging the power of the strict-identity assumption, might do the same job as the example of notes' identity and might do it as well or better. Sometimes the jejune, concrete examples may make a desired point more evidently, so more effectively. Sometimes less simple, less concrete examples may make a point more strongly and impressively, so more effectively. In either case, the examples may have more than merely rhetorical, pedagogical, or psychological significance. They may serve an important methodological purpose.

Aquinas suggested that even after the intellect has abstracted a concept from sensible particulars, it must return to those particulars in order to understand what is stated by means of the concept. From an essentialistic viewpoint, it is not clear why this should be so. In that perspective, what one says about blue, one says about blue and not specifically about cobalt, turquoise, or aquamarine. If, however, these particulars are precisely what one is talking about, under the general heading "blue," it is no mystery why we must attend to them in order to understand blueness. And the like holds for the rest of language in a nonessentialistic understanding of its functioning.

The particulars attended to may be as concrete as blue or as abstract as the distinction between essence and existence. They may be samples, paradigms, models, or parables. They may be as trivial as high C or as profoundly significant as Abraham on Mount Moriah, the exodus, the tale of Job, or the paschal mystery. Thus the present discussion, focused on examples, points to a broader perspective such as Michael Novak evokes: "In between imaginative literature and academic theology there is a form of intelligence which is precise, discursive, and analytical, but also in touch with concrete experience and with the imagination. *That* is the model for academic intelligence."[5]

For Further Reflection

Though I have encountered no discussion of this chapter's topic, the following passages bear some relation to it. The most pertinent materials for critical reflection would be whole chapters, or perhaps entire theological works, that proceed without use of examples.

1. "There is a paradigmatic content of 'demonstrable continuities' within Christianity, but of such generalizability that it can and must take many different forms. It is not primarily what one can say in a general way about Christian faith that is interesting or important; what are interesting and important are the particular metaphors, models, and concepts which make God's saving power a concrete reality for particular peoples in particular times and places"[6] (Sallie McFague).

2. "Consequently a theory of language of a general kind, intended to be comprehensive in its range, must be based upon concrete issues and concerned with specialist aspects. Otherwise it runs the risk of becoming empty and saying nothing, the more general it becomes"[7] (Gerhard Ebeling).

3. "If theology becomes overly abstract, conceptual, and systematic, it separates thought and life, belief and practice, words and their embodiments, making it more difficult if not impossible for us to believe in our hearts what we confess with our lips. There is a way to do theology, a way

that runs from the gospels and Paul through Augustine and Luther to Teilhard and the Berrigans, that one could call intermediary or parabolic theology, theology which relies on various literary forms—parables, stories, poems, confessions—as a way from religious experience to systematic theology"[8] (Sallie McFague TeSelle).

Chapter 15

Important Linguistic Distinctions

Only later did I realize the full significance of a comment dropped long ago by the instructor at the end of a course in traditional logic. We had just reviewed half a dozen rules required for valid inference, and the teacher remarked that only one of the rules was violated with any frequency, namely the rule requiring that the "middle term" in a standard syllogism (the term occurring in both its premises) have the same sense in both of its occurrences. Thus, for instance, we may not argue:

> The *end* of a thing is its perfection.
> Death is the *end* of life.
> Therefore death is the perfection of life.

Here, the conclusion itself tips us off that something has gone wrong, and the difficulty is not hard to spot, even without the italics. In the first premise, "end" means "goal" or "aim," whereas in the second premise it means "finish" or "last event." So the premises fail to connect as they need to and as they do when the same sense is maintained from premise to premise, as, for instance, in the following valid inference:

> The end of a thing is its perfection.
> The beatific vision is our end.
> Therefore the beatific vision is our perfection.

Sample illustrations such as these, good and bad, populate logic texts because they are obvious. But in real-life argumentation, our professor was suggesting, matters are not so simple. Crucial distinctions are often not as easy to spot as that between the two senses of the word *end*, and reasoning falters as a consequence.

The implicit admonition was clear: watch out for such pertinent, hidden distinctions! However, for that purpose, I later realized, our rules for valid syllogisms would be no help, since they offered no tips on how to spot pertinent shifts of sense from premise to premise. Hence, if such changes of sense were the only cause for serious concern, the rules were of little practical utility. The important thing was to spot crucial, invalidating variations of meaning. But how could these be guarded against, aside from the mere warning to beware of them? Most words have more than one meaning. Some words have dozens of different senses. Clearly, then, the warning cannot be made more explicit by running through all possible meaning-variations in advance. A partial, practical solution is the one this chapter will adopt: some of the most important *kinds* of meaning shift can be reviewed, by means of specific illustrations.

Verdict or Value?

Aquinas's supreme moral principle can illustrate a first important distinction of senses. In reply to the query "Whether the natural law contains several precepts, or only one," Aquinas writes: "[T]his is the first precept of law, that *good is to be done and pursued, and evil is to be avoided*. All other precepts of the natural law are based upon this: so that whatever the practical reason naturally apprehends as man's good (or evil) belongs to the precepts of the natural law as something to be done or avoided."[1] In this principle—"good is to be done and pursued, and evil is to be avoided"—the key terms *good* and *evil* veil a basic ambiguity. In one reading, they would express moral verdicts and the principle would be saying: "Whatever is right to do should be done; whatever is wrong to do should be avoided." In another reading, the terms *good* and *evil* would have a broader sense, indicating varied values and disvalues, and the principle would be saying: "Good of whatever kind—food, life, pleasure, knowledge, virtue, God—should be pursued; evil of whatever kind—pain, hunger, error, war, disease, injury, ignorance, confusion, poverty, estrangement—should be avoided." Amplified, this latter version might then be taken to suggest that the right action is the one that maximizes good and minimizes evil. The principle would point in this general direction and provide this general guidance. Understood the other way, it would, on the contrary, furnish no practical guidance. It would just say to do what is right, whatever that may be, and to avoid what is wrong, whatever that may be and however it may be determined. So understood, the principle would be compatible with any theory of right action, whereas the other version would compete with a variety of alternative approaches. Hence, the distinction between these two readings holds basic methodological significance.

Some have read Aquinas one way, some the other. This is not surprising, for weighty evidence in Aquinas's writings points in each of these different directions.[2] This example therefore illustrates an important principle of interpretation. Scholars often call attention to such difficulties in determining "the" sense of a text but do not see the difficulties as telling against the existence of a sense. Surely the author meant one thing or the other (when meaning both makes no better sense than here), and what the author meant is what the text means. It may be doubted, though, that Aquinas clearly envisaged both readings of his principle, recognized how importantly they differ, and intended just one sense rather than the other, yet made no clearer than he did which sense he had in mind. Further examples in this chapter will illustrate the same point: when the sense of a passage is unclear to the reader, it may have been unclear to the author; that is, the author may not have noted the necessary distinction and, not noting it, may not have meant one thing or the other.

This is a tip for interpreting others' sayings. What, though, of our own use of words? How can we effectively be forewarned or forearmed against such basic ambiguities in our thinking and reasoning? As already noted, the general advice "Watch out for important distinctions lurking beneath the surface of words" has very limited usefulness. Instead, attention can be drawn to certain recurring distinctions that prove troublesome—for example, to the one apparently not noticed by Aquinas and clearly overlooked by many commentators on his principle. For this is no isolated example. I have cited it because, being overlooked, the same distinction between verdict and value has frequently caused difficulties elsewhere.

A notable illustration is the dictum "A good end does not justify an evil means." This principle is often cited against a teleological, value-maximizing approach in Christian ethics, of the kind suggested by the second reading of Aquinas's supreme norm. In confirmation of the criticism, Romans 3:8 is often invoked: "And why not say (as some people slander us by saying that we say), 'Let us do evil so that good may come'? Their condemnation is deserved." Here, if the words "Let us do evil" referred to nonmoral evil (death, suffering, destruction of property, etc.) of the kind teleologists would permit for the sake of greater good, Paul would be condemning their position, but the reason for the condemnation would not be evident. (What is wrong, for example, with legal sanctions to maintain law and order, or with amputations to save people's lives?) If, instead, the words meant "Let us do moral evil, let us sin, that good may come of it," no condemnation of teleology would be implicit in Paul's words; for no Christian ethician, whether teleologist or other, would condone sinning. This latter, exonerating reading makes excellent, evident sense, for the dictum that Paul rejected might then be understood as saying : "Let us do moral evil so that nonmoral good may come of it." Sin, Paul would rightly be objecting, cannot be justified by any nonmoral good, however great—not even the greater glory of God! Once Paul's likely meaning (the one that makes most evident sense and does not contradict anything else he says) is thus made explicit, a second likely source of confusion appears. Not only do the words *good* and *evil* and their near-equivalents in other languages have moral and nonmoral senses, but in this instance the sense shifts quickly from one to the other—from moral to nonmoral ("Let us do *moral* evil so that *nonmoral* good may come of it"). There is nothing wrong with this shift; it captures the criticized viewpoint. However, it can cause problems; and so it has, for readers too little attentive to the distinction between moral and nonmoral senses of evaluative expressions.

Neutral or Normative?

Terms such as *cheat, lie, robbery, theft, mutilation,* and *adultery* illustrate a second major distinction to watch out for, since, as already noted, they can have either a neutral, descriptive sense, or a moral, more than purely descriptive sense. A "lie," for example, can be a knowingly false utterance or it may be a knowingly false utterance that, in addition, is morally objectionable. The word can have either meaning. This distinction, too, between neutral and non-neutral senses, can easily be overlooked or lost sight of, with unfortunate consequences.

Consider the word *natural,* for instance in this influential saying of Aquinas: "Since good has the nature of an end, and evil, the nature of a contrary, hence it is that all those things to which man has a natural inclination, are naturally apprehended by reason as being good, and consequently as objects of pursuit, and their contraries as evil, and objects of avoidance. Wherefore according to the order of natural inclinations, is the order of the precepts of the natural law."[3] In a neutral, merely descriptive sense of "natural inclination," common human tendencies to vanity, pride, greed, resentment, and the like might qualify as natural; but they would not be "apprehended by reason as being good." Contrariwise, in a normative, more than descriptive sense of "natural inclination," no bad inclinations would qualify as "natural" and all good inclinations would. Hence, as claimed, all natural inclinations would be "apprehended by reason as being good." Yet this tautology would provide no guidance of the kind the passage suggests, discriminating good inclinations from bad by their naturalness or unnaturalness and thereby indicating which ones should be acted on.

Failure to note this distinction between neutral and non-neutral senses of "natural" or "unnatural" can have notable consequences. In one major illustration, Germain Grisez has detected a basic ambiguity running through traditional natural-law arguments against artificial contraception; for the arguments' core contention, he notes, can be stated as follows:

> Major Premise: To prevent any human act from attaining its natural end is immoral.
> Minor Premise: Contraception prevents sexual intercourse from attaining its natural end.
> Conclusion: Contraception is immoral.[4]

The problematic expression in the premises is "its natural end." In a neutral, descriptive sense, the act's natural end would be the one it typically or frequently attains. In a normative, non-neutral sense, the act's natural end would be one it should attain and should be allowed to achieve. The argument's first premise is made evidently true by the normative reading of "natural end." The second premise is made evidently true by the neutral, descriptive reading. And the argument derives its apparent force from a failure to note this shift of sense from premise to premise. Given this oversight, both premises have looked true and have seemed, between them, to entail the conclusion.

Verbal or Nonverbal?

The preceding dichotomies are important, yet are often overlooked. A further significant distinction is still more important because it is still more frequently relevant and still more frequently missed. Since thinkers often attend little to the familiar usage of the expressions they employ, the question constantly arises: in their statements, what is factual assertion and what is personal definition of terms? In illustration, consider an example from Kant. When he states that "[t]hought is knowledge by means of concepts" ("Denken ist das Erkenntnis durch Begriffe"),[5] is he making a factual assertion or implicitly defining the subject term ("thought," "Denken")? There is no telling. For consider the alternatives.

On the one hand, an utterance such as "Thought is knowledge by means of concepts" has the appearance of an assertion of fact but, taken as such, with no change in the terms' meanings, it is false. Most thinking is not knowledge of any kind. Neither "think" nor "denken" is used that way. (Indeed, in English, "think" is often employed in contrast with "know": we "think" that something is so, but do not "know" it is.) So the principle of charity suggests that Kant's assertion be taken in a way that avoids falsehood, namely as an implicit redefinition of the word rather than a statement of fact. But, for different reasons, this reading appears no more satisfactory, either here or in countless similar instances, in Kant and in other thinkers. Surreptitiously redefining terms, without warning, explanation, or justification, typically makes no sense in the context of discussion. And the speaker's nonlinguistic cast of mind, centered on the object of discourse rather than the medium, makes such an interpretation appear doubly unrealistic. So the principle of charity offers no solution, one way or the other, but leaves us in irresolvable uncertainty. Thus, the utterance, being unrecognizable either as an assertion of fact or as a definition of meaning, does not function either way. It conveys no decipherable message.

This looks serious, for Kant's nonchalance about established word uses is extremely common; hence the problem his sample statement poses is equally prevalent. Time and again, in philosophy, theology, and elsewhere, there is no telling what is factual claim, what is implicit redefinition of terms, and what is neither the one nor the other since the difference between them has not been considered or clarified. Methodologically, it matters little how we label the faulty statements that frequently result—whether we call them false or, applying the principle of charity, refrain from labeling them either true or false. The important lesson is to pay more heed to language ourselves and avoid making such statements.

Verdict versus value, neutral versus normative, verbal versus nonverbal: left abstract, such contrasts as these would be mystifyingly vague. But now, as the preceding chapter recommended, specific examples—from Aquinas, Saint Paul, Grisez, and Kant—have illustrated and clarified these basic yet often-blurred distinctions. I could go on to indicate how it is sometimes necessary to distinguish, not between just two alternative readings of a text but between three: factual, linguistic, and evaluative. All three perspectives can and sometimes do get conflated. (A classic illustration, I suggest, analyzed elsewhere, is Plato's discussion of justice in the *Republic*.)[6] However, the simpler, either-or cases here examined furnish the wherewithal to sort out these more complex configurations, not only in others' statements but also in one's own. Discriminating interpretation makes for more discriminating practice. The alternative senses one comes to distinguish in other people's utterances, one is more likely to keep distinct in one's own thinking and verbal communication.

The illustrations cited in this chapter, chosen for their special aptness, have been more broadly philosophical than strictly or narrowly theological. Such mixing has an incidental advantage worth noting. To focus too consistently on linguistic difficulties that arise in theology could convey the impression that theological practice is uniquely, disreputably problematic. It isn't. Theology has no monopoly on linguistic problems of the kinds noted here, in previous chapters, or in those to come.

For Further Reflection

1. "But, when the works themselves are already sins, such as theft, impurity, blasphemy, and the like, who would say that they should be done for good reasons so as either not to be sins or else, still more absurd, to be just sins?"[7] (Saint Augustine).

2. "Insight is more than intellectual understanding—it is knowledge through and through, knowledge to which the whole person can say Yes. It is understanding that pervades man from head to heart, from top to toe, from brain to guts"[8] (Henri Nouwen).

3. "Human knowing, then, is not experience alone, not understanding alone, not judgment alone; it is not a combination of only experience and judgment, or of only understanding and judgment; finally, it is not something totally apart from experience, understanding, and judgment. Inevitably, one has to regard an instance of human knowing, not as this or that operation, but as a whole whose parts are operations. It is a structure and, indeed, a materially dynamic structure"[9] (Bernard Lonergan).

4. "And here we must always remember that a mystery is not something still undisclosed, which is a second element along with what is grasped and understood. This would be to confuse mystery with the still undiscovered unknown. Mystery on the contrary is the impenetrable which is already present and does not need to be fetched: it is not

a second element unmastered only provisionally. It is the indomitable dominant horizon of all understanding, that which makes it possible to understand other things by the fact that it is silently there as the incomprehensible"[10] (Karl Rahner).

Chapter 16

Verbal Disagreement

It was God, we read in Genesis, who brought about the multiplication of languages at Babel. How, though, are we to account for the confusion of tongues, less obvious so more insidious, of those who speak the same natural language? Though most disagreements are genuine, many are merely verbal. A principal explanation of this latter, unfortunate phenomenon is that, intentionally or not, people often pay slight attention to language as a determinant of truth or assertability. Sometimes one party heeds language's authority while the other party does not; sometimes neither party does.

Several pages in C. S. Lewis's *Mere Christianity* nicely illustrate the first possibility. Objections have been expressed, Lewis writes,

> against my use of the word *Christian* to mean one who accepts the common doctrines of Christianity. People ask: "Who are you, to lay down who is, and who is not a Christian?" or "May not many a man who cannot believe these doctrines be far more truly a Christian, far closer to the spirit of Christ, than some who do?" Now this objection is in one sense very right, very charitable, very spiritual, very sensitive. It has every amiable quality except that of being useful. We simply cannot, without disaster, use language as these objectors want us to use it.[1]

Lewis explains fully, with his customary clarity and style, why we cannot:

> Now if once we allow people to start spiritualizing and refining, or as they might say "deepening," the sense of the

word *Christian*, it too will speedily become a useless word. In the first place, Christians themselves will never be able to apply it to anyone. It is not for us to say who, in the deepest sense, is or is not close to the spirit of Christ. We do not see into men's hearts. We cannot judge, and are forbidden to judge. It would be wicked arrogance for us to say that any man is, or is not, a Christian in this refined sense. And obviously a word which we can never apply is not going to be a very useful word. As for unbelievers, they will no doubt cheerfully use the word in the refined sense. It will become in their mouths simply a term of praise. In calling anyone a Christian they will mean that they think him a good man. But that way of using the word will be no enrichment of the language, for we already have the word *good*. Meanwhile, the word *Christian* will have been spoiled for any really useful purpose it might have served.[2]

Not only does Lewis's position agree with and illustrate the Principle of Relative Similarity, but it admirably suggests the virtues of the principle and its corresponding norm. People do not customarily call virtuous Moslems, Buddhists, Taoists, agnostics, or atheists "Christians." In English, as in other languages, "Moslem," "Buddhist," "Taoist," "agnostic," and "atheist" are rival expressions, conflicting with "Christian." To be understood and to say what you wish to say, it is best to leave both them and "Christian" as they are.

Lewis, wise in the way of words, does not simply contradict those who speak in the way he critiques, for he is aware that his disagreement with them is verbal, not factual. The people they call Christians may indeed be as spiritual and fine as alleged. When, however, neither side in a debate is attentive to language, neither side may heed the established use of words and thicker verbal fog may then descend on the proceedings. The samples we will now examine illustrate this possibility. More specifically, they reveal the following recurring configuration: (1) Verdicts differ on some debated question. (2) The disagreement is made possible by the fact that neither side in the debate has regard for the authority of language. (3) In place of language, the conflicting answers are dictated by conflicting values or commitments. (4) Were the disputants to consult the language they speak, they would find that it backs neither side in preference to the other. (5) Indeed, they would discover that it backs no answer, or no single answer, to the debated question. (6) Hence, according to chapter 4, there is no answer, or no single answer, to the question. (7) In an important sense, then, the debate is merely verbal. (8) Attention should therefore shift to underlying substantive considerations and away from the empty verbal altercation. The following samples exemplify all these points. However, disputes that agree in these eight respects do not simply duplicate this common pattern, but may differ in their structure as well as in their subject matter. Thus, in the first of the following examples clashing assertions target a single reality, whereas in the second example they do not.

Fetal Status

From its different perspective, chapter 6 suggested a relatively clear example of an apparently factual dispute that, on inspection, can be seen to be verbal. The question of fetal status appears to be a matter of life and death: if the fetus is not a human being or person, it may be aborted; if it is a human being or person, it may not be aborted. Hence, opponents of abortion assert and proponents of abortion deny the fetus's status as a person or human being. In support of these conflicting verdicts, proponents of abortion stress how far the fetus falls short of full human development, while opponents stress the fetus's potential for such development and the human characteristics it already possesses. The verbal nature of the debate is clear from the fact that neither side denies the evident facts alleged on the other side (for example, the fetus's lack of speech, on the one hand, or its possession of human DNA, on the other). They just differ in their use of words. And, as their very altercation makes clear, neither side can claim the backing of the shared language they speak. Familiar usage establishes you, me, and Napoleon Bonaparte as human beings and excludes our pets or kitchen utensils; but in the zone between the clear instances on either side the dividing border is not sharp, and neither present linguistic usage nor the mere stipulation of new senses for the contested terms supports the claim that the fetus is or is not a person or human being.

This case differs from that of the fabled elephant, palpated by the blind in different parts (trunk, tail, tusks, etc.), hence differently described. It is not readily conceivable that two sighted speakers of the English language would take hold of the same part of the elephant and describe it in diametrically opposed terms (smooth and rough, soft and hard, thick and thin, etc.); but a comparable altercation, with regard to the selfsame fetus and its status, is not only possible but widely realized. It is not readily conceivable in the case of the elephant because no motivating source of disagreement is evident; it is readily conceivable in the case of the unborn because such a source is amply apparent. The life of the fetus is at stake. The health, wealth, or reputation of the mother may be threatened. So the descriptive term *person* or *human being* is tugged this way and that, back and forth across the no man's land where language gives no answer one way or the other. And where language gives no answer, I suggest again, there is no answer; for no reality by itself validates its own description in any language. Those blinded to this fact in the ways chapter 6 itemized are not likely to recognize the verbal nature of the debate that still rages over the status of the unborn.

Substantive issues, whether factual or moral, cannot be decided by the simple expedient of giving terms whatever meaning one wishes. Drawing attention to this fact, the Principle of Relative Similarity highlights its own significance. Judged by PRS's standard, the issue that is widely viewed as crucial in the abortion debate is in fact not even relevant: there is no answer to the question "Is the fetus a person or human being?" For the fetus alone cannot dictate an answer, in English or any other language. The backing of language is also necessary, and where that backing is lacking, there is no answer.

I have cited this as a relatively clear example of a verbal, nonfactual dispute. Yet I do not expect all readers to be satisfied with these brief remarks. Some will undoubtedly feel that I have reduced a crucial factual issue to a mere matter of words. This likely reaction attests the importance of the present discussion and suggests the desirability of dwelling a moment longer on this illustration.

It may be suggested, for example, that I have said nothing about the soul. One reason is that most contemporary disputants do not cite the possession or nonpossession of a human soul in their arguments for or against the fetus's status as a human being. And it is understandable that they don't, for the argument would have to go the other way round: whatever soul the fetus might possess, the only evidence for its being a human soul would be its possession by a human being.

This is not the place to suggest how, once the verbal question of fetal status has been set aside, the issue of abortion should be addressed. I can just observe that the factual questions—e.g., ensoulment, actual development, or potential growth—that do not decide the fetus's status do, nonetheless, have moral significance. Indeed, only they, and not the application or refusal of the label *person* or *human being*, have moral significance. My limited purpose here is to illustrate how conflicting values and commitments can prompt the acceptance or rejection of terms and thereby beget disputes which, in the sense explained, are purely verbal. There is no answer to the debate about fetal status, yet people give an answer, one way or the other, and suppose that they are making conflicting factual claims. On inspection, their clashing assertions reveal no factual disagreement.

A second issue, no longer debated as vigorously as heretofore, may for that reason more readily be accepted as illustrating the possibility here being examined, of verbal disagreement not recognized as such.

Faith

In the foregoing example, it is relatively clear what single reality the disputants are describing when some call the unborn zygote, embryo, or fetus a "person" or "human being" and others deny it that status. In other instances, it is much less evident what single reality, if any, is the object of dispute. In illustration, consider chapter 1's example. Some describe "theology" one way, some another, and, although a single reality may correspond to each of the descriptions, it is far from evident that the competing accounts target any single reality and describe it differently. Each description, it seems, picks out its own referent and therefore cannot fail to be true—for that referent. And so it often is, or has been, for "revelation," "justification," "faith," and other possible illustrations.

Take faith. Vatican Council I states that by faith, "with the inspiration and help of God's grace, we believe that what he has revealed is true—not because its intrinsic truth is seen with the natural light of reason—but because of the authority of God who reveals it, who can neither deceive nor be deceived."[3] Such has been the Catholic emphasis: "[A]s a general description, the specific notion of Christian faith appears essentially as a personal acceptance of a divine attestation, announcing to men that the possibility of salvation has now been given to them."[4] Protestant accounts have differed from this one in their emphasis or focus. For Luther, as for others, faith is more than "believing things revealed"; it is, above all, *fiducia*—"personal trust, reliance, a grasping or taking hold of Christ."[5] More recently:

> Friedrich Schleiermacher analyzed the ground of religious faith in what he called the experience of absolute dependence. Schleiermacher did not mean by this a psychological feeling nor an experience mediated through a distinct religious faculty. Arrived at by a form of transcendental analysis, it refers to an underlying experienced condition of being dependent in one's being. For Kierkegaard, the preeminent theologian of faith of the nineteenth century, faith is a more intentional

"infinite passion," where both terms underscore the intensity of commitment to its object that constitutes faith. Paul Tillich, in his classic *Dynamic of Faith*, has taken these two themes and woven them together in his definition of faith as "ultimate concern."6

These are just a few examples of the varied claims made about faith. The polemics of centuries reflected by these divergences have shifted of late to attempts at reconciliation. These can take either of two forms. It may be surmised that, as for the palpated elephant, disputants have been describing the same thing (faith) from different perspectives, with different emphases. Or it may be suggested that disputants, variously motivated, have been applying the same term to different things, without noting the lack of a common reference or the persuasive, nondescriptive nature of their conflicting accounts. Remarks of Dulles on a related debate illustrate the first approach:

> As Louis Bouyer points out, Luther himself understood faith as a loving response to the God who bestows his gifts upon us. Comparing the doctrines of Aquinas and Luther, Otto Pesch contends that the latter, in rejecting *fides caritate formata* [faith informed by charity], misunderstood the Thomistic formula as though it meant that charity were something extrinsically added to faith. In reality, Pesch maintains, charity is an inner moment of living faith, and thus the Thomistic thesis that justifying faith must be enlivened by charity does not really contradict the Lutheran thesis of justification by faith alone.7

One account complements the other, Dulles and Bouyer suggest; the disagreement is merely apparent. This approach may be extended: bundle various salvific realities together under the single honorific title "faith," and the single reality thus designated may be described in a variety of ways—sometimes as assent, sometimes as trust, sometimes as hope, sometimes as charity, and so forth. The elephant has all these parts. However, one may doubt the aptness of such an analysis. A single moon circles the Earth and a single sun shines in the sky, but no single reality called "faith" runs through Scripture and Christian tradition, inviting ever more accurate, adequate characterization. Attempts to capture the single (though perhaps ample) essence of faith make no better sense, I suggest, and have no greater significance, than the attempts described in chapter 1, to define the essence of language or the essence of theology. The real, nonverbal issues lie elsewhere.

Verbal disputes of the kinds suggested by these examples—fetal status and faith—would be less worrisome were they mere aberrations, perverse departures from normal rationality. However, they are not. It is natural to focus on the things we describe rather than the words with which we describe them. It is natural, thus fixated on the things, not to notice the words' essential role as codeterminants of truth. Without this recognition, it is easy for value preferences of various kinds—for incipient human life or for women's welfare, for trust or for doctrinal assent—to override the authority of language. For influences such as these can be strong, their workings may be subtle and complex, and their claims may appear obviously superior to those of mere words.

What, then, can be done about verbal disputes such as those here examined? Attention to language can reveal them, and attention to language can prevent them. Babel breaks out when the role of language in determining truth is ignored. However, people can talk at cross-purposes in more ways than one. As the next chapter will indicate, their agreements, too, as well as their disagreements, may be more verbal than real.

For Further Reflection

1. "Once when he was praying by himself, with only the disciples near him, he asked them, 'Who do the people say that I am?' They answered, 'John the Baptist, though others say Elijah, and others that one of the old prophets has come back to life.'

    And he said to them, 'But who do you say that I am?' Peter answered, 'The Christ of god!' " (Lk 9:18–20).

2. "Now it might be argued that, when Jews say Jesus is not the Messiah and Christians say Jesus is the Messiah, this is not a full-fledged disagreement. Because, we might say, even though the same sentence is being used by both, they do not mean the same thing by it. Jews mean by 'the Messiah' a nondivine being who will restore Israel as an earthly community and usher in the consummation of history. Christians mean a promised savior of mankind from sin. Two different Messiah concepts are being expressed; hence two different propositions are being asserted"[8] (William Christian).

3. "Prudence, for pagans, is a purely intellectual virtue equivalent to knowledge. Christians have made of it a practical virtue that judges an action's conformity with

the demands of the Gospel.... The Stoic's patience was submission to an implacable destiny; for the Christian it has become the courageous expectation of God's hour, in communion with the passion of Christ. Humility was a little-known value or at least little esteemed. It has become one of the most characteristic Christian attitudes"[9] (Philippe Delhaye).

4. "[A]nyone who reflects on the history of epistemology ... can hardly fail to notice that there are two very different ways of analysing belief. In the traditional way of treating the subject, it is assumed that believing is a special sort of mental occurrence (sometimes described as a 'mental' act). This mental occurrence need not necessarily be introspected by the person in whom it occurs; but it always *could* be.... The modern way of treating belief is quite different. Believing something is now generally regarded not as an occurrence, introspectible or otherwise, but as a disposition"[10] (H. H. Price).

5. "Rahner presents faith as the handing over of oneself to ultimate mystery; Lonergan describes it as 'falling in love unrestrictedly,' without necessarily or clearly knowing with what one is in love; for Tillich, faith is the profoundly personal experience of 'the courage to be,' whereby we simply 'accept the fact that we are accepted.' For the Buddhist, faith is the new awareness and new way of being that overwhelms one in enlightenment"[11] (Paul Knitter).

6. "We must admit, at the very least, that the embryo can as well be considered a person as not. And therefore, in the second place, ethics must proceed on the supposition that abortion does kill a person ... we cannot consider ourselves blameless if we are willing to kill what may or may not be a person, even if it is not"[12] (Germain Grisez).

Chapter 17

Verbal Agreement

In Genesis, babel arises when people start speaking different languages. In theology, philosophy, and elsewhere, a worse form of confusion occurs when people speak the same language so differently that they no longer communicate effectively. One result may be the sort of verbal disputes reviewed in the last chapter. There, unconcerned about linguistic backing for their claims, people talk at cross-purposes: they argue for and against the humanity of the fetus, for and against conflicting descriptions of the supposedly single referent "faith," and so forth. However, this is only half of the story. As verbal disagreement may mask factual agreement, so too, the other way round, verbal agreement may veil significant factual, nonverbal disagreement. This chapter's examples illustrate important ways in which this latter situation may arise and the similar significance it may have.

Fidelity to Tradition

Of traditional dogmas, George Lindbeck has written: "In practice they appear to be relatively empty shells which can be filled with any one of a number of concrete religious meanings; they can be given an indefinitely large variety of theological interpretations."[1] Lindbeck would not speak this way of scriptural texts and their accurate exegesis, as faithful as possible to the original. The theological "interpretations" he has in mind are more creative: they do not attempt to determine the actual meaning of a doctrine, but a possible, preferable reading among many. No doubt, in order to count as at least a candidate reading, an interpretation must be compatible with traditional formulations of the doctrine in question. And to qualify not only as a possible but also as a preferable reading, it must be faithful to more than just the words. But how much leeway does a dogma leave for theologians who wish not merely to repeat it but to "interpret" it?

Here, the doctrine of transubstantiation, as formulated, for example, by the Council of Trent, can serve as a trial case. The Council condemned the view "that in the most holy sacrament of the Eucharist the substance of bread and wine remain along with the body and blood of our Lord Jesus Christ."[2] To the contrary, for the Council, at the words of consecration, one substance replaces the other. Now, according to the reading proposed some years ago, by Protestant as well as by Catholic theologians, in the Eucharist nothing happens, empirically, to the bread and wine: their molecules, atoms, and the rest remain. However, according to these interpreters, things are not defined empirically or physically, but by their finality or significance. And in the Eucharist the words of consecration, "This is my body, this is my blood," impart a new finality and significance to the Eucharistic elements. So the elements' identity is altered, and the words of Trent are therefore verified: the bread and wine do not remain but are replaced by the body and blood of Christ.

There can be little doubt that the Council's members did not view matters in this light. So it may appear that these new "interpretations" (in terms of "transfinalization" or "transignification") are simply statements of dissimilar views in similar terms, and that the apparent agreement is therefore merely verbal. The new readings are not readings at all; they state different doctrine using the same or similar words. This could suggest a weak understanding of Lindbeck's talk about "relatively empty shells" and of the sense in which they "can" be filled in endlessly varied ways. Understand the words of a dogma as you please and the words can, of course, be given an indefinitely wide variety of "interpretations." However, Lindbeck's suggestion might be given a stronger sense. To see how and why it might, recall Wittgenstein's example, "Moses," and imagine the following scenario.

Two people, who hold very different views about other details of Moses' career (date, birth, upbringing, flight, marriage, etc.) agree in saying that Moses led the Israelites out of Egypt. If, however, you ask them what person they mean by "Moses," they offer very different answers. Yet the truth or falsehood of their disparate beliefs need not affect the truth or falsehood of their common statement, that Moses led the Israelites from Egypt. For, as chapter 4 explained, the truth of their common statement is not determined by their individual beliefs but by the established uses of the words they employ. Their personal beliefs about Moses—the beliefs of these two speakers—do not define the name "Moses" in the language.

There are two ways, then, of understanding Lindbeck's "empty shells": (1) People may use the same doctrinal formulae (for instance, those of Trent) but give the words different meanings, with the result that their similar-sounding statements in fact differ and their agreement is purely verbal; or, (2) People with very different views may use the same words to make the same statement, with the same word meanings and the same truth-conditions; for their different personal beliefs do not determine either the meaning or the truth of the statement. In this latter case, their agreement is factual; they are not talking at cross-purposes. Offered these alternative accounts of their enterprise, interpreters of the Tridentine doctrine (like the interpreters of other doctrines) would no doubt choose the second option. "Yes," they might agree, "we hold different views about substances than the Council Fathers did, but we agree with them in our common statement that a substantial change occurs in the Eucharist. Our beliefs differ but our statement is the same." If this response is correct, it strikingly illustrates Lindbeck's thesis, and suggests how "indefinitely large" theological interpretations can be. So let us examine our Eucharistic example more closely, to see if this analysis fits it.

Specifically, we can take a closer look at the key premise that permits the new theories to employ the same terms as Trent. Things, we are told, are defined by their function, finality, or significance. "The final reality of things is not in themselves, not in what they convey to our senses, even when those are improved by the most intricate laboratory instruments. In order to apprehend the substance of reality, it is necessary to have a knowledge in depth, attaining, beyond what the things are, the why of their existence."[3] So it is for chairs, bicycles, and binoculars, and so it is for bread and wine. Change their purpose, their finality, and you change what they are. They are no longer chairs, bicycles, or binoculars but something else. They are no longer bread and wine but the body and blood of Christ. So goes the reasoning, with some plausibility.

In response to this underlying rationale, consider an episode from the Charlie Chaplin film *Modern Times*. When Charlie arrives at his girlfriend's ramshackle house and, grabbing a broom, starts to do some sweeping, the house almost falls down. The broom was a pillar. Notice how I put that, naturally: the *broom* was a pillar. In its new function as a pillar it did not cease to be a broom. Similarly, I suggest, bread and wine do not cease to be bread and wine simply because they acquire new, Eucharistic significance or finality. In support I cite countless other examples—books used as doorstops but still called books, white shirts used as flags of surrender but still called shirts, smoke used for signals but still called smoke, and so forth. That is, I cite usage, not a theory. No theory can flout usage without running the risk of vacuity ("To be sure, people still call the broom a broom, but it really isn't, you know"). Trent did not flout usage, but the new theories do. Thus, what Trent denied, the new theories admit. The disagreement cannot be papered over.

Lindbeck might find this verdict too facile, for he writes:

> To say that two positions are possibly compatible means no more than that they have not been proved contradictory. Contradictions, however, are notoriously difficult to establish. One must show that "x" is denied on the one side in precisely the same sense that it is affirmed on the other, but this can rarely be done in any rigorous way outside of mathematics and the exact sciences. In other areas, including theology, irreconcilability is often undemonstrable.[4]

Push the degree of precision required, and a rigorous proof of incompatibility might not be feasible even in the exact sciences. However, I need not attempt such a demonstration in the present instance. For the only thing that makes the new interpretations of transubstantiation appear at all plausible as readings of Trent is their underlying theory of what makes things what they are, and that theory ignores the authority of language. As tin cans do not cease to be tin cans when used in place of soccer balls (I recall some noisy street play in Rome) and forks do not cease to be forks when used as weapons (I recall one that landed, quivering, in my brother's youthful head), so bread does not cease to be bread when given some new finality or significance besides its ordinary one. Things are not so defined in French, German, English, or any other tongue spoken by transfinalists or transignificationists. These theorists might, of course, propose this new way of speaking ("Let us say that the cans are no longer cans, that the forks are no longer forks, and so forth"), were the futility of such a move not evident. Interpretations cannot be legitimized either by redefining the terms employed in them or by redefining the terms of the text interpreted. Dogmas are not *that* empty.

I therefore view this present, Eucharistic example as illustrating the first alternative above: when people offer interpretations of a text, they may use the same words to make very different statements, in which case their agreement with the text is purely verbal. The example not only illustrates this alternative but explains it and demonstrates its real-life relevance. This, too, is a genuine possibility. For when people offer theological interpretations, they may do as they often do when making their own assertions: intent more on the theories proposed than on the established uses of the words employed to state the theories, they may ignore the authority of language. Doubtless they would hesitate to assert, for example, that the broom is no longer a broom when used to prop up the shack or that the smoke is no longer smoke when used to send a message. The conflict with usage would then be too blatant. But when engaged with higher, more theoretical concerns, they may see no need to consider or heed linguistic usage.

Returning to our starting point with this paradigm case in mind, we can gloss Lindbeck's remarks as follows. Dogmas, he says, "can be given an indefinitely large variety of theological interpretations." If this is taken as a comment on theological practice, the example just considered can illustrate how indefinitely varied proffered "interpretations" may in fact be. If it is taken as a comment on how varied legitimate interpretations, genuinely compatible with a text, can be, our example suggests that there are limits: the possibilities are not "indefinitely" large and varied. There can come a point when the alleged or apparent agreement is merely verbal.

Another example, now, raises similar issues but does so very differently.

Moral Agreement/Disagreement

Christian ethicists and others long supposed basic invariance in the meanings of moral terms, and often still do. If, for example, church teaching consistently called artificial contraception "wrong," the teaching was ipso facto invariant. No need to inquire very seriously whether "wrong" ("evil," "immoral," etc.) always meant the same thing. Wrong is wrong, as red is red and rain is rain. Thus, Hans Küng has written: "The theological history of contraception, comparatively speaking, is sufficiently simple, at least with regard to the central question: Is contraception always seriously evil? For in answer to this question there has never been any variation and scarcely any evolution in the teaching. The ways of formulating and explaining this teaching have evolved, but not the doctrine itself."[5] The act was always judged to be "evil"—whatever that might mean.

Küng's words reflect a double supposition, typically unexamined: first, of basic similarity between moral terms and others; and, second, of basic invariance in the terms' meanings. In the way previously noted, this widespread assumption found classical expression in G. E. Moore's *Principia Ethica*. Seeking to identify the property that the word *good* denotes and failing in the effort, Moore concluded that the property in question is too simple to define. In this respect, he thought, *good* is comparable with *yellow* or *sweet*. It apparently did not occur to Moore that his failure might be due to the word's varied meanings or to the more than descriptive richness that attaches to it, invalidating any equivalence between *good* and a purely descriptive defining formula.

Both of these explanations are now commonly accepted in preference to Moore's. Evaluative words such as *good* add emotive and dynamic dimensions to the descriptive, and they vary more in their descriptive content than do most other expressions. Thus, people may, for instance, differ notably in their account of what makes an action "right" yet agree, emotively and dynamically, in approving it and supporting it, or may differ notably in their description of what makes an action "wrong" yet agree, emotively and dynamically, in condemning and opposing it. In such a case, the strong noncognitive content of the moral expressions employed could easily suggest total agreement in pronouncements which, in fact, notably diverge in their cognitive content. For the noncognitive content is relatively constant ("right," for example, is used to urge or approve and "wrong" to oppose, regardless of underlying theory). The case of contraception nicely illustrates this abstract possibility and its significance.

The encyclical *Casti connubii* employs strong language to characterize artificial contraception: it is "shameful," a "nefarious crime," a "base sin"; those who do such a thing are "stained with the guilt of serious sin." These loaded expressions do more than describe; they condemn, castigate, deter. They pack more emotive charge and exert greater pressure for conformity than do milder, though still condemnatory terms such as "wrong" or "immoral." And that, no doubt, is why they were employed. But what do these expressions say descriptively? What is their cognitive content? No explicit definitions being provided in the encyclical, we must look to the arguments briefly adduced, and behind them to the tradition from which these and other arguments and their negative verdict derived—the tradition traced by John Noonan in his monumental work *Contraception*. Impressive uniformity, he there writes, marks that tradition from the start. Yet here, briefly, is what we find in his account.

At the outset Christians already possessed important answers on marriage but no worked-out rationale. The antinomians were wrong, on the one hand, in sanctioning promiscuity, and the Gnostics were wrong, on the other hand, in condemning all use of marriage. But why they were wrong was not immediately evident. For pleasure or the satisfaction of desire was not seen as a legitimate motive for intercourse, with which to answer the rigorists; nor, in answer to the promiscuity of the laxists, was marriage, in those days, viewed as a mutually supportive relationship in which sexual intimacy fostered union and affection. Exclusive emphasis was therefore placed on procreative purpose. Here was a clearly legitimate value, excluded by the purists and threatened by the libertines, which could therefore serve to legitimize the traditional middle position. This solution, clearly excluding contraceptive intercourse, was the one adopted, for example, by Augustine and by St. Gregory the Great.

By the time Pius XI reiterated the condemnation, much had changed or was changing. Pleasure, especially others', was now more readily (though sometimes still grudgingly) acknowledged as an acceptable motive, along with control of the sexual instinct. And stress was increasingly laid, as in the encyclical itself, on love as the prime concern of marriage and central to the meaning of conjugal union. Yet the condemnation of contraceptive intercourse persisted; for in the meantime a different rationale had risen to dominance, one that abstracted from such considerations. Onanistic intercourse was now judged "unnatural" and therefore "intrinsically evil." As Noonan observes, this Thomistic analysis "put enormous emphasis on the *givenness* of the act of insemination; the act was invested with a God given quality not to be touched by rational control or manipulation."[6]

From stress on purpose to stress on manner—such, very broadly, is the movement Noonan traces. Earlier moralists tended to condemn even intercourse of the pregnant or sterile, since it lacked the justifying end that distinguished legitimate conjugal coitus from extramarital license. Today these same forms are approved, since they do not contravene "nature," as the forbidden procedures do. "It is, no doubt, piquant," notes Noonan, with reference to Augustine, "that the first pronouncement on contraception by the most influential theologian teaching on such matters should be such a vigorous attack on the one method of avoiding procreation [namely, periodic continence] accepted by twentieth-century Catholic theologians as morally lawful."[7] Instructive as well as piquant, I would say. The contrast suggests how different was the rationale behind Augustine's teaching on contraception.

So, does the recent teaching agree with the ancient teaching? Yes and no. In its condemnation of artificial contraception, yes; in its reasons and underlying moral theory, no. The cognitive content has shifted while the noncognitive content has remained the same. This difference deserves more attention than the little it has received, for it relates importantly both to the morality of contraceptive intercourse and to the authority accorded to the tradition that has condemned it. Both these issues, however—the ethical and the ecclesial—lie outside the scope of the present discussion on verbal versus nonverbal agreement. Here, I will just make clear how this example differs from the preceding, Eucharistic one.

In that case, I surmised, there was only verbal agreement between the pronouncement of Trent and its recent transfinalist or transignificationist interpreters: once the cognitive content differed, so did the total meaning; for "bread" and "wine" are descriptive, not moral, expressions. In the present example, the agreement is largely verbal but not entirely, for expressions such as "sin," "wrong," and "evil," adding noncognitive content to the cognitive, thereby permit noncognitive agreement even where there is little or no cognitive consensus.

To carry conviction, this analysis requires one further step. For it may seem to assume that where reasons differ, so does the cognitive content of what is asserted. This is surely wrong. People may, for instance, agree in saying "It's raining" but differ in their reasons: one may hear the rain, another may see it, another may hear about it from others, in person or by radio, or may see someone come in dripping from outside. Yet here the cognitive content of the assertion "It's raining" does not differ, person by person or reason by reason. That is the same for all the speakers: their different evidence leads them to assert, in effect, that drops of water are falling from clouds roundabout. There is the descriptive core. Now, given this common combination of semantic sameness with epistemological differences, it is easy to suppose that moral expressions function similarly. But they do not: "right" and "wrong," "moral" and "immoral" reveal no comparable descriptive core unaffected by wide divergence in the reasons for applying the terms. This difference is veiled in multiple ways: by the fact that in a given society at a given time the divergence of reasons may not be as notable as in the history just sketched; by the presence, at a deeper level than shared descriptive criteria, of what might be termed the logic of moral concepts; by the presence of an emotive and prescriptive core which is constant; by the fact that this noncognitive core typically has cognitive backing of some sort (people have reasons—often strong, fully thought-out reasons—for favoring the actions they call right and opposing the actions they call wrong).

I could amplify this thumbnail account, adding further details, but already the contrast drawn can illustrate a massive phenomenon not previously noted a propos of earlier examples. Simpler, less complex expressions tend to influence our thinking about more complex expressions. For instance, proper names ("Lincoln," "Newark," "The Statue of Liberty"), with their single, easily identified referents, influence our thinking about general terms: they, too, we suppose, designate single referents—the essences hidden among all the varying, accidental features of the things covered by the terms. Again, the "is" of strict identity (say, between George Washington and the first president of the United States) is simpler than other kinds (say, the identity between the high C sung by a soprano and that written in the score); so that simpler use of the word acts as a default setting for our thinking about many matters, including central doctrines of Christian faith. Similarly, here, descriptive terms ("rain," "house," "human being"), though more complex than proper names, are simpler and more perspicuous in their functioning than moral expressions. So we conceive the latter on the model of the former. Reasons may differ, we think, but not the descriptive core. In this respect, we suppose, moral expressions basically resemble descriptive expressions.

I have challenged this assimilation. For the contrary view obscures the fundamental disagreement often hidden beneath verbal agreement in moral discourse—for instance, in debates concerning the morality of artificial contraception. Though my analyses of this particular example and of that in the preceding section may have erred in detail or overall, the analyses can serve their purpose nonetheless. They illustrate ways in which the surface appearance of agreement might, on closer scrutiny, prove importantly deceptive.

With one problem-centered chapter following another, a word of explanation and reassurance may not be amiss before we continue. In the preceding chapters, mixing negative and positive, the negative may seem to have predominated. For even when the overall thrust of a chapter has been positive—the role of language in thought, the nature of linguistic truth, the corresponding norm of predication, its feasibility, its transcendent possibilities, and so forth—negative examples have served to highlight the significance of the points being made. The impression might therefore arise that the linguistic practice of theologians is widely, deeply flawed. However, it is here, I suggest, as with the gospel saying about the healthy and the sick, and the greater need, if not the greater numbers, of the latter: whatever the ratio of failure to success may be in theology with regard to the issues here being canvassed (and doubtless success is more frequent than failure), it is the problems that merit attention more than the successes. The healthy have no need of a physician.

For Further Reflection

1. "There is a complexity about the logic of doctrinal statements which means that they have their meaning only in relation to a total world-view of God and his relation

to the world. And that total world-view is emphatically subject to change in differing ages. It therefore seems inescapable that what Cardinal Mercier regarded as a powerful objection to Tyrrell's modernism ought to be accepted as a simple statement of fact—'the dogmas of the Church . . . change their sense, if not necessarily their expression, with the ages to which they are addressed' "[8] (Maurice Wiles).

2. "It is also possible to claim that sometimes where the formulas have remained unaltered their meaning has significantly changed. Thus 'no salvation outside the church' meant something very different to Cyprian from what it meant to Jacques Maritain, who reinterprets it in terms of 'the soul of the church' and understands it to mean that 'there is no salvation outside the truth' or 'for those who sin against light' "[9] (Maurice Wiles).

3. "The author of this philosophy was spoken of at the end of the eighteenth century as a 'God-intoxicated man.' There is no page of Spinoza's *Ethics* on which the name of God does not appear many times, but this God is the antithesis of the Christian God. It is a Deity without personality or moral attributes, nothing more than the inexorable, indwelling principle of order and necessity in nature. Descartes' mathematically and mechanically ordered cosmos has become God"[10] (Ralph Eaton).

4. "The name of this infinite and inexhaustible depth and ground of all being is *God*. That depth is what the word *God* means. And if that word has not much meaning for you, translate it, and speak of the depths of your life, of the source of your being, of your ultimate concern, of what you take seriously without any reservation. Perhaps, in order to do so, you must forget everything traditional that you have learned about God, perhaps even that word itself. For if you know that God means depth, you know much about Him. You cannot then call yourself an atheist or unbeliever. For you cannot think or say: Life has no depth! Life itself is shallow. Being itself is surface only. If you could say this in complete seriousness, you would be an atheist; but otherwise you are not. He who knows about depth knows about God"[11] (Paul Tillich).

5. "An ecclesiastical anathema of the form 'If x says p, *anathema sit*' states that a particular formula p is false. With Whitehead, I want to distinguish a verbal statement or 'form of words' from a 'proposition.' A form of words can symbolize 'an indefinite number of diverse propositions.' . . . Since for the most part the propositions into which the condemned statement is analyzable will be significantly similar, common sense suggests that *many* of them will lie within the range of meaning of the condemned statement. But it is not logically necessary that *all* the propositions into which the condemned statement is analyzable are false. The most an anathema *need* say is that a certain verbal statement is analyzable into at least *one* false proposition"[12] (Anselm Atkins).

Chapter 18

Interfaith Dialogue

"If a lion could talk," Wittgenstein remarked, "we could not understand him."[1] The lion and its world are too foreign to us. So it is, it sometimes appears, for dialogue between believers of disparate faiths. According to one current perception of religious pluralism, the comparison is only too apt:

> There is no possible bridge to span the gap between religions. Also, there is no common core, including an underlying theism or ethics to unite them. Therefore, they are incommensurable. With the possibility of translation ruled out *a priori*, it would seem that there is no hope for a dialogical middle, no potential for deep conversation between persons practicing different religions.[2]

The purpose of the present chapter, in continuity with the preceding two—on agreement and disagreement, real and apparent—is to facilitate this deep conversation, or at least explore the possibilities. (The description of this study as a quick reconnaissance holds especially for the rapid tour, in this chapter and the next, through the complex topic of interfaith dialogue.)

It may be acknowledged to begin with that, as Michael Barnes has remarked, "a model of dialogue as a purely intellectual activity is no longer valid. Dialogue is, first and foremost, something more profoundly religious and therefore more profoundly human."[3] Nonetheless, as Barnes further observes,

> if dialogue is not to degenerate into a cosy exchange of vague imponderables, concentrating on the bland and uncontroversial,

it must be prepared to accept *all* aspects of a religion, including many which may well make us feel uncomfortable and distinctly puzzled. More than that: we must recognize that all religions have certain truth-claims which are a significant part of the tradition; to ignore them is to take the religion less than seriously.[4]

Theology, to be sure, does not ignore them and neither, therefore, will the present discussion.

Of all the problems of religious dialogue, those concerning truth are the thorniest. Customs, rites, symbols, languages, stories, metaphors, traditions—these may differ notably without their contradicting one another or some being better than others. Truth, however, is partisan. Where two doctrines conflict, both can't be true, and true beliefs are superior to false. As such, they should be preferred. Yet, "Claims to uniqueness or normativeness on the part of Christianity, or any religion," it may be urged, "are simply an inappropriate response to the problems raised by the pluralism of modern religious culture."[5] One solution is to downplay truth and its significance. Another is to make truth relative to individual traditions, religions, or believers. Neither of these options looks promising in the light of previous chapters on the nature and normativity of truth. Hence, the present chapter, in continuity with the next-to-last, will take a different tack and consider whether, when, and how different-sounding doctrines of different faith traditions really contradict one another.

Apparent conflict, as we have seen, may be largely or entirely verbal. Yet the possibility cannot be ignored that the conflict is real and that one side or the other may be closer to the truth than the other. Hence, there arises a psychological, moral, and religious dilemma:

> "Is it possible to speak as a *committed* believer and still participate in genuine religious dialogue?" More concretely: "Is it possible for a committed Christian to have real dialogue with a Hindu?" For it is the essential character of genuine dialogue that it is an *open* exercise, in which each participant is prepared to meet the other as the adherent of a sacred tradition valid in its own right and enshrining valuable insights that one's own religion perhaps lacks but would do well to share.[6]

However they are formulated, in Barnes's view the problems surrounding any serious interfaith conversations ultimately reduce themselves to some version of this loyalty-openness dilemma. "Holding both values means appreciating the other tradition for its own sake and appropriating that tradition without losing touch with our roots. Such an ideal is fraught with difficulty."[7]

Essential for dealing with the difficulty is the sort of linguistic analysis sampled in the last two chapters, on genuine versus merely verbal agreement and disagreement. Whereas the comparison between Trent's teaching on transubstantiation and recent doctrines of transignification or transfinalization showed that fidelity to traditional doctrine demands something more than employing the same words, the comparison between apparently conflicting accounts of faith attested that disagreement between doctrines may be more verbal than real. Since interfaith examples inviting similar scrutiny are far too numerous to review and analyze here, the present treatment will focus on a single illustrative topic of paramount interest and importance for interfaith dialogue: God, the supreme being.

Perhaps no issue of interreligious dialogue stands in greater need of clarification, and, as a passage such as the following illustrates, the needful clarification is largely linguistic:

> [M]an is related to a power or reality "above" or "beyond" himself, i.e., beyond his material life. This reality is referred to in different religions as Brahma, Allah, "Buddha"—life, or even *Nirvāna*. Religion is therefore an expression of man's relation to the limits of his own existence. That ultimate frontier of human existence, in whichever way religions may conceive it, is what the word "God" signifies.[8]

One wonders. Is this really what the word "God"—the English, Western word "God"—signifies? And are all these expressions, drawn from various traditions, really names for one identical reality? So do all the world's religions really venerate the same deity? How much truth do, or may, such claims contain? Such questions as these will take us beyond the examples and analyses of the last two chapters.

A Chart of Possibilities

A few guidelines will be helpful at the start. In everyday discourse, for the most part statements that appear to agree do agree and statements that appear not to agree do not. In interfaith dialogue, however, across linguistic, cultural, and doctrinal boundaries, appearances are more deceptive and agreement or disagreement is harder to ascertain. Discernment may be aided by distinguishing four general possibilities:

1. *Apparently conflicting assertions, same reality*. This characterization is suggested by an example such as the debate about fetal status, scrutinized two chapters back. The same reality—the fetus, zygote, or embryo—is described as a person or not a person, a human being or not a human being. These apparently clashing descriptions do not assert and deny some feature or set of features commonly conveyed by the expression *person* or *human being*. Rather, they surreptitiously (though usually unwittingly) redefine the expression. The difference is verbal.

2. *Apparently conflicting assertions, different realities*. Here claims about "theology" or "faith," examined in previous chapters, can serve in illustration. Thus, the assertion that faith is "believing things revealed" and the assertion that faith is "personal trust" appear to conflict but do not; rather, they accord the same honorific title to different things, whose existence and desirability neither side contests. It is good to believe and it is good to trust, and people do both. The word *faith* just gets selectively attached to one or the other.

3. *Conflicting assertions, same reality*. This common configuration is illustrated by Wittgenstein's example. People may differ widely in what they say about Moses. One may assert that Moses was in fact fished from the Nile as a child and another may deny it; one may assert that Moses received the tablets on Sinai and another may contest it; and so forth. Yet the name "Moses" may still refer to the same historical individual, who did some of the alleged things and not others. The like holds for any proper name of a single person, place, nation, race, or other referent about which speakers hold and express conflicting beliefs. Their assertions clash, but the reality referred to is the same.

4. *Conflicting assertions, different realities*. This configuration, completing the set of logical variations, may cause puzzlement. If two speakers are not talking about the same reality, how can they make conflicting statements about it? Think, though, of the conflicting assertions that the Earth is the center of our planetary system and that the sun is the center. The assertions speak of different realities, the Earth and the sun, yet they do conflict.

In this listing I have used the word *reality* or *realities*, which suggests the things' existence, as do the illustrations I have cited; but I might complicate matters further by distinguishing between existent and nonexistent referents. Thus, if no such person as Moses existed, we might wish to accommodate this situation by varying the third characterization to read: "conflicting beliefs, *no* reality." However, the chart is sufficiently complex as it stands. Refinements can be added as they arise.

God

The more assertions diverge about some apparently single referent, the more doubts they occasion about their having a common referent, hence about their genuine incompatibility. I shall therefore pass over divergent Christian sayings about God, with their significant but lesser discrepancies, and consider first, more generally, the God of Western tradition.

The God of Jewish, Christian, and Muslim Belief

Jews, Christians, and Muslims believe in a personal god, creator and sustainer of the universe, supremely worthy of worship and obedience. Their god "is not an abstract idea but is a living and loving Person."[9] For Christians, the sameness of the Christian with the Hebrew god has been a basic, very significant assumption. In their gospels,

> The God to which both the speaker and the listeners relate is God as manifested in the religious tradition of Israel, and because this is so the Old Testament has been foundational for the Christian doctrine of God. In the second century AD a figure arose to contest this. Marcion said that the God of the Old Testament was not the same God as that of the New Testament, that the former was responsible for this world and its prevalent suffering, while the latter God came as a stranger into this place bringing kindness and love. But early Christianity rejected this teaching as heretical. It was held that "the God and Father of our Lord Jesus Christ" was the God of the Old Testament.[10]

Jews have been more reluctant to recognize this identity. As C. Schoeneveld notes: "For Israel God cannot be man or become man. For the Church, God can be man and does become flesh. Here is the deep gulf: for Judaism God's holiness and power, so to speak, forbid him to be man; for Christianity God's holiness and power, so to speak, enable him to be man. Two different understandings of God are here at stake; which understanding of God is the true one?"[11] Going farther, we may ask: are these two different understandings understandings of the same god? Where does this confrontation fit within our fourfold scheme of possibilities?

In the light of chapter 3, the third classification ("conflicting assertions, same reality") looks most apt. Jews and Christians acknowledge the same god but they disagree about the relationship of that god with the man Jesus. Just how they disagree is far from evident, for the nature of the relationship of Jesus with God is, by Christian admission (indeed, by Christian insistence), deeply mysterious. The conflict is made to seem sharp by the frequent though often unspoken assumption, by Christians as well as by Jews, that the relationship asserted and denied is one of strict identity, excluding any difference between the terms, human and divine, of the relationship. Yet the assumption is merely that—an assumption. For the strict identity that a word such as "is" (as in "Jesus is God") too readily suggests, neither Christian scriptures nor authoritative Christian teachings (e.g., of the Council of Chalcedon) support.[12] Thus, the gulf Schoeneveld speaks of is not as deep as it appears—not deep enough, in its mystery, to indicate that the "God and Father of our Lord Jesus Christ" is any other than the god of Jewish belief.

With regard to Christian Trinitarian doctrine, where disagreement with the other major monotheistic faiths seems most profound, a similar assessment may be warranted. Here, observes David Brown, for the Trinity as for the Incarnation, "[t]he central difficulty concerns what is commonly labeled the problem of identity, namely the question of what would justify us in speaking of one entity rather than of a plurality of entities; that is to say, talking of one person rather than two in the incarnational case and of one God rather than three in the trinitarian instance."[13] If Christians believed that the three divine "persons" were such in the full, familiar sense of the term, then, despite the singular expression "God," they would use it as the name for three gods. Communitarian theologians sometimes veer in this direction before stopping short, but Christian doctrine in general does not countenance or imply such a view.[14] So comparison with Moses seems apposite. As people can hold widely varying views about Moses and still be talking about the same historical individual, so too, perhaps, Christians, Jews, and Muslims—indeed Christians among themselves—may hold widely varying views about God and still be talking about the same divine being.

Nevertheless, the theoretical, much-debated question will intrude: How notably can people diverge in their beliefs and still be talking about the same reality? The question becomes more pressing if we pass from a comparison of Western beliefs that we do not hesitate to call beliefs about God and compare them with the most comparable beliefs of Eastern religions. Are these latter, that often sound so different, still beliefs about *God*?

The God of East and West?

John Hick, the most prolific writer on this topic, employs a more comprehensive expression, "the Real," and draws the following distinction: "The two main concepts in terms of which religious experience is structured are the concept of deity, or of the Real as personal, and the concept of the absolute, or of the Real as non-personal."[15] The first, personalist conception, dominant in Western faiths, appears also in the East: "In quite a different strand of history deity became concretized as the Vishnu of India, God of a thousand names who has become incarnate on earth in times of human crisis."[16] Other religious cultures, however, "have experienced the Real in non-personal terms, which have become specific as the Tao, or as the Brahman of advaitic Hinduism, or as the *dharmakaya*, or *sunyata*, or *nirvana* of Buddhism."[17]

The epistemic parity of these varying views is important to Hick, for if some views were truer than others, the difference should show: it should manifest itself in the lives and virtues of their adherents. However, he detects no such differentiation. "While there are all manner of fascinating cultural differences, Muslims and Jews and Hindus and Sikhs and Buddhists in general do not seem to be less honest and truthful, or less loving and compassionate in family and community, or less good citizens, or less religiously committed, than are one's Christian neighbours in general."[18] Three different solutions to this problem—three ways of placing the major faiths on a par with respect to their truth—can be discerned in Hick's writings. Adapting our fourfold scheme of possibilities, we might state them as follows, bringing out the parity preserved in all three:

1. *Apparently conflicting assertions, different realities, and the assertions equally true about those realities.* In Hick's words: "These different and incompatible truth-claims are claims about different manifestations of the Real to humanity. As such, they do not contradict one another."[19] The Real is one, but its manifestations are many, and it is these that we are characterizing, aptly enough, when we make our apparently conflicting faith-claims.[20]

2. *Conflicting assertions, same reality, and the assertions equally false about that reality.* This alternative results when Hick combines the view that "the different world religions are referring, through their specific concepts of the Gods and Absolutes, to the same ultimate Reality"[21] (not just to its manifestations) with his repeated assertions that the Real in itself lies so far beyond human understanding that "it cannot be said to be one or many, person or thing, conscious or unconscious, purposive or non-purposive, substance or process, good or evil, loving or hating."[22] All such claims are mistaken.[23]

3. *Apparently conflicting assertions, same reality, and the assertions equally (but selectively, imperfectly) true about that reality.* "Speaking very tentatively," Hick has written, "I think it is possible that the sense of the divine as non-personal may indeed reflect an aspect of the same infinite

reality that is encountered as personal in theistic religious experience."[24] Think, he suggests, of the fabled elephant palpated by the blind and of the differing descriptions that result when one blind person feels a leg, another the trunk, and a third a tusk. To be sure, "The suggestion is not that the different encounters with the divine which lie at the basis of the great religious traditions are responses to different parts of the divine. They are encounters from different historical and cultural standpoints with the same infinite divine reality and as such they lead to differently focused awareness of the reality."[25] In illustration of this viewpoint, we might note how differently even Christian thinkers may characterize the Christian God: in a philosophical context as "first cause," "ground of being," or "last end" and in a liturgical, homiletic, or theological context as "creator," "judge," or "God and Father of our Lord Jesus Christ." The first way of speaking is impersonal, the second personal. Yet one way does not contradict the other, nor is one truer than the other; so problems of superiority or inferiority do not arise.

A problem for each of these three hypotheses, as stated, is its uniformity. Is it realistic to suppose that any such single account fits the relationship between all major faiths?

Consider a comparison. A half-dozen pages in William Manchester's *The Glory and the Dream*, recounting the days before Franklin Roosevelt's election in 1932, contain the following diverse perceptions of the president-to-be: "a magnificent leader," "no leader," "wishy-washy," "another Hoover," "another weak man," "an apostle of progress," "a great borrower," "the only politician in the country who thought of economics as a *moral* problem," "not a man of great intellectual force or supreme moral stamina," "corkscrew candidate of a convoluting convention," "magnanimous and sure of himself," "too soft," "too eager to please and be all things to all men," "the image of zest, warmth, and dignity," "weakness and readiness to compromise," "a kind of universal joint, or rather a switchboard, a transformer," "a pill to cure an earthquake," "a vigorous well-intentioned gentleman of good birth and breeding."[26] No two of these descriptions are identical. Some are contradictory. Others differ greatly yet are mutually compatible. Others are neither clearly compatible nor clearly incompatible. Furthermore, the descriptions, reflecting the diversity and fallibility of those who proffer them, are more or less true, more or less plausible, more or less objective and unbiased. Nonetheless, despite their disparities, the descriptions are all of the same person; all have the same referent. Is it likely, though, that similar uniformity of reference prevails where cultural conditioning is still more diverse, where descriptions are still more disparate, where no common name picks out or even suggests a common referent, where the reality or realities in question lie far beyond our shared, sensible experience, and where not even the existence of all and sundry is assured?[27]

Thus, a further possibility besides those so far envisioned may be more realistic. Various of the four suggested configurations listed above, plus perhaps others, and not just one, may be pertinent for interfaith dialogue, and various of them may in fact be instantiated.[28] Even comparison of just the major Eastern and Western faiths, case by case and variant by variant, may not suggest a single configuration or lead to a single verdict. Indeed, no verdict may emerge; the mystery may be too deep for human discernment. In any case, whatever the outcome, it will depend largely on considerations hardly touched on thus far. What criteria determine that a given entity is the object of a person's belief or assertion? What criteria determine that that entity is the same as some other? These questions we can save for a separate chapter, carrying farther the same inquiry: Do the world's major religions, in their different ways, all name a common supreme reality?

For Further Reflection

1. "No one can communicate the gospel without using the word 'God.' If one is talking to people of a non-Christian religion, one is bound to use one of the words that the language of that people provides to denote 'God.' Plainly the content of the word as heard by the non-Christian will have been furnished by religious experience outside the Christian faith. By using the word, the missionary is taking non-Christian experience as the starting point. Without doing this, there is no way of communicating"[29](Lesslie Newbigin).

2. "[M]any Christians have maintained that the stories about Abraham, Isaac, Jacob, and Jesus are part of the referential meaning of the word 'God' as this is used in biblical religion and have therefore concluded that philosophers and others who do not advert to these narratives mean something else by 'God.' The God of the philosophers may or may not exist and may or may not in some respects be assimilable to the God of the Bible, but faith in the biblical

deity, according to this view, is logically independent of philosophical arguments over these questions"[30] (George Lindbeck).

3. "If, however, the insight is gained that, as a human being, one cannot really talk about the divine and ultimate truth, but nevertheless can talk about human understanding, a common basis for a human dialogue is attained. Then only human persons, who can talk with one another about their understanding of the ultimate unknown, face one another in a discussion between the various religions. They can talk about their human understanding, but not about that which lies beyond human understanding"[31] (Karl-Erich Grözinger).

4. "Thus, says the relativist, religions are particular frameworks of belief and behaviour which have a certain *internal* coherence. One can therefore raise questions about the truth or falsity of individual assertions within the framework. What one cannot do is ask whether the framework *as a whole* is true or false. This is because a religion is by definition culture-relative; it can only be understood in relation to particular cultures and customs which are appropriate to particular people"[32] (Michael Barnes).

5. "For the outsider, the language of another religion is like a foreign language, which is at first unintelligible to the other person without a process of translation. This means that the themes to be treated in such a dialogue must be taken out of their particular clothing and formulated in a universal way, before they can become intelligible to the other party. In other words, it is necessary to create an abstract, comparative language, into which both sides translate their statements"[33] (Karl-Erich Grözinger).

Chapter 19

Interfaith Identities

According to Peter Byrne, "The doctrine that all major religious traditions refer to a common sacred, transcendent reality is at the heart of [religious] pluralism."[1] In this doctrine, which Byrne endorses, two points can be distinguished: (1) the traditions all refer to a sacred, transcendent reality; (2) the reality referred to is the same for them all. Both of these claims have been contested and both stand in need of confirmation. So, continuing the last chapter's inquiry, let us explore these two questions of broad linguistic and methodological interest: first the alleged reference (for the question of sameness does not arise unless there are instances of transcendent reference to compare), then the alleged sameness.

Reference

We have noted Hick's ambivalence concerning the reference of "Vishnu," "God," "Allah," and other sacred names. Sometimes he says that they refer to "the same ultimate Reality," sometimes that they refer to "different manifestations of the Real to humanity."[2] Now, it seems he can't have it both ways—both transcendent reference and nontranscendent; and it is not clear, from his viewpoint—or rather, from his varied viewpoints—which way the verdict should go.

Suppose, for comparison, that one person, looking skyward, spots a plane and calls it tiny while another spots a plane and calls it huge. If we surmise that the plane they are thus describing is the same, we may explain the discrepancy of their reports in either of two ways: (1) They are talking about plane-appearances, not about the plane; for the plane-appearances do differ in size, whereas a single plane cannot, in itself, be both tiny and huge. (2) They are talking about the plane but (perhaps not noticing the difference) are describing it as it appears and not as it is in itself. The plane itself is neither that tiny spot in the distance, as it appears to one viewer, nor the body filling the other's visual field. It transcends all such subjective representations.

As an explanation of Hick's ambivalence, this sounds plausible. For, on the one hand, believers typically speak the language of being and not of appearing: Yahweh *is* loving and does not just *look* loving; God *is* triune and does not just *seem* triune; and so forth. Yet, on the other hand, in Hick's oft-stated, most characteristic recent view, the transcendent Real is not loving, triune, or any such thing; only the appearances—the beings of religious faiths—are. This, then, may explain his sometimes taking the appearances, and not the transcendent Real, as what is spoken of. Still, even from such an agnostic perspective, a verdict against transcendent reference does not follow automatically. For even a Kantian can admit that when we say objects *are* blue or spherical, not merely that they *look* that way, we are speaking of the objects and not merely of their appearances. The populace may not note any noumenal-phenomenal distinction, but a Kantian need not correct their assertions about what physical objects are (hot, round, heavy, etc.), or cease to speak that way himself. He can analyze what is said without rejecting it; and his analysis can identify the things themselves as what are referred to when people talk about pokers, mushrooms, locomotives, and the like. Such, in fact, is an ordinary Kantian way of speaking.

Given his views, another possible source of Hick's ambivalence are familiar theories of reference. One such theory would require accurate description for successful reference. If, for example, I have a sister and only one, and I speak of "my sister," that description pinpoints the person referred to. Likewise, if there is a creator of the universe and only one, and I speak of "the creator of the universe," that description, too, pinpoints the being referred to. If, however, I had no sister, or if there were no creator of the universe, reference would fail. Yet, according to Hick's favored recent view, such is the actual situation: there is no transcendent being that "creator of the universe" or any other religious characterization accurately describes. Only our phenomenal, cultural divinities are "merciful," "wise," "powerful," "judge," "creator," or the like. The Real itself transcends all such characterizations.

A "causal" account of reference, less dependent on accurate description, might therefore appear more promising, from Hick's agnostic perspective, for transcendent reference. Here, "What connects a name to what it names is not the latter's satisfying some condition specified in the name's definition. Names, instead, are simply attached to things, applied as labels, as it were. A proper name, once attached, becomes a socially available device for making the relevant name bearer a subject of discourse."[3] Thus, an infant is baptized "Rebecca" or a ship is christened "Admiral Simms," and thereafter people know what person or ship is intended when that name is used. So it may have been long ago, we might surmise, for "Brahman," "Yahweh," "God," and the names of other major world divinities: first, direct experience of the transcendent reality; then the naming; then a complex causal chain maintaining the original reference down to our day. Yet, abstracting from other difficulties, how would the initial labeling succeed without any implicit or explicit description of the intended referent—any *true* description, of the kind Hick typically disallows?

Near the start of his *Blue Book*, Wittgenstein imagines meaning being imparted to the word *tove* by our pointing to a pencil and saying "This is tove." This definition, he observes, could be interpreted in all sorts of ways: "This is a pencil," "This is round," "This is wood," "This is one," "This is hard," etc.[4] And indeed, for all that the defining formula alone indicated, it might serve, not to define a descriptive term but to identify a referent. "Tove" might be a proper name for that particular object. To remedy such ambiguity, we would need to become more specific and say, for instance, "This *shape* is tove," "This *color* is tove," or "This *size* is tove." Thereupon, the same problems would return as above, for a descriptive account of reference. Suppose that the indicated object only appeared to have the property (shape, color, or size) in question. Suppose, in our instance, that the Real has none of the properties—goodness, wisdom, power, etc.—we ascribe to it. To what, in that hypothesis, are we referring, if not to the mere appearances?

There is no need to pursue this line of inquiry more closely, for the main source of these recurring problems, for both descriptive and "causal" accounts of transcendent reference, is the supposition that none of our descriptions aptly characterize the Real itself. That is why the names have difficulty getting attached to it. And in Hick's thought, a principal reason for this supposition, it seems, is his failure to make place for analogy: he repeatedly assumes that if what we say about the Real is not "literally" true, then it must be merely "figurative." Once this obstacle is removed, via the elephant analogy, PRS, or the like, the difficulties for transcendent reference do not entirely disappear, but they do greatly diminish.

Byrne argues, realistically, that our conceptions of the transcendent need not be entirely accurate in order for reference to succeed. Consider, he suggests, the broadly analogous problem in the philosophy of science:

> Interpreters of science may, for good reason, want to say of earlier scientific theories that they genuinely refer to things and stuffs that our present theories commit us to (for example, viruses, atoms, genes) even though these theories disagree with current definitions of these entities and thus are largely mistaken in their characterization of them (when judged by the norm of present theories). The answer to the conundrum from recent semantic theories is that reference is for the most part not a function of descriptive success, but of causality and context.[5]

Thus, "the name 'virus' was coined before researchers had the ability to observe viruses with the aid of the electron microscope. The word was coined to refer to the cause of a range of effects—symptoms of disease. 'Virus' referred to whatever it was that was the explanation of these effects."[6]

In *Prolegomena to Religious Pluralism*, Byrne develops this comparison at length, in support of his assertion that the major religious traditions all refer to a sacred, transcendent reality. However, even if such reference were discernible in each of the major religions, individually, it would not follow that they all referred to a "*common* sacred, transcendent reality," as we have seen Byrne assert. So let us now turn to this second, more troublesome aspect of his claim.

Sameness

Purely verbal truths aside, the truth of assertions of sameness or oneness is determined no differently than that of other statements: partly by the things described and partly by the language employed in describing them. However, in the language to which "same" and "one" belong (which in this respect is not idiosyncratic), these words function differently than do terms such as, for instance, "blue" and "rectangular." Shown a pair of objects—say, a pair of books—and asked to describe their color or shape, one can readily comply: it suffices to see their color or shape. Shown the same pair of objects and asked to say whether they are one and the same, one cannot reply without more ado.

First, it is necessary to distinguish (in the way the phrase "one and the same" can either suggest or obscure) between what I will call the question of individuation and the question of identity.[7] The identity question starts with an x and a y (e.g., the book in my right hand and the book in my left) and asks if they are identical. The individuation question asks the prior question, what makes the x *an* x (e.g., *a* book in my left hand) and the y *a* y (e.g., *a* book in my right hand). Why the singular?[8] This more fundamental question is easily conflated with the other, since both can be discussed in terms of "sameness," and often are. It is necessary, then, to be clear about what type of sameness is under discussion. Here I will focus first on the individuation question, because it is more basic.

Within this focus, it is necessary to distinguish between terms that have individuating criteria and those that do not. For the former, the criteria vary from term to term. Thus, the "same" lake can dry up then return whereas the "same" puddle cannot. A club can change all its members over time and remain the "same club," whereas a book cannot change all its words and remain the "same book." Class by class, category by category, the criteria of individuation differ widely. Clearly, however, words such as "thing," "being," or "reality," which pluralist identity claims employ, lack such criteria. As they stand, therefore, these claims look empty.

Suppose someone holds up two books and asks, "Are these the same?" The answer must be, "The same *what*?" If the questioner replies, "the same copy," the answer must be "No." If the questioner replies, "the same novel," the answer may be "Yes." The individuating criteria differ for copies and for novels. So, too, if someone asks, for example, whether God and nirvana are the same, the answer will have to be, "The same *what*?" If the questioner replies, "the same thing," there can be no answer; for there are no individuating criteria for things in general.

Since this kind of objection is not widely familiar,[9] let me dwell on it for a moment. An expression such as "three rivers" does two things: it counts and it describes. So, too, does the expression "a river"; it just changes the number. Such numbering is based on reasons so familiar that we may not advert to them or notice their variation from class to class. Thus, whereas water can return to the same river bed after a dry spell and still count as the "same river," water cannot crest later on in the same spot and still count as the "same wave." It might be otherwise. Indeed, the criteria might conceivably be reversed: the "same river" might have to fill the river bed continuously, without temporal break, and water repeatedly cresting in the same place, no matter how discontinuously, might still count as the "same wave." The single river might get counted as many rivers; the many waves might get counted as a single wave. However, for whatever intriguing reasons, such is not English usage. And the language spoken determines truth conditions for expressions used in that language.

Now, a river and a wave are both "things." So, clearly, temporal continuity does not figure among the criteria of individuation for things in general. To count as the same, some things, like waves, must be temporally continuous, whereas other things, like rivers, need not be. Similarly, some things, such as people, must be spatially continuous, whereas other things, such as societies, need not be. Yet all are "things." And so it is for any other individuating criteria we might cite. No such criteria hold for all classes of things. Accordingly, it seems that the only sense it might have to say, for example, that God and nirvana are the same thing would be that they satisfy the criteria of sameness for some more specific term. So the question returns: *What* term?

A remedy that might suggest itself would be to restate the claims of sameness using a more definite word than "thing" or "reality." Within the Western tradition one might, for instance, try "god" or "spirit"; but these terms, too, are problematic. What criteria of individuation does the language reveal for gods or spirits, and how might such criteria conceivably arise, language-wide? For much of our history, notes Nicholas Lash, "gods" were simply what people worshipped. "In other words, the word 'god' worked rather like the way in which the word 'treasure' still does," and there is no class of objects known as "treasures." [10] ("There is no use going into a supermarket," Lash observes, "and asking for six bananas, a loaf of bread, two packets of soap and three treasures.") Besides, pluralists have a reason for their choice of less definite expressions: thanks to their greater generality, "thing" and "reality" more readily accommodate the full range of religious referents—Tao as well as sunyata, Brahman as well as God, nirvana as well as Vishnu. Such, then, are the terms pluralists favor, and such are the terms they need.[11]

A solution to this problem of individuation might first be sought in the following direction. For many terms (e.g., "time," "part," "sky") there are no individuating criteria. However, criteria or no criteria, descriptions can also explain and justify the singular. They, too, can pick out individuals. And once individuation is effected either way, by criteria or by descriptions, a basis may exist for judgments of sameness.

In illustration of these abstract remarks, think of a river winding through a forest. A swimmer speaks of the widest stretch of the river, a fisherman of the shallowest stretch, and a traveler of the sunniest stretch. Upon investigation, it turns out that all three are speaking of roughly the same stretch of the river. So we might naturally state the situation. Despite the absence of any criteria of individuation for "stretches," individuation does here occur, it seems, via the descriptions ("the widest stretch," "the shallowest stretch," and "the sunniest stretch"). Each time, the phrases identify, roughly, the stretch in question—the same, single stretch.

In the light of this example we can ask: Suppose one transcendent being were described as the most powerful being there is, another as the wisest, and a third as the best; and suppose that all three coincided much as do the three described stretches of the river. Mightn't we then be justified in saying that all three are one and the same being? Granted, there are no criteria of individuation for "beings," but neither are there for "stretches." And, given the transcendence of the realities in question, what better term is there to describe the imagined common referent than "being," "thing," "reality," or the like?

This comparison has two problems. One concerns the singular. Any stretch of the river consists of many stretches, and if all, for example, are equally, maximally sunny, then all may be described as the sunniest stretches of the river (e.g., one from the bend to the boulder, another from the boulder to the pier, and so forth). "Sunniest stretch" does not suffice to individuate. A second difficulty concerns the comparison's simplicity. It seems most readily applicable within a single religion, or with regard to kindred religions such as Judaism, Christianity, and Islam. All three superlatives—"most powerful," "wisest," and "best"—apply to the God of Jew, Christian, and Muslim. However, even within this kinship cluster, some characterizations diverge. Most notably, the Christian God is triune whereas the Jewish and Muslim God is not. So, does the river comparison still work? If one person spoke of the widest, *slowest* stretch of the river and others spoke of the widest, *fastest* stretch of the river, would they be talking about the same stretch? How could that be determined, even by the most knowledgeable observer, given the contradiction in their descriptions (slowest versus fastest)?

Perhaps it could not, and the like might hold for the comparison, say, between Christian and Buddhist beliefs, which diverge still more sharply. However, for the three Western monotheistic faiths, a different, somewhat richer comparison might be substituted for the river. One person speaks of his encounter with a woman who is middle-aged, brunette, *the mother of three*, and president of the local college. Another person speaks of his encounter with a woman who is middle-aged, brunette, *childless*, and the president of the same local college. Though both speakers cannot be right about the number of children (three versus none) for a single woman, if all the rest of their descriptions are correct, then doubtless both are speaking about the same woman: the president of the college. So it may be, perhaps, for Jew, Christian, and Muslim. Despite their differences, they may all be talking about the same being—the same omnipotent, omniscient, holy creator of the universe.

Such is the frequent suggestion. Thus, Hendrik Vroom writes:

> It is remarkable to note, for example, that in English translations of Christian, Islamic and Hindu treatises similar predicates are attributed to the Divine, such as "eternal,"

"omniscient," "blissful," "gracious" and "unchangeable." This similarity provides a firm ground on which to defend the claim that two or more traditions have the same idea of transcendence. If there are indeed enough commonalities, it would be right to conclude that these traditions are referring to the same 'god.'[12]

This solution via converging descriptions looks plausible, but notice how its plausibility is achieved. More than one woman might be middle-aged, brunette, and the president of a local college; hence, those traits would not suffice to individuate. Individuation was assured by adding the crucial word "same" (the individuals described were president of the *same* local college), together with the reasonable assumption that, though there might be more than one local college, individual colleges do not have more than one president. Now, neither that saving word, *same*, nor that saving assumption of singularity appears in the theological listing just quoted (which in this respect is typical of others that might be cited). Vroom notes that in English translations of Christian, Islamic, and Hindu treatises similar predicates, such as "eternal," "omniscient," "blissful," "gracious," and "unchangeable," are attributed to the Divine; and he sees this descriptive agreement as warranting a judgment of identical reference. However, neither individually nor collectively do these terms assure individuation (any more than do "middle-aged," "brunette," and "president"): there might be more than one being that was eternal, omniscient, blissful, gracious, *or* unchangeable, and more than one that was eternal, omniscient, blissful, gracious, *and* unchangeable. And if we make the supposition that there is only one such being, it seems we will need criteria of individuation to give the supposition sense. There are individuating criteria for presidents but none for sheer "beings."

As at least a partial solution for a restricted range of religions, in place of converging descriptions we might envisage some one description, common to kindred faiths, which can have no more than one referent. Thus, Levenson, for example, cited omnipotence, foreknowledge, justice, and mercy as among the attributes of the God of Jews, Christians, and Muslims. For reasons already noted, the last three traits, even if maximized, would not suffice to individuate, since they might be shared by more than one being; and the supposition of a single possessor would be empty without criteria of individuation for "possessors." The first trait, however, could not be shared: the hypothesis of multiple all-powerful beings is incoherent, since the power of each would be limited by the power of the others.

This line of reflection may, like others, mitigate somewhat the misgivings stirred, incidentally, by the challenge here raised to pluralist claims; but, given the breadth of those claims, it does not save them from the charge of emptiness. They embrace, for example, both Christians and Buddhists; and Christians and Buddhists give very different accounts of the transcendent. However, implicit in the suggestion of convergent descriptions, an alternative response may lie dialectically concealed. Rather than asserting that the transcendent referents of the major faith traditions are all the same single reality, we might take a cue from the Principle of Relative Similarity and look for comparisons that come closer than alternative comparisons. Perhaps the river comparison, or the comparison with the woman college president, could serve this way. Or, citing the homely comparison of multiple faith traditions with several blind men feeling a single elephant, we might suggest: if this comparison comes closer than does a comparison with several blind men feeling parts of different elephants in the same herd, in the same elephant population, or in the same museum collection of elephant parts, the single-elephant comparison is preferable. The resemblance may still be distant, as it is for descriptive expressions applied to the transcendent; and other comparisons might be still more appropriate. However, whatever the comparison, if it appears apt, it may replace the corresponding identity statements relating the same faith traditions. For in the absence of criteria of individuation, the assertions look empty, whereas the comparison or parable is not.

True, the assertions may not be psychologically empty. Fuzzy images, indefinite phantasms, flitting through our minds, may accompany the words, especially if the assertions are challenged. Advised that claims of transcendent sameness are empty, we may call up a phantom thing, imagine that single thing being experienced or mentally targeted by multiple thoughts or thinkers, and—without recognizing the emptiness of such image-mongering—dismiss linguistic objections as sophisticated obfuscation of the obvious. Where is the problem? Viewed in the way I have suggested, a parable, such as that of the elephant, can serve to articulate and give intelligible form to vague thoughts such as these.

We know what the blind men are feeling; they don't. We know criteria of individuation for such things; they don't. We know that, by these criteria, what they are feeling is one and the same elephant; they don't. We can contrast one and the same elephant with one and the same elephant herd, elephant population, or collection of elephant parts; they can't. Yet, with sharing and reflection they might form some educated surmises in the manner David Krieger has suggested:

What if the blind men were able and willing to listen to one another and to perceive that they all had, indeed, experienced some truth? What if, instead of condemning each other, each took the other by the hand and led him to that point where he had touched the elephant? Each would then see that the description which the other had given was justified. It would turn out that the elephant really was as each had described it. All could now admit this. For each would find not only his own description of the elephant confirmed, but also *completed* through the description of the other.[13]

In some such way as this, I suggest, we can make sense of the pluralist hypothesis that all the world's major religions refer to the same transcendent reality. For notice that Krieger here says nothing, explicitly, about *sameness*.

The elephant parable might tempt us to do so; for, like most comparisons, it is not apt in all respects. Filling it out, we may plausibly imagine that the blind men know some language and some linguistic criteria of individuation, just not the ones we know for visible objects such as elephants. So the men's surmises might become semantic as well as ontological. That is, they might surmise that sighted people have a word for the sort of thing that they, the blind, can only nonvisually surmise. And they might further conjecture that by the criteria of individuation for that sort of thing, what they are palpating counts as one and the same individual of that kind. At this point, however, the parallel with our theological situation breaks down. We, in our darkness, may be ontologically blind, but we are not semantically deprived. No transcendent facts of language lie beyond our ken. Figuratively speaking, transcendent elephants there may be, but not unknown words for such creatures or unknown criteria determining their sameness or difference, oneness or multiplicity. No Platonic realm of Forms remains to be intuited or recollected to tell us what we should say. The parable, therefore, or some variant, appears irreplaceable; this may be the best we can do.

Claims of "sameness" may appear more definite than the fuzzy parable, but the reverse seems in fact to be the case. Two people feeling different parts of a single, living elephant might be said to feel the "same thing," but so, too, for example, might two people feeling similar items in a single collection of elephant parts. That, too, the whole collection, could count as the "same thing." Given these alternative examples of sameness (same elephant versus same collection), which would pluralists choose as approximating more closely, though still distantly, to what they wish to say? Making a choice (no doubt in favor of the elephant), they would move beyond the empty indefiniteness of assertions of sameness. "This," they might say, "comes closer to what we have in mind."

Let this rapid reconnaissance suffice. Its aim has been, not to complicate a simple, straightforward question ("Same or not?"), but to dispel the deceptive impression of the question's simplicity, which apparently accounts for the fact that the semantic dimension of the pluralist debate, underlying the epistemological, has received so little attention.

For Further Reflection

1. "Direct reference to God is made possible by a person's perceiving God, and attaching the name 'God' to what she thus meets in experience"[14] (Joe Houston, on William Alston).

2. "In I Kings 18, the prophet Elijah, confronted with widespread defection to Baal among his countrymen, poses a stark challenge: 'If the LORD [the conventional English rendering of the four-letter Hebrew name of the God of Israel] is God, follow Him; and if Baal, follow him!' . . . Elijah does not accuse his hearers of polytheism or atheism; he accuses them, rather, of catastrophically misidentifying the one particular being who alone is worthy of the title 'God.' The prophet readily acknowledges that the apostates believe in God, but insists that they do not properly or adequately know the LORD"[15] (Jon Levenson).

3. "Consider the following analogy. I am sitting in my office. Six people come in with different accounts of an incident they have seen take place on the Strand. Their differences mean that I cannot be sure that anyone of them has the whole, detailed truth, but I may be able to be sure that they did collectively see something, and I may be able to construct a minimal account of what happened, surrounded by much agnosticism, from their witness. I do not need to claim a vision they lack. The above example gives the essential form of pluralism"[16] (Peter Byrne).

4. "Can one rule on philosophical grounds alone that all religions focus on the same transcendent reality? Such a conclusion lies at hand more readily if one takes a single

religion as starting point. Then maybe one can state that the other religions have the same transcendent reality in mind. If one tries to argue as neutrally as possible, however, this becomes more difficult"[17] (Hendrik Vroom).

5. "When a Hindu or Sikh prays to God, how can we know that in his intention it is the same God we worship? Even in the case of a pious Muslim this is not clear, because his way of turning to God is informed by his belief in Muhammad, although in part we share the same 'cumulative tradition.' Is it nevertheless the same God? This is a question to be decided by God, not us"[18] (Wolfhart Pannenberg).

6. "What enabled Paul to say that he worshipped the God of Abraham was the fact that although many changes had taken place in the concept of God, there was nevertheless a common religious tradition in which both he and Abraham stood. To say that a god is not the same as one's own God involves saying that those who believe in him are in a radically different religious tradition from one's own"[19] (D. Z. Phillips).

Chapter 20

Theological Language

It is frequently suggested that, in a sense of the word *language* often left unclear, theology needs new, better language than our mother tongues provide. The scientific conduct of theology, or more effective communication with a diverse, contemporary audience, is said to require it. This alleged need can be viewed, roughly, under two chief headings: theoretical adequacy and precision.

Theoretical Adequacy

In *Method in Theology*, Lonergan makes claims worth quoting rather fully, since they suggest so aptly the focus of the present chapter's interest. Lonergan concedes that much progress can be made even if "thought and speech and action remain within the world of common sense, of persons and things as related to us, of ordinary language." However,

> if man's practical bent is to be liberated from magic and turned towards the development of science, if his critical bent is to be liberated from myth and turned towards the development of philosophy, if his religious concern is to renounce aberrations and accept purification, then all three will be served by a differentiation of consciousness, a recognition of a world of theory. In such a world things are conceived and known, not in their relations to our sensory apparatus or to our needs and desires, but in the relations constituted by their uniform interactions with one another. To speak of things so conceived requires the development of a special technical language, a language quite distinct from that of common sense.[1]

Lonergan adds: "Such speech, however, is found clear and accurate and explanatory only by those that have done their apprenticeship. It is not enough to have acquired common sense and to speak ordinary language. One has also to be familiar with theory and with technical language."[2] Physics, chemistry, biology, astronomy, and the like have need of "technical language" distinct from "that of common sense"; and so does theology, Lonergan believes, if it, too, is to be scientific.

Other theologians have spoken similarly, but I have not discovered any halfway adequate assessment of their claims. Here, if anywhere, in a methodological study of theology and language, is an appropriate place to assess the claims' merits somewhat more carefully. Why, if these theologians are right, does theology need its own technical language distinct from that of everyday discourse?

Crucial here, as throughout this study, is the distinction stressed at the start, between two senses of the word *language*. By "language" theologians typically mean discourse, not the medium of discourse, and such is often Lonergan's use of the term.[3] However, in the above quotation, it is not at all clear that the special language Lonergan recommends, distinct from that of common sense, is more technical discourse; for it is hardly necessary to stress the need for scientists or theologians to go beyond common sense in what they *say*. Such is their calling, their *raison d'être*. If, however, Lonergan is urging the need of technical *terminology*, that claim clearly is worth stating; for the need is not obvious. Without technical terminology, Mendel counted his peas and reported the results, Copernicus suggested that the earth went around the sun rather than vice versa, Darwin proposed the evolution of species, Pasteur postulated living things too small to observe with the naked eye, and so forth. They went far beyond common sense but did not leave their native tongues behind. Why may not theologians do likewise?

In his own work on theological method, *La théologie parmi les sciences humaines*, Georges Tavard appears to address this query. "It seems to me," he writes, "that the following principle is required: no natural language, written or only spoken, constitutes a medium of revelation that does entire justice to that revelation."[4] For Tavard, a new, better, more technical system of signs is required. For, in general, "Every organized science creates its own language. Within a natural language, given or chosen, it specifies a more particular language, both more adequate to its object and also more secret, more intimate, demanding an initiation that may be arduous."[5] So, too, for theology. "If revelation and the kerygma it transmits should adopt everyday language to avoid becoming a sectarian doctrine reserved for a small number, theological language, for its part, must become highly specialized; otherwise it will never express the inner intelligibility of the revealed mystery."⁶

The key word here may be "organized": every "organized science" creates and has need of its own technical terminology. Copernicus may not have needed a technical terminology, but contemporary astronomy does ("galaxy," "light year," "dwarf," etc.). Mendel may not have needed a technical terminology, but contemporary genetics does ("gene," "chromosome," "DNA," etc.). And so for physics, chemistry, physiology, cybernetics, and the rest. But why include theology? Is theology really so comparable to astrophysics, crystallography, genetics, or the like that what suits them, methodologically, automatically suits it, too? "What is important for theological language," replies Tavard,

> is less the form it adopts than the reason for which it prefers one form rather than another. Thus, in Trinitarian language it is not all that important to speak of the Word [*Verbe*], of processions, of persons; but it is extremely important to know the reason for *Verbe* rather than *mot*, of processions rather than emanations, of persons rather than individuals.⁷

It may be similarly important, no doubt, to know the reason for calling the snorting creature approaching me a bull rather than a peaceable cow, or the creature slithering beneath the porch a copperhead rather than a harmless garter snake. But that does not indicate the need for a new, more adequate terminology. As "bull," "cow," "copperhead," and "garter snake" may do fine, so may "emanation," "procession," "word," "person," and "individual." What need is there of a "new particular language," with new words or new meanings for familiar words (Tavard does not indicate clearly which of these alternatives he has in view)? How might either newly minted terms or redefined terms be more "adequate to their objects" than the present stock of words with their familiar senses? How *could* they be?

"When I talk about language (words, sentences, etc.)," remarked Wittgenstein, "I must speak the language of every day. Is this language somehow too coarse and material for what we want to say? *Then how is another one to be constructed?*"⁸ The same query applies to talk about persons, words, processions, emanations, and the like. How can a technical sense of such terms, or technical terms to replace them, be tailored save by means of existing terminology? So if that terminology, with its existing senses, is not adequate to theology's objects, how can the technical terminology do any better, content-wise? The new terminology may be handier, as it is handier, for example, to speak of a "light year" rather than "the distance light travels in a year." But if the latter, longer expression is not adequate to the reality, neither is the shorter. And the like holds for even the most technical and sophisticated theological terminology. It is parasitic on less technical, sophisticated terminology. What it can say, the other can say. Let us turn, then, to the other alleged advantage of more refined theological language.

Precision

In theology as in philosophy, some have stressed the need of special terminology for the sake of greater exactness. Theology, observes Albert Keller, "has developed its own technical language. No science can function without such a language if it wishes to speak with both brevity and precision."[9] With regard to brevity, we have just noted the handiness of some technical expressions, encapsulating longer definitions. What, though, about precision?

The indefiniteness of our unrefined natural languages would be a defect only if our utterances needed to be sharper than such languages permit. But they allow much precision. If an individual word is fuzzy, modifiers can sharpen it. And what modifiers do not achieve, context often can. If neither context nor modifiers nor both together achieve the desired exactness, we may define an expression more precisely by picking out one existing meaning as the intended one (as chapter 1 did for "language"). Even if we occasionally feel the need for something sharper and stipulate new word meanings, that still does not demonstrate the inadequate precision of our mother tongues. For the argument just made with regard to accuracy holds also for precision. Whatever a technical term can say precisely, nontechnical terms can say with equal precision. For the nontechnical terms used to define the technical term give it whatever precision it possesses. "Light year" may be handier than "the distance light travels in a year," but it is not more precise—not if such is the meaning given the expression "light year."

In view of these reminders, what should we make of a strong assertion such as the following:

> Theology, or sacred science, has also to define and elaborate the ideas which it constantly uses. The concepts of revelation, inspiration, credibility, faith, mystery, dogma, magisterium, tradition are first categories, implied in every theological process, categories, therefore, which need to be identified and made precise. It is a question of a sort of theological semantics.[10]

At first reading, this claim appears reasonable. What would become of geometry, say, if the word *circle* were used with popular abandon, for social circles, circles under people's eyes, circles in the sand, and the like? Geometry has need of a more exact notion, namely: "plane curve everywhere (exactly) equidistant from a given fixed point." So too, perhaps, if theology is to be a sacred science and not mere empty vaporing, its first categories must, like those in geometry, be made more precise. Once, however, we consider the suggested theological categories to be sharpened—e.g., "revelation," "inspiration," "credibility," "faith," "mystery," "dogma," "magisterium," "tradition"—we experience misgivings. Or at least we should, in the light of preceding discussions.

Recall chapter 16's account of the theological battles that have been waged over such basic concepts as "person" and "faith." Recall chapter 13's distinction between verbal and theoretical definitions and the unfortunate characteristics that typify so many of the latter. Recall the same chapter's discussion of value-driven definitions, and, for instance, Ormerod's words: "What are our criteria for determining *faith*? What is *faith*? Is it simply an intellectual assent to what is proposed by divine authority? Or does it involve a fully existential commitment, not only of mind but also of heart? How we understand faith will greatly influence how we do our theology." From all this, the contrast should be clear between a concept such as "circle" and a concept such as "faith." The former is theoretically neutral, available for common use, whereas the latter frequently (especially in theological discourse) is not, but is both theoretically loaded and value-driven.

Consider, then, whether and how a concept such as "faith" might be defined in a way that was both precise and generally acceptable, since it begged no substantive theological issues, and could therefore serve as common linguistic currency. First, see if you can discern some neutral nucleus of meaning that might be enshrined in a technical definition of the term. Then, if you spot anything of the kind, consider whether the resulting definition would have the kind of significance Ormerod envisages for "how we do our theology." That is, try to do for "faith" what chapter 1 attempted, unsuccessfully, for the similarly debated, value-laden term "theology." Leave out the "intellectual assent to what is proposed by divine authority," leave out a "fully existential commitment," leave out all debated characterizations, and isolate a precise, neutral core at the heart of the debates about faith. The enterprise looks as chimerical for "faith" as it does for "theology."

Theology and faith are not natural kinds, neatly delimited by nature, ready to be characterized precisely. To highlight the difference, consider the word *water*. Once that concept was fuzzy, then it acquired greater scientific precision through scientific inquiry. Chemists analyzed water's atomic constituents, the analysis was accepted, and the word *water* acquired this new, shared content, H_2O. If, similarly, theologians analyzed faith and their analysis was generally accepted, the word *faith*, too, might acquire new, more precise content. There would be no need to propose a new sense of the term; the enrichment would occur automatically. The fact that no such development has occurred for "theology," "faith," "revelation," or any other basic theological expression is not a sign of theology's immaturity or arrested development. More indicative of its incomplete maturation, I suggest, would be the notion that any of its expressions designate theological natural kinds, waiting to be precisely identified, as in the natural sciences.

Philosophy has faced similar problems for "meaning," "truth," "causality," "reference," "identity," and other basic concepts. These terms, too, do not designate natural kinds. Yet many philosophers, like many theologians, have felt that, in order to be scientific, their discipline required more precise definitions of such concepts. In response to this sensed need, Rudolf Carnap proposed the procedure he labeled "explication." "By an explication," he wrote, "I understand the replacement of a pre-scientific, inexact concept (which I call 'explicandum') by an exact concept ('explicatum'), which frequently belongs to the scientific language."[11] Here, he explained, "The only essential requirement is that the explicatum be more precise than the explicandum."[12] Accordingly, "The interpretation which we shall adopt . . . deviates deliberately from the meaning of descriptions in the ordinary language. Generally speaking, it is not required that an explicatum have, as nearly as possible, the same meaning as the explicandum."[13] Rather, it suffices that the explicatum satisfy the following four requirements, "to a sufficient degree":

1. The explicatum is to be *similar to the explicandum* in such a way that, in most cases in which the explicandum has so far been used, the explicatum can be used; however, close similarity is not required, and considerable differences are permitted.

2. The characterization of the explicatum, that is, the rules of its use (for instance, in the form of a definition), is to be given in an *exact* form, so as to introduce the explicatum into a well-connected system of scientific concepts.

3. The explicatum is to be a *fruitful* concept, that is, useful for the formulation of many universal statements (empirical

laws in the case of a nonlogical concept, logical theorems in the case of a logical concept).

4. The explicatum should be as *simple* as possible; this means as simple as the more important requirements (1), (2), and (3) permit.[14]

This detailed account still leaves much unclear. It is evident, however, that none of its prescriptions, with regard to similarity, exactness, fruitfulness, and simplicity, restricts the account to any one discipline. Such explication can work in science (think, for example, of the scientific redefinition of "fish"). If it can also succeed in philosophy, perhaps it can succeed in theology, too. However, in philosophy I have never encountered a successful Carnapian explication,[15] and in theology I have never encountered an explicitly formulated attempt to do any such thing. I doubt that many theologians, once they saw what was involved, would adopt the Carnapian formula for rendering their enterprise truly scientific. After all, even Carnapian explication results only in a handier expression, not one more precise than its defining formula; the familiar, unexplicated expressions of which the explication is composed might be used, though perhaps less conveniently, to say the same thing.

The recommendations that emerge from the discussion to this point can be stated simply as follows:

1. Accept and follow current usage until some clear advantage suggests a different use for a term.

2. Weigh this advantage against possible disadvantages (including, in every case, the new use's unfamiliarity).

3. To do so, take a realistic look at current usage and its possibilities.

4. If the revision still seems desirable, introduce the new sense explicitly as a new sense (not a theory), explain the reasons for it, and indicate the contexts and types of discussion for which it seems desirable.

5. Distinguish clearly between the new meaning of the word and any theory or factual claim stated by its means.

6. Recognize that, even in the contexts indicated, people who employ a different terminology may nonetheless be making true statements.

For Further Reflection

1. "Theology has to develop intelligible concepts for the articulation of its subject-matter, but it has to do this without falling into sheer abstraction and without infringing the mystery of God"[16] (John Macquarrie).

2. "There has been a temptation—which some Christian thinkers have found hard to resist—to allow reflection concerning the difficulties posed by our knowing and speaking about God to go forward independently of the conviction, based in faith, that he has spoken to us in his Word and that, in a real sense, the words to speak about him are already his gift to us"[17] (J. Augustine Di Noia).

3. "D'Costa . . . argues that the definitions of 'God' and 'human' are hardly givens, and that, for the Christian, they are disclosed decisively only through Jesus Christ. However, Hick's incompatible definitions are somehow known by him prior to the incarnation. For many theologians, this is simply not a properly Christian approach to the question"[18] (Paul Rhodes Eddy).

4. "In other words, theology creates and reveals itself as language. It does not only state God and God's action in history (a valid but inadequate view of the theologian's task!). Rather, just as the thought is never separate from the word, just as one does not reflect save to the extent that one uses a language from which to draw the symbols of one's reflection, so theology is inconceivable save in the measure that it is language. . . . To theologize is to invent a new language"[19] (Georges Tavard).

5. "Lonergan calls such an aberration of understanding a 'scotosis,' derived from the Greek word *skotos*, which means 'darkness,' and the resultant blind spot a 'scotoma.' By introducing these terms, he has helped us to come to a better understanding of the massive resistance against learning. For it is exactly this scotosis that prevents us from really dealing with those factors that are crucial today in our human struggle"[20] (Henri Nouwen).

6. "The language of the churches and of scripture, as we have seen, including their so-called religious or theological

terms, is common language in the societies and cultures where church and scripture are found. It is this common language and these ordinary uses that theology always presupposes, and with which, therefore, it should begin, not with special or technical meanings alleged to be authoritative because 'revealed' by God. All special and technical meanings are variations or developments of the ordinary language, building upon it, refining it, transforming it. They are thus parasitic upon it and cannot be understood apart from it . . ."[21] (Gordon Kaufman).

Chapter 21

Metaphor

Once accepted as a norm, the Principle of Relative Similarity enjoins that, on most occasions, a statement's use of terms should resemble the established use of terms more closely than would the substitution of any rival, incompatible expression. The resemblance may be distant—indeed, the points of dissimilarity may outnumber those of similarity; but if the dissimilarities would be still greater for any rival expression, the principle may be satisfied. Such analogy may therefore appear comparable to that in a good metaphor. For example:

> Christians speak of God as "Father." That's simple enough, but it's not clear or unambiguous. Christians use it of God as creator of the universe; they use it of his relation to the whole human race made in his image, of his particular relation to Christian believers made his sons and daughters by adoption and grace, and more specifically still of his special relation to Jesus.[1]

Here, multiple similarities validate the term "Father," as multiple, perhaps fewer, similarities validate many a PRS extension of a term. So metaphor and PRS analogy may seem to merge, and in that case metaphor may pose no challenge to PRS and its norm. It may not be an exception to their requirements. However, since in fact even the best metaphors typically do not satisfy the Principle of Relative Similarity, the challenge cannot be so easily finessed.

To take a simple example, it is not evident how the Psalmist's declaration "You are indeed my rock and my fortress" (Ps. 31:3) can pass the PRS test. "Rock" and "fortress" are rival expressions, for different sorts of things; and if tested for closer similarity with established word-uses, neither term appears preferable to the other as a description of God. God is rock-like and God is fortress-like. Furthermore, "god" competes with both "rock" and "fortress" and clearly does better by the same test of established word-use: "god" is used for gods, whereas "rock" and "fortress" typically are not. So, has the Psalmist said something false or unacceptable, as PRS and its norm would seem to suggest?

We here confront the issue postponed earlier, as we passed from truth and its norm to other, related questions. As a necessary condition of truth, I acknowledged, PRS may appear too restrictive. Though the principle may rightly resist a statement such as "Atoms love one another," does it rightly exclude "The Lord is my rock"? Is such a declaration false? May it not be true? Whatever the answer to this question, the legitimacy of such utterances can hardly be contested, at least in some contexts for some purposes. However, if admissible in poetry, psalms, preaching, and the like, are they equally acceptable in theological discourse? Are they perhaps, as some have claimed, not only suitable there, but necessary? In the light of the answers to these queries, we may need to ask, in addition, whether preceding discussions, citing PRS and its norm but ignoring metaphor, should be reconsidered.

For reasons apparent from chapter 13, on defining and saying what things are, we need not first address the further question, "What is metaphor?" Clearly, "The Lord is my rock" qualifies as a metaphor. And clearly, as just noted, it differs importantly from PRS extensions such as those considered earlier ("God is good," "God is wise," etc.). But no sharp criterion discriminates metaphor from non-metaphor. As Max Black observed, " 'Metaphor' is a loose word, at best, and we must beware of attributing to it stricter rules of usage than are actually found in practice."[2] Some theorists apply the term narrowly, whereas others apply it broadly, to any verbal extension by similarity, so that metaphor appears an all-pervasive, unavoidable aspect of discourse. I need not here debate the felicity of thus stretching the term *metaphor* to cover both "The Lord is my rock" and "God is good." I need only indicate that the present discussion of metaphor will focus on the former type of utterance ("The Lord is my rock") rather than the latter ("God is good"), and will use the words *metaphor* and *metaphorical* accordingly.

True?

Chapter 4 defended the claim to truth of statements that satisfy the Principle of Relative Similarity. What, now, of metaphorical utterances that do not satisfy that principle? What of "The Lord is my rock" or

"The Lord is my fortress"? Can such utterances qualify as true? Verdicts differ. "Although literal and metaphorical sentences have different types of meaning," writes Timothy Binkley,

> when they are used to make claims those claims can be true or false in roughly the same way, i.e., without the mediation of an additional expression of their meanings. It is usually (though not always) somewhat more involved to explain to someone the meaning of a metaphor or other trope than of a literal expression. But once the meaning is clear, the truth of the claim can be established without the assistance of translations into literal meanings.[3]

Others attach more significance to the difference between literal and metaphorical assertions. According to Stephen Phillips, "[A]ll figures of meaning appear to flout what Grice calls a 'maxim of quality'—that one should try to say what is true."[4] For in a metaphor, notes Wim de Pater, whereas "the subject is not really F (Achilles is not really a lion), in the case of literal talk it really *is* F (God is really good and wise, etc.)."[5] And, as Aristotle observed, truth correlates with what things are: "[H]e whose thought is in a state contrary to that of the objects is in error."[6] Accordingly, if asked whether it is true that Achilles is a lion or God is a rock, I think most people would at least hesitate before giving an affirmative answer, and their hesitation would suggest that, judged by its own standard of established word use, the Principle of Relative Similarity may not need to be amended so as to admit metaphorical utterances as "true."

Thus, back and forth, the debate might go. However, I shall not continue this dispute in fuller detail, for it may not matter greatly whether metaphors can qualify as "true." Regardless of their labeling, they may be perfectly apt. What, then, can be said more generally about the utility, perhaps even the necessity, of metaphor in theology?

Precise?

We can focus first on the much-prized virtue of precision. For what Daniel Cohen writes of philosophy might also be said about theology:

> I think what many philosophers have found most objectionable about metaphors is that they are obscure—i.e., semantically indeterminate. The discourse of philosophy is

so often caught up in the confusions of language, that quite naturally—and quite rightly!—philosophers valorize clarity and precision.... Ambiguity and obscurity [are] anathema to clear philosophizing.[7]

Reading this assessment, thus reported, one may wonder: Is it anathema in philosophy to say (metaphorically) that obscurity is anathema? Cohen himself notes the pervasiveness of figurative speech, even in philosophy: "For example, we speak of *clear* texts, texts whose *points* can be *seen* immediately, as opposed to *dense*, *heavy*, or *impenetrable* texts."[8] When we speak this way, we do not speak obscurely. What, then, is the complaint against metaphor?

The charge of semantic imprecision might be urged as follows: "To say that God is a father is to say that God resembles a certain kind of human being. To say that God is a rock is to say that God resembles, say, a hunk of granite. But the resemblance between God and a father is greater than that between God and granite. So the former predication is more perfect than the latter, though of course both are very imperfect. If we say for instance that God is a being, we must make allowance for the analogy of being, but the statement is more accurate than when we call God a father, and far more accurate than when we call God a rock. That is a mere metaphor."

The idea here is that there are levels of predication which correspond to grades of being. The rock is at the bottom, then comes the human being, and far above is the divine nature. Thus, the rock term is least appropriate in theology, the human term comes closer, and a term applied quite generally to angels, God, and human beings is highest and best of all. Accordingly, if we would speak about the constancy of God, "rock" is the least apt description, "steadfast" is somewhat better, and "unchanging" is preferable to either.

To see where the error in all this lies, consider the contrast between "rock" and "steadfast." The supposed advantage of the latter lies in its being applied to people, not to rocks. But the pragmatic consequence of this difference is that "rock' is, if anything, a better term than "steadfast" with which to describe God. For human character is not granitic in its constancy, but notoriously chalk-like and crumbly. To call a man a rock is to say he is *exceptionally* strong and steadfast. The figure is hyperbolic. And since a typical scriptural or liturgical setting in which we call God a rock indicates a moral sense as clearly as in this human application, the term *rock*, being hyperbolic, comes *closer* to the divine reality than does a more human term, suggesting mere human steadfastness.

In the context of the present study, the charge of imprecision might be urged against metaphor somewhat differently. Granted, it might be said, even the most "literal" sayings are typically imprecise; for example, a "red" car may be crimson, salmon, scarlet, or some other shade within an indefinite penumbra. Granted, too, extensions by PRS analogy (e.g., statements about the "calculations" of autistic savants or the "wisdom" of God) may be still more imprecise. But typical metaphorical utterances, which do not satisfy even the elastic requirements of PRS, are still more inexact. They ignore competing terms. They ignore greater or less similarity in comparison with those terms. Anything goes!

No, not really. Whereas "The Lord is my rock" is fine, "The Lord is my bent reed" is not. What can be acknowledged and may affect reactions to metaphor is the fact that some metaphors are more open to varied interpretations than are others. Thus, contrast "The Lord is my rock" with Richard Swinburne's sample, "Cynthia proved to be a hedgehog." This, he suggests,

> may be a description of how Cynthia looks, or how she behaves in her personal relations. . . . It could be saying that in her sexual relationships or in her relationships with employers, or in her relationships with her friends, she "clams up" unless approached with extreme gentleness and tact; or alternatively that she is very "prickly," takes remarks the wrong way, if that is possible, is quick to resent the slightest suggestion that there is anything wrong with her.[9]

Uttered in a specific context, the hedgehog metaphor would probably acquire greater definiteness. If it didn't, clarification might be necessary. And the like might hold for equally indefinite theological metaphors.

This brings us to the further question, of evident methodological interest, whether such clarification is always possible or whether some things can only be stated metaphorically.

Untranslatable?

On this question, too, opinions split. On one side, as Mark Johnson reports, "One view of metaphor has, with a few brave exceptions, dominated philosophers' thinking on the subject. That view can be summarized as follows: A metaphor is an elliptical simile useful for stylistic, rhetorical, and didactic purposes, but which can be translated into a literal paraphrase without any loss of cognitive content."[10] The "brave exceptions" on the other side of this disagreement include, for instance, Gerald O'Collins and Daniel Kendall, who write: "Metaphors use and build on literal utterances and literal meanings but go beyond them, at times saying things that can be said only in metaphor."[11] What examples, one wonders, might illustrate this claim?

Consider again "The Lord is my rock." Although "I can rely on the Lord" seems to say much the same thing, the equivalence is not perfect. Thus, as William Alston observes, "[i]t may be that in a metaphorical statement there is no sharp line between what is being asserted and what is only more or less explicitly suggested, so that propositions asserted metaphorically possess a kind of fuzzy boundary that is not shared by propositions expressed literally." Nonetheless, adds Alston, "even if that is so it would not prevent the propositional content from being partially expressed in literal terms."[12] And such a partial rendering, he believes, is always theoretically possible. "If we can make any assertion about God definite enough to have truth-value, it will be in principle possible to say the same thing literally, at least partially, even if that requires introducing new terms (or new meanings for old terms) into the language for that purpose."[13] If we are sufficiently astute, we can pull it off.

Here Alston covers his bases so carefully that it may be difficult to find any counterexample. "The Lord is my rock" is not such, for surely "I can rely on the Lord" is at least *part* of what the metaphorical saying conveys. However, if, as Alston recognizes may be the case, the rewording states only part of what the metaphor states, O'Collins and Kendall's claim may still hold for this and other examples. Metaphors may go beyond literal utterances and say things that can only be thus figuratively stated, and the difference may have methodological interest.

How significant, then, is Alston's distinction between "what is being asserted" and "what is only more or less explicitly suggested"? To illustrate the distinction, consider a nonmetaphorical example. Suppose someone says, "Americans enjoy sports." Though the statement does not mention football, basketball, or baseball, to anyone acquainted with the American scene these are surely suggested, rather than bocce or sumo wrestling. The statement carries this cognitive plus, without asserting it. So the question is this: Does any metaphor have as rich a suggestive fringe as does "Americans enjoy sports"? And can that fringe, unlike the one for "Americans enjoy sports," only be stated metaphorically? The very wording of the question suggests why no such examples come to mind: to identify such a fringe would be to state it nonmetaphorically. "Here is the asserted core," we would have to say, "and here is the suggested fringe—stated nonmetaphorically."

Thus, consider, for example, the following passage from Swinburne:

> Creeds still contain living metaphors, such as the Nicene Creed's statement about Christ that he is "light from light." In the literal sense Jesus Christ, the second person of the Holy Trinity, is clearly not light. He doesn't consist of photons of zero mass, such as stream out of the light bulb when you turn on the light. Nor is he being said to be something similar thereto. "Light" does have an analogical meaning—as when we talk of some discovery "throwing light" on something else, we mean that it helps us to understand the something else, in the way that light helps us to see things. But when Christ is said to be Light, something much more is meant than that he helps us to "see" deep things as they really are—although that is certainly involved. It's rather that he's everywhere at once; just as light seems to travel from one place to another with infinite velocity. As the original light seems to spread itself without ceasing to illuminate somewhere else—and so there [seems] not to be just a finite quantity of it, so too, there is no limit to the power and wisdom of Christ.[14]

The creedal metaphor does not say all this, but for Swinburne (and he believes for other knowledgeable recipients as well) it casts this suggestive halo. And doubtless no single literal saying would be as richly suggestive. However, as Swinburne's own rendering indicates, what the metaphor suggests—"he's everywhere at once," "there is no limit to the power and wisdom of Christ"—can also be stated nonmetaphorically, in those words. So a further question now arises.

Indispensable?

If metaphor can always be translated nonmetaphorically, and the nonmetaphorical version typically spells out the sense more clearly, it might seem that metaphor is dispensable, even undesirable, in theology, which aims at greater clarity. However, several considerations might be urged against this verdict and against what Johnson terms the "mainstream philosophical tradition," that metaphors are, for example, simply "more pleasing, forceful, or striking than ordinary literal discourse."[15]

"I have argued," Alston writes, "that the propositional content of any metaphorical statement issued with a truth claim is, *in principle*, capable of literal expression, at least in part."[16] Alston italicizes the phrase "in principle" because, as he explains, his claim is quite compatible with the possibility that one who makes or grasps the statement may not be in a position to bring off even a lame and inadequate literal version. One may have the property "in mind" in too implicit or intuitive a fashion to know whether any term in the language signifies it, or to associate it explicitly with a new term. Or perhaps the most we can come up with is a paraphrase into other metaphors. The "in principle" possibility for which I have argued may not be a real possibility for anyone at this point, or, perhaps, at any point.

In its indefiniteness, such a metaphor would then resemble many a PRS analogy—for instance, "God knows our hearts" or "God is loving." No one can identify just what similarities between divine and human knowing or between divine and human loving justify our speaking thus of God and using the words *know* and *love* in preference to competing expressions (*doubt, surmise,* etc., or *hate, dislike,* etc.).

Given its openness to varied interpretations, many theologians regard metaphor not only as stylistically and rhetorically advantageous but also as heuristically desirable. Metaphor is valued "as a source of hitherto unnoticed insights into the nature of the subject."[17] A good metaphor, it is said, "places things in a new light, so that we can see them in a way we have never seen them before."[18] It can " 'set the scene before our eyes' . . . with a vividness that induces an alternation of perspective that lets us 'get hold of new ideas.' "[19] Again, it may carry "an evocative and associative power, an openness to new interpretations, and a lack of specificity which enables it to express and evoke feelings and thoughts in new and subtle ways."[20] If any of this is true, not only generally but specifically in theology, then, though perhaps dispensable, metaphor should not be dispensed with. Heuristically as well as stylistically, it may be a valuable medium of theological discourse. In any case, we have seen no reason to exclude metaphor, as PRS and its norm might suggest. So the moment has come to reexamine that principle and norm and the validity of the discussions in earlier chapters that invoked them.

Retrospective Reassessment

It is not clear that metaphors may be true. It is not clear that they may be untranslatable. It is not clear that they are indispensable in theology. It is also far from evident, however, that theologians should eschew them. For metaphors may be as precise as nonmetaphorical equivalents, may be stylistically more pleasing and effective, and may be intellectually more stimulating. They therefore pose a major challenge, if not to the Principle of Relative Similarity, which concerns truth, then at least to the corresponding norm, which concerns what we should say, and specifically to the norm's validity in theology.

In defense, it might be suggested that metaphorical utterances do in fact conform to PRS's norm, for the norm speaks of established word-uses and metaphor is such a use. Granted, metaphor is not an aspect of individual word-use, but neither is grammar, and surely grammar affects the truth and aptness of utterances. (The verb *rain* may be as appropriate as you please, but if you reverse the word order and say "Raining it's" rather than "It's raining," the utterance won't be true, or even readily intelligible.) The chief problem with this saving suggestion is that it overlooks the rest of PRS, with regard to rival expressions. In "It's raining," the verb *rain* may win out over incompatible expressions such as "snow" and "sleet" and the utterance may therefore qualify as true. But in "The Lord is my rock," the noun *rock* does not similarly prevail over incompatible expressions such as "fortress" and "shepherd." "The Lord is my rock" does not satisfy PRS any better than does "The Lord is my fortress" or "The Lord is my shepherd," so does not satisfy PRS's requirement of closer resemblance. It appears, then, that there is no escaping the conclusion that, though the norm derived from PRS may hold for nonmetaphorical statements, it does not cover metaphorical assertions.[21]

True, PRS was proposed as only "roughly right" and its normativity was stated with corresponding caution: "When making statements, we should, *as a rule*, employ words in the way described." However, metaphor now appears such a major exception that the norm looks overly restrictive. This can now be remedied by confirming the possibility earlier envisaged: the norm holds for nonmetaphorical utterances, not for metaphorical ones. This restriction does not cast doubt on preceding chapters' invocation of the norm, for the utterances they considered and assessed were not metaphorical. Neither does it call in question the ready applicability of the norm to nonmetaphorical rather than to metaphorical statements, for, on the whole, it is not difficult to distinguish the former from the latter. The very difference that blocks application of the norm to typical metaphorical statements distinguishes adequately between the utterances for which the norm holds and those for which it does not. "The Lord is my rock" *clearly* does not satisfy the norm, and is not so intended or understood. No one supposes, or is tempted to suppose, that the predicate *rock* comes closer than "fortress," "shepherd," "salvation," "god," or any other term which, in nonmetaphorical discourse, would pose as a rival expression.

Contrast this example with earlier ones, for instance with Aquinas's denial that unjust laws are laws, Ebeling's assertion that only love is true, or conflicting claims for and against fetal personhood. These sayings, too, disregard the Principle of Relative Similarity, but that is where the resemblance ends. If we asked the Psalmist whether God is really a rock (hard, heavy, etc.), he might simply regard us askance, or, tolerating our imbecility, he might explain: "No, of course not; I'm speaking metaphorically." A similar query would elicit no such response from Aquinas, Ebeling, the fetal disputants, or the multitudes they represent. They mean what they say. They are not speaking figuratively. Here, then, in such instances as these, there arises the kind of quandary chapter 15 described, concerning what is statement of fact and what is implicit redefinition of terms. And here, with regard to such claims, there arise the sorts of verbal disagreements chapter 16 recounted, with only one party or neither party heeding any PRS-like norm. Metaphorical utterances such as "God is my rock" or "God is my fortress" do not elicit such incomprehension or communicative breakdown. However, metaphorical sayings are the exception in theology. That is why I have dwelt on PRS, which applies to the majority of theological assertions.

For Further Reflection

1. "The point is that *everything* we say of God, whatever our style or register of discourse, is anthropomorphically, metaphorically said, and that, perhaps paradoxically, habits of speech which, as it were, carry their metaphorical character on their sleeve, may be *less* likely than more abstract expressions to lead us into the trap of supposing that *now*, at last, we are getting nearer to getting a 'fix' on God, to grasping 'what God looks like' "[22] (Nicholas Lash).

2. "Whatever Christians find apt—for example, the language of the Psalms and such traditional metaphors for God as shepherd, fortress, and rock—is apt. What is apt for some—for example, Bernard of Clairvaux's (1090–1153) image of the Holy Spirit as 'the Kiss of God,' the kiss between Father and Son—may not be apt for all"[23] (Richard Lennan).

3. "Furthermore, we challenge any suggestion that one metaphor can regularly replace another without changing

or losing the meaning. Switching metaphors will normally mean saying something different; in that sense one metaphor is not as good as another"[24] (Gerald O'Collins and Daniel Kendall).

4. "The metaphor 'God is a father,' for example, does not obey the rules governing propositions, but a metaphor does have a structure and a function of its own. Plato noticed that a metaphor has a structure; it has the structure of a proportion. To illustrate, this metaphor says that 'God is to a man as a father is to his child' "[25] (Bowman Clarke).

5. "According to Tilley, 'doctrines are live or dead metaphors'; but metaphors are not true, nor are they false; therefore the question of whether doctrines are true or false becomes meaningless. Tilley is led to conclude: 'The truth of a religious tradition . . . is borne, not in its doctrines, but in its stories.' But is this an acceptable solution?"[26] (John Thornhill).

6. "To speak of love in God, of sin in humankind, or of nature as divine creation, is perforce to make mystery meaningful while keeping meaning finally mysterious. If theology should fail in one of these tasks it must also fail in the other. A metaphor, wisely and fitly chosen, does both at once, which makes it eminently useful for theological purposes"[27] (Roger Hazelton).

Chapter 22

Mystery

All of reality—not just antimatter or distant galaxies, but familiar things we take for granted—is deeply mysterious. Light, for instance, is notoriously mystifying, but we succeed sufficiently in handling it if we treat it sometimes as waves and sometimes as particles. When it strikes our eyes and impulses reach our brain, there results, somehow, a spangle of colors (reds, greens, browns, purples, etc.), but we have no clue how such a transmutation from neural stimulus to sensible appearance takes place. The genesis of sweet and sour, soft feel and hard, violin notes and blaring horns—all this is equally mysterious, as is the brain's ability to store the persons, scenes, and events of a lifetime, available for conscious recall. To be sure, we accumulate ever more physiological and neural information about ourselves, but such data do nothing to bridge the gap between the neural and the experiential. In the other direction, from the experiential to the neural, we decide to walk and, lo, in some mysterious fashion, our intention gets translated into motion: our legs obey. As for our legs and other parts, we imagine them made up of muscles, cells, molecules, atoms, a whole menagerie of subatomic particles, and so on down into mysterious depths where energy and mass are somehow convertible and any resemblance to our sensations is beyond surmise. In the universe around us, all is equally mysterious. Surrounded by dogs, squirrels, moles, sparrows, catfish, turtles, bats, and countless other sentient creatures, we have no idea how much consciousness they possess or how they experience the world. As for nonsentient beings, apples fall, clouds float, and planets spin, all in accordance with the laws of gravity, yet we have no insight into the regularities we label "laws"; we see no reason why they hold. Billions of years back, before all such familiar patterns, we envisage a pinpoint from which this staggering universe erupted, but why and how there was such a point is as mysterious to us as was human conception to our ancestors. And even though we should arrive some day at similar, scientific understanding of that cosmic seminal moment, Hume's conclusion would still carry through: we do not and cannot perceive the necessity of anything occurring as our science says, or surmises, that it does. For us human inhabitants of the cosmos, mystery is all-pervasive.

It has widely been felt, however, that theology, to its credit or discredit, somehow specializes in mystery. And this impression has repeatedly, variously been related to theology's linguistic situation. William Power has suggested, for example, that "the sentence 'God is a mystery,' like the sentence 'God is the inexpressible,' is actually a second order statement about what we cannot do or have not done with our language about God."[1] In a similarly linguistic vein, Gordon Kaufman has written:

> [T]o say, "It is a mystery" does not yet tell us anything specific about the subject matter we are seeking to grasp or understand. "Mystery" is, rather, a grammatical or linguistic operator by means of which we remind ourselves of something about ourselves: that at this point we are using our language in an unusual, limited, and potentially misleading way. The word "mystery," thus, is a warning to ourselves not to mistake what we are now doing for our ordinary ways of speaking and thinking.[2]

The preceding paragraph's many examples raise doubts about this assessment, with its linguistic emphasis, as do the typical dictionary entries for "mystery" they exemplify: both highlight our limited knowledge or understanding rather than any oddity of verbal expression. Preceding chapters, too, cause misgivings with regard to Kaufman's claim of linguistic idiosyncrasy. The Principle of Relative Similarity and its norm apply to all areas of discourse, including theology, and to all factual claims, no matter how mysterious their subject matter. Closer scrutiny may reveal a kernel of truth in assertions such as Power's and Kaufman's, but for the moment they can illustrate how murky and how badly in need of elucidation is the relationship between mystery and language in theology.

The very word *mystery* may obscure the relationship. As Gareth Jones has noted, " 'Mystery' is a term used in many different ways in many different theological discourses; often it is ill-defined, confusing to the reader, and impossible to interpret in any meaningful fashion."[3] To be "entirely clear" about his own employment of the word, Jones adds his personal entry to the list of conflicting definitions: he will understand mystery, he explains, as "the first principle by means of which one understands the presence and absence of God with/from the world."[4] The need for such an esoteric meaning is itself far from clear. For present purposes it will suffice and will be preferable to employ the word *mystery* in the familiar, broad, more readily intelligible dictionary sense of "something not fully understood or eluding the understanding."

In this sense, everything qualifies as mystery, for nothing is fully understood. Still, there are degrees, and in theology mystery is particularly pervasive and profound. This creates both fewer linguistic problems than are often alleged and more than are frequently realized. The aim of this chapter, therefore, will be to suggest a balance between excessive diffidence, on the one hand, and excessive confidence, on the other, with respect to the use of language in theology.

Excessive Linguistic Diffidence

Deeply religious people, particularly mystics of various religious traditions, have long voiced doubts about the ability of words to express the transcendent mysteries of faith. Through the centuries they have echoed the refrain of Justin Martyr: "God so far surpasses our powers of description that no one can really give a name to him."[5] According to Augustine, "God is not even to be called ineffable, because to say this is to make an assertion about him."[6] Understandably, such linguistic diffidence has posed a quandary:

> Each time we attempt to say something about God, or about God's action in the world, we fail. The reality we name God cannot be put into words. All of what we say about God is always too much and not enough: too much because we cannot grasp the divine reality in words and not enough because that reality is always more and transcends what is said about it. But even if all our words for God are incompetent to name Him, Her, or It—and we know that our attempts to name necessarily do not succeed—we cannot stop naming God; we feel compelled to do it.[7]

And yet, as Alvin Plantinga has noted, Christians cannot, consistently and in all seriousness, admit *total* failure in their attempts to speak of God:

> It is a piece of sheer confusion to say that there is such a person as God, but none of our concepts apply to him. If our concepts do not apply to God ... then our concepts of

being loving, almighty, wise, creator and Redeemer do not apply to him, in which case he is not loving, almighty, wise, a creator or a Redeemer. He won't have any of the properties Christians ascribe to him.[8]

A response can go farther than such dialectical rebuttal and note possible sources of excessive diffidence about our ability to "grasp the divine reality in words."

It is helpful, first, to distinguish between adequately describing God and speaking truly about God. The distinction is not difficult to grasp. If, for instance, we do not know the cause of a disease or the function of whale vocalizations, we cannot adequately describe the cause or the function, but we may truly say that the disease has a cause (or causes) or that the vocalizations have a function. So too, if we do not know how God loves or knows or creates, we cannot adequately describe the manner but we may truly say that God does these things. The terms *love*, *know*, and *create* may be as adequate as words can be. They may satisfy the Principle of Relative Similarity.

Such comparisons may appear unrealistic, since our familiar words leave out so much when applied to God. "All talk about God has to be implemented in an attitude of knowing that no expression can contain God."[9] In what sense, though, might any expression conceivably "contain" the reality it serves to describe or pick out? Perhaps, as was long and widely supposed, it might do so in the sense of indicating some single, invariant, sharply defined essence, so that whenever the expression was applied we would know exactly what reality it indicated. But words seldom if ever do function in this fashion. If, for instance, I say that the Allies defeated the Axis powers in World War II, none of these expressions—"Allies," "defeated," "Axis," "powers," "in," or "World War II"—expresses a single, invariant essence, and the specific details left out, with respect to the countries, the war, and its outcome, would fill whole libraries. In any area of discourse, on any topic, the notion of one-to-one correspondence between words and the realities they "capture" is an illusion.

Besides, how can we assert the inadequacy of our language for its intended transcendent object without claiming, or assuming, knowledge of both terms of the relationship—of the transcendent object as well as of the linguistic medium? To illustrate the difficulty, consider a passage such as the following:

> The "negative theology" of Aquinas, for instance, was alive to the fact that, whatever may be truly said of the divine

mystery is said only by way of analogy—an insight which carries the inescapable implication that what is proper to the divine analogue infinitely transcends the meaningfulness which may be derived from created analogies in the making of theological assertions.[10]

Such talk of infinite transcendence poses a problem. If the dissimilarity between the divine and created analogues was infinite, the Principle of Relative Similarity would have no application in theology. God would, for example, be infinitely unlike both a wise person and a foolish person; the resemblance would not be greater in one case than in the other. If it was, then God would be less unlike one human person than another, and the dissimilarity would not be infinite with regard to that person, but finite, limited. And the like would hold for any other predicate we might think of applying to God. So, in defense of PRS analogy, we may ask the linguistic pessimist: "How do you know that the dissimilarity is infinite?" It seems that any attempted answer to this query would negate itself, by saying things about God it had no right to say.

In general, agnosticism about God entails agnosticism about the relation of language to God, hence about language's limitations in speaking of God. In the words of one theologian: "When you're on the low end of an analogy, be very slow to decide you know what the upper end is all about."[11] Or, as another author has put it: "[I]f an individual finds himself engaged in this sort of discourse, he had better find a way of speaking which exhibits due reverence by constantly reminding listener and speaker alike that they know little of which they speak."[12] Unavoidably, they know equally little about how closely their speaking approximates its object. (You can't know how close you have come to hitting the bull's-eye, linguistically or otherwise, if you have a very hazy idea where the bull's-eye is located.)

Excessive Linguistic Confidence

Paradoxically, then, excessive diffidence about the theological use of language derives in part from excessive confidence about such use. We think we know enough about the object of theological discourse to know how far short such discourse falls of its object. We have previously noted important indications of similar overconfidence and can here add others. The image they suggest is that of people skating confidently over an ice-covered lake, unaware how perilously thin the ice may be in some places. The surface, which looks the same all over, gives no warning where not to skate or where to skate with caution. The imperfection of this comparison is that skaters quickly learn where ice is weak (they hear it crack, or crash through it), whereas theologians who skate on thin linguistic ice, hearing no such warning and experiencing no such dousing, typically do not realize when the ice has given way beneath them. What this "giving way" means and how it occurs, unnoticed, we can consider under the following four headings. In doing theology, we may too readily assume that:

Apparently Meaningful Utterances Are Meaningful

In this connection, I think of the notorious experiment that a sly miscreant once performed of writing some unintelligible gibberish in the most impressive, sophisticated, up-to-date style—and getting it published. There is a lesson here, I suggest, even for serious thinkers not given to writing nonsense. For, despite the apparent rashness of the suggestion, I still believe, as I once put it, that "Some of the best minds have fallen, unawares, into incoherence or have failed to provide meaning for their words."[13]

Surely Aquinas's was one of the very best minds, yet recall his famous dictum "Good is to be done and pursued and evil is to be avoided," discussed in chapter 15. Since much textual evidence backs one reading ("Moral good is to be done") and much backs another ("Good of every kind is to be done"), it may be doubted, I suggested, whether Aquinas clearly envisaged both readings, recognized how importantly they differ, and intended just one sense rather than the other, yet made no clearer than he did which sense he had in mind—the empty tautology or the substantive norm. Recall, too, the same chapter's equally radical quandary with regard to the Kantian saying "Thought is knowledge by means of concepts" ("*Denken ist das Erkenntnis durch Begriffe*").[14] Such an utterance, I proposed, being unrecognizable either as a factual assertion or as a linguistic recommendation, does not function either way. It conveys no decipherable message. And since, I further suggested, Kant's nonchalance about established word uses is common, the problem his sample statement illustrates is also widespread. Time and again, in philosophy, theology, and elsewhere, there is no telling what is factual claim, what is implicit redefinition of terms, and what is neither the one nor the other since the difference has not been considered or clarified.

It is natural to assume that apparently meaningful statements make sense, for the vast majority of statements do; and to question statements' meaningfulness may seem to cast doubt on the intelligence or sanity of those who utter them. According to a popular conception, in order for an utterance to be meaningful, it need only express a thought, where "thought" means "mental representation." Provided that this condition is met, even if the words are unfortunately vague or ambiguous, or one assertion conflicts with another, each individual statement retains a sense. But surely, it is felt, this condition is typically satisfied, for surely any intelligent person who makes a statement means something by it. On this view, then, to claim that a theological statement lacks meaning would be equivalent to saying that its author merely set pen to paper, without a thought in his or her head. And surely that is absurd.

Yes, but so, on reflection, is this conception of language. For if representation in the mind of the speaker were the necessary and sufficient condition for meaningful utterances, it would follow that any series of sounds uttered by a thinking person would automatically be meaningful. If, for instance, someone said "Walla walla boo," while thinking about the weather or the stock exchange, the words would be a statement about the weather or the stock exchange. If, however, as chapter 2 suggested, the words we speak are the medium of the thought expressed and not merely a coded public translation thereof, the thoughts that may accompany our words cannot assure their meaningfulness. "Only in the stream of thought and life," as Wittgenstein remarked, "do words have meaning."[15] That stream is so vast, varied, complex, and dimly perceived that it is not surprising if words sometimes fail to have meaning when immersed in it, and if we are often unaware of the failure.

Any Statement That Makes Sense States a Genuine Possibility, at Least for an Omnipotent Agent

This second supposition, too, is ever so natural. Most meaningful statements—"Brutus admired Caesar," "Air pollution causes global warming," "The Earth's core is composed of iron"—do state possibilities. Yet, as chapter 8 noted, we should not too readily assume that what is usually the case is always the case. What makes sense is not ipso facto possible. The significance of this discrimination can be sensed from familiar ways of speaking. We read, for example: "To say that God is infinite is to say that God is able to do anything that it is logically possible that God do, that God knows everything that it is logically possible that God know, and that God depends on nothing else for existence."[16] Typically, such "logical" possibility and impossibility, determining divine options, are equated with what can or cannot be meaningfully, coherently stated. Chapter 8 questioned this equivalence. If, for instance, someone proposes to trisect an angle using just ruler and compass, an appropriate observation may be, "That has been shown to be impossible," but not, "Your proposal does not make sense." What the proposal states, meaningfully, is what has been shown to be impossible.

Valid Deductive Inference Is Feasible in Theology

Chapter 9, on inference and analogy, questioned this third supposition, and used Eucharistic debates to illustrate the problems with it. In further illustration, consider Rahner's deductive reasoning about the divine nature. Starting with the premise that God is spirit, he argues:

> [A]n authentic metaphysics of the spirit tells us that there are two (and only two!) basic activities of the spirit: knowledge and love. On the other hand, in harmony with the threefold distinct manner of subsisting of the one God, we know of two (and only two!) processions or emanations within God. . . . We are allowed, then, to combine these two data and to connect, in a special and specific way, the intra-divine procession of the Logos from the Father with God's knowledge, and the procession of the Spirit from the Father through the Son with God's love.[17]

Still, Rahner acknowledges, mystery remains: "[W]e cannot further explain *why* and *how* these two basic actuations of God's essence, as present in the unoriginate Father and, on account of God's simplicity, essentially identical within him, constitute nonetheless the basis for two processions and thus for three distinct manners of subsisting."[18]

Rahner's reasoning merits scrutiny, since it exemplifies a common format—a theological conclusion deduced from a premise of faith and a premise of reason—and illustrates the problems for such an approach. Specifically, its stress on "only two" basic activities and "only two" processions evokes chapter 10's warnings. "All," "none," "never," "only," "always"—such are the words that valid deduction requires; a mere "most," "usually," "typically," "seldom," or the like will not do. But universal claims, employing such terms, typically encounter linguistic difficulties. To be true, such claims need the backing of language, backing that the language employed typically does not provide, since the meanings of its terms are too open, indefinite, and varied to fit within any such straightjacket. So it is here.

Concerning Rahner's premise of faith—"we know of two (and only two!) processions or emanations within God"—we may wonder how it is possible to pass from "we know of only two" to "there are only two"—especially in view of the way the number two was arrived at. His premise of reason, alleging two and only two "basic activities of the spirit," appears still more problematic. Ignoring the dubious characterization of knowledge and love as "activities" (see chapter 3), we can ask, with similar latitude: What about enjoyment? What about regret? What about hope, expectation, thought, remembrance, contrition, frustration, intention, desire, compassion, hate, doubt, belief, interest, gratitude, repugnance, and the rest? "Not basic," might be the reply. "If we hope for something, it is because we *love* it. If we doubt something, it is because we *know* reasons for uncertainty. And so for all the rest." Well, similar dependence cannot be asserted at all evidently for all remaining "activities of the spirit." Furthermore, this reasoning might be reversed. Knowledge, the first of Rahner's two "basic activities of the spirit," has been defined as justified true belief, and can be traced to other beliefs, which may not qualify as knowledge. Love, his second "basic activity," can arise from gratitude, belief, imagination, expectation, admiration, desire, . . . Perhaps, amid the welter of interconnecting psychological concepts, some sense of the term *basic* might be discerned that would allow us to identify "knowledge" and "love" as the only two basic psychological concepts, but I doubt it. However, it does not matter. For certainly all other psychological states or activities, however derivative, cannot be *reduced* to just these two. And if all the rest remain possibilities, then the divine persons might be characterized by admiration, awe, generosity, gratitude, enjoyment, respect, compassion, concern, or what have you, alone or variously combined (as for human persons). Or they might be differentiated in transcendent ways for which we have no appropriate terms.

These are not the only difficulties for Rahner's demonstration, but they suffice to suggest again how problematic are theological arguments that, like his, rely on universal premises employing "all," "only," "never," and the like. Thus, I think Rahner's own words might have been a helpful reminder in this instance: "[W]hen I do not perceive [God] as the absolute mystery, then I have to say: Stop! You're on the wrong track, this path certainly does not lead to the true God of Christianity, the God of eternal life. If you intend to 'explain' God with a certain rationalistic clarity, as is done sometimes even in Catholic theology, then you have certainly failed in your task."[19]

Fuller Analysis Assures Fuller Clarity

This assumption, too, is natural and common. Rahner's account typifies countless efforts to achieve greater clarity through closer analysis. The present work is full of such attempts, both mine and others', and often they succeed. Frequently, however, the result may be the reverse of that desired and supposed: rather than bring greater clarity, added words may only deepen the initial mystery. In suggestive illustration, consider the deeply mysterious utterance, "Jesus is God." In the New Testament, the saying that comes closest to this declaration is Thomas's confession "My

Lord and my God!" And John's prologue suggests a possible explication of these words when it states that the Word is God and Jesus is the Word. There, we might surmise, lies the secret of Jesus' divinity; that is how Jesus is God. However, each of these two new identities—of the Word with God and of Jesus with the Word—is as mysterious as the identity explained. Hence, despite the appearance of greater definiteness, the initial mystery is deepened rather than clarified by this conjectural analysis. Two mysteries replace the original one.

It appears that Chalcedon in fact reveals such an inverse relationship between analysis and understanding. To the Johannine account it adds greater apparent precision: in Jesus two natures, human and divine, coalesce to form a single *prosopon*, a single *hypostasis*. Yet, how the natures coalesce without confusion, in full integrity, and how they form a single *prosopon*, is left mysterious. Indeed, what in this context is meant by the term "*prosopon*" is equally unclear.[20] So here, as in the suggested explanation of Thomas's confession, despite apparently greater definiteness the mystery deepens.

In most instances, a more definite-sounding account does clarify. Consider, for comparison, the statement "Ice is water" and its explication. As one author has observed, "If one assumes as background the theory which identifies various ordinary substances with chemically precise compounds and mixtures, then in the appropriate circumstances, the fact that ice is water can be fully explained by the fact that ice is H_2O."[21] Here, the general nature of the identity is understood, and its specific nature is indicated by identities whose nature is likewise understood: ice is H_2O and water is H_2O. Suppose, however, that we understood neither the nature of the original identity, "Ice is water," nor the nature of the explanatory identities, "Ice is H_2O" and "Water is H_2O." Indeed, suppose we did not even know whether water "is" H_2O in the same sense that ice "is" H_2O. In that case, the proffered explanation would only deepen the original mystery. So it is, it seems, with regard to the suggested analysis of John 20:28. The nature of the identity expressed by Thomas's confession is unclear; the nature of the identities in the Prologue is unclear; and it is not evident whether any of these identities is of the same general kind as any other. Thus, in an explanation of the confession by means of the Prologue, multiple mysteries would replace the single mystery.

Striking a Balance

The significance of the preceding two sections' balancing between excessive diffidence and excessive confidence can be sensed from Chenu's historical overview:

Does not our respect for the mystery weaken our efforts at reasoning to the extent of imposing upon us a mute adoration and an admission that all we can say must be equivocal? It is here that we find, throughout the history of Christian thought, a tension between those whom we call mystics, that is, theologians with a greater awareness of the ineffability of the mystery, and those whom we call scholastics, that is, theologians devoted to expressing the tenets of their faith in a rational and structural form. On the one hand this tension can lead to a dangerous agnosticism and a lapse into nominalism of which Thomas à Kempis and Gerson, for example, were suspected, and, on the other hand, to a "theologism" in which the mystery of the Word of God is obliterated behind dialectical scaffolding.[22]

To the charge of ineffability or equivocation brought against theological practice I have responded optimistically: thanks to the Principle of Relative Similarity, we may speak both meaningfully and truly of realities far beyond our reach. To the charge of rationalism or theologism, I have replied less optimistically, since the possibility of speaking truly does not guarantee our statements' truth, our knowing their truth, their stating a genuine possibility, or our understanding what makes them true. Thus, these present "efforts at reasoning," distinguishing between making sense and achieving truth, on the one hand, and achieving knowledge and understanding, on the other, may make us both more confident and more diffident in addressing the mysteries of Christian faith.

Although the chapter's illustrations have come from Christian theology, all its main points apply, to a greater or lesser extent, beyond the bounds of Christian faith. There, too, in other faith traditions, there are mysteries. There, too, PRS analogy has an essential role to play in expressing the transcendent. There, too, we may too readily assume the meaningfulness of apparently meaningful utterances, the genuine possibility of what can be meaningfully stated, the feasibility of deductive theological inference, and the link between closer analysis and genuine clarification. There too, accordingly, a difficult balance needs to be sought, this way or that, between excessive diffidence and excessive confidence in the face of transcendent mystery.

For Further Reflection

1. "How can mere human words even approximate to, let alone do justice [to], the infinite and transcendent reality

of God? Is not all human speech about God bound to distort and limit and thus misrepresent the reality with which it is concerned?"[23] (Colin Gunton, Stephen Holmes, and Murray Rae).

2. "Human words, were they to be pronounced by God himself, must fail to exhaust God's reality"[24] (Jacques Dupuis).

3. "The pluralist idea seems to be that none of the positive claims a religion makes about God are true, but that they are all equally groping towards the truth, which none of them has yet attained. But unless the pluralists have some privileged epistemic access to the nature of God, it is hard to see on what basis they would know such a claim about the world's religions to be true"[25] (Eleonore Stump).

4. "It is to be noted that the human word receives concrete content and concrete form from God, and becomes capable of saying something, by the fact, and only by the fact, that it is spoken on the strength of God's permission and command, and therefore has the definite similarity with its object which is promised and bestowed by God's revelation, and is not arbitrarily discovered and affirmed"[26] (Karl Barth).

5. "Moreover, it would seem that any and every theological explanation is doomed to be reductionist in that it replaces a revealed truth that expresses an aspect of the divine mystery (for example, of God as creator) with a humanly accessible truth or explanation (for example, a theory of divine causality). This reductionist tendency will apply as much to nonphilosophical explanations as to philosophical explanations, since the uniqueness and transcendent reality of the mysteries of faith imply that the truths of faith cannot, in principle, be explained in any other terms"[27] (Gerald Gleeson).

6. "Modern philosophers of language have enunciated a principle of expressibility, according to which it is held that for anything that a speaker wishes to communicate, there are words in the speaker's language that can express it"[28] (Bimal Krishna Matilal).

Epilogue

This work's opening chapter cited a predicament. Because the methodological implications of language for theology, though numerous and basic, are not obvious, the need to study them seriously is not evident. Because the need is not evident, the study is not undertaken. Because the study is not undertaken, the need is not recognized. And so the unfortunate circle spins, round and round. To break out, I could do no better at the beginning than to offer a promissory note: the significance and value of such an inquiry, I predicted, would become increasingly evident in the course of the inquiry. And so, I trust, it has turned out. The paths taken, the areas reconnoitered, the issues addressed are too numerous to review, but collectively they may have had the desired effect: they may have convinced the reader (if convincing was necessary) that language, the medium of theological discourse, deserves all this attention.

Collectively, they also suggest the reply to an objection this summation is likely to elicit. It may appear that in order to highlight the contribution of the present study, I have drawn an exaggerated contrast. Surely theologians have said a great deal about language! Yes, but as chapter 1 noted, the "language" spoken of has typically been linguistic discourse, whereas in the summary just given and throughout the work thus summarized the focus has been on language in the sense of the medium of discourse. *That* has been slighted. Again, surely theologians have said much about analogy! Yes, but as chapter 7 noted, fixation on the objects of analogical predication and inattention to the language spoken, with its competing expressions, has resulted in the absence of any such formulation as the Principle of Relative Similarity, without which traditional accounts of analogy will not work. Again, surely theologians have said much about definition! True, but as chapter 13 indicated, they have devoted far more attention to linguistically dubious theoretical definitions than to linguistic definitions. Such contrasts could be multiplied, but I will just suggest, more broadly, that comparison of the present work's coverage with typical works of fundamental theology or theological method reveals what I mean by *serious* attention to the methodological implications of language, on the one hand, and by the lack thereof, on the other.

However, all this attention to language, though justified, may have had two unfortunate side effects that now need to be addressed. One is the impression that, as Macquarrie has put it, "The jungle of theological verbiage stands badly in need of some cleaning up."[1] To some extent, this negative impression was unavoidable. In order to demonstrate and explain the need for linguistic attentiveness in theology, and to profit fully from the demonstration, it was necessary to suggest, through numerous, varied examples, the unfortunate consequences of linguistic inattentiveness. However, I should now note that such negative samples, though far from rare, are the exception rather than the rule, not only in theology generally but even in the writings from which I have drawn my cautionary illustrations. Theological discourse may be a linguistic danger zone, but linguistic problems do not appear on every page. Far from it.

The following, then, may be a more apt comparison than Macquarrie's. In most parts of the world, people walk freely without worrying about quicksand. When, however, they enter areas where quicksand is present, they need to be warned. Even in those areas, solid ground is more extensive than treacherous, and people need not watch their every step. Where, then, should they be on their guard? The general warning "Watch out for quicksand hereabouts!" does not suffice. Descriptive clues may serve somewhat, but a tour of actual sites is still more helpful, to convey the look and feel of danger spots. Throw in a stone, or try a step or two, and see what happens! Such has been the tactic of the present study—or at least of enough chapters to create the impression, which now may need correction, that danger spots lurk everywhere: the whole of theology is quicksand![2]

A second likely impression was also unavoidable if the study was to make its case convincingly. Theology, it may appear by now, is confined, hemmed in, imprisoned within the bounds of language. There is no escape. At every moment, in every utterance, language must have its say. Misgivings on this score may merge with others, concerning the philosophical source of all this linguistic emphasis, and may coalesce, more broadly, with misgivings regarding such heavy reliance on philosophy of any variety. For, as Paul Avis has observed:

> Christian theology has tended to be ambivalent in its attitude to philosophical speculation. On the one hand, it has been

felt that speculative philosophy constitutes a threat to theology, invading its province, usurping its functions, and enticing it away from its true object. On the other hand, theology exists in a philosophical and cultural climate, and the great advances and discoveries of theology have often come about through its enrichment with philosophical thought.[3]

Here, then, is matter for retrospective reflection, now that this survey has run its course. How threatening or intrusive has its dependence on linguistic philosophy been? To what extent has the overall message been unduly restrictive, and to what extent, perhaps, has it on the contrary been more liberating than confining?

Linguistic Philosophy and the Autonomy of Theology

Of Karl Barth, notoriously jealous of theology's autonomy, the English-language editors of his *Church Dogmatics* write: "Instead of binding theology to the philosophy of one age, like an Aquinas or a Schleiermacher, Barth has sought to give theology such an expression in our thought that the living Truth becomes the master of our thinking, and not thinking the master of the truth."[4] On this Barthian agenda Avis comments: "The position is perfectly clear: Christian theology stands above the fray, untainted by merely human thought-forms and any involvement will be entirely on its own terms."[5] Avis rightly receives such claims with skepticism. "Barth himself teaches that revelation comes to us clothed in the garments of creaturely reality. I would go further and suggest that the faith is not merely clothed with, but actually merges with the thought-forms borrowed from human philosophies."[6] And not just from human philosophies, I would add, but from human languages: the thought-forms are necessarily linguistic.

As remarked, this dependence of theology on language can appear confining. By contrast, how free Plato was, for example, to consult his eternal, nonlinguistic Forms for guidance. How free subsequent thinkers, for whom thought was equally nonlinguistic, felt to go their speculative ways, untroubled by linguistic restrictions. But then came Wittgenstein, with his negative, therapeutic message: "The results of philosophy are the uncovering of one or another piece of plain nonsense and of bumps that the understanding has got by running its head up against the limits of language. These bumps make us see the value of the discovery."[7] Some results of the preceding survey might be characterized similarly. Language sets limits against which theologians, too, have often run their heads, and we have repeatedly observed what sizeable bumps have sometimes resulted. Thus, we have noted, for example:

> how language's typical role as medium, not object, of thought inclines us to maintain this natural, non-linguistic focus and how, thus fixated, we fail to recognize with what pervasive power the linguistic medium affects our thinking;
> how powerfully, for example, language can suggest the existence of essences shared by all and only members of a class of things denoted by a single term (e.g., "theology");
> how fundamentally belief in essences, matched with words and things, can falsify our conception of the relationship between language, thought, and world;
> how this traditional conception can blind us to the role of language as the co-determinant (or occasionally sole determinant) of the truth of our statements, in theology and elsewhere;
> how pervasively this blindness undermines the authority of language to co-determine what we say;
> how such disregard for the authority of language affects our thinking with regard, say, to privileged paradigms, theoretical definitions, universal claims, and deductive inferences based on them;
> how, in these and other ways, inattentiveness to language can beget excessive confidence in the face of mystery.

This is just a sampling. Drawing on previous chapters, the list might continue still more impressively, and depressingly. And yet, the tale also had a more positive side. Once recognized and accepted, reliance on language proves liberating as well as confining, for our words can reach much farther than can our mental representations. Although the Principle of Relative Similarity does set limits, limits that are frequently ignored and contravened, the principle may be satisfied by realities far beyond the reach of nonlinguistic thought. For the truth of even the most transcendent utterances, it suffices that the realities described bear adequate PRS resemblance to realities customarily so described. And for the meaningfulness of such utterances, it suffices that they have determinate truth-conditions, so specified. Thus, to regret the control that comes with language's assistance is like regretting the need to keep contact with the earth in order to walk, to live in earth's atmosphere in order to breathe, or to look through a telescope in order to view distant planets. How confining!

Blindness is not liberating. Neither, though ever so natural, is blindness to language. In this respect, linguistic awareness may be compared with the historical awareness now strongly stressed by theologians. "For the first time," it has been said, "theology is acutely aware of being conditioned by history and of the impossibility of avoiding this conditioning. . . . This is a new theological situation, parallel to that created by the chronic pluralism of modern thought, and it has serious implications for our understanding of Christian doctrine and dogma."[8] Substitute the word *language* for *history* and none of this would need to be changed, save for the part about theology's "acute awareness." Theologians are not yet conscious to an equal extent of the unavoidable conditioning of theology by language and of the weighty implications that this conditioning has for their discipline. Limited linguistic awareness has importantly affected the way even eminent theologians have conceived their whole enterprise.

System Versus Straightjacket?

As previously noted, theologians have sometimes stressed the importance of the question, "What is theology?" and have conceived the query in basically Platonic fashion. The reality itself, by itself (this valued activity, this estimable form of life), if adequately analyzed and scrutinized, would yield an adequate answer to the question about its nature and thereby lay a solid foundation for subsequent theological inquiry. How, it has been felt, can theologians proceed scientifically if they do not know what they are doing, and how can they know—precisely, accurately—what they are doing if they have no sound, scientific answer to the query, "What is theology?"

Chapter 1 suggested difficulties for the "scientific" approach thus illustrated, and chapter 13, on defining and saying what things are, developed them more fully. The problems' seriousness appears if we consider, with regard to this example (theology), the alternatives set out in chapter 5. First, in saying what theology is, we can either ignore the word *theology* or recognize the relevance of the word and its meaning. In the former, word-ignoring alternative, we will be free to define theology any way we please—say, as the study of the world's divinities, of mystical experience, of life's most important questions, or of whatever other content most catches our fancy. (Indeed, on the same supposition of language's irrelevance, we may define theology, not as any kind of study, but as a hobby, habit, pastime, profession, or what have you.) How liberating!—but also how confining, once a single, specific definition of the discipline is chosen and imposed. In the other, more reasonable alternative, attentive to the word *theology* and its meaning, we may either accept the guidance of existing word usage or stipulate a substitute sense for the word *theology*. If, seeing no point in redefining the word, we accept the guidance of existing usage, with all its fuzzy diversity, we will come up with no definition of the clear, unified, discriminating—and restrictive—kind Nygren and others have aspired to. Theology will be anything that falls within the term's ample reach as circumscribed, say, by the Principle of Relative Similarity.

Here, then, is the choice suggested by these alternatives: we can free ourselves from the restrictions of language, or we can free ourselves from a narrow, restrictive conception of theology. A similar choice arises for the conduct of the discipline as well as for its definition. In illustration, recall, for instance, from the preceding chapter how Rahner conducted his treatment of Trinitarian processions. Noting "two (and only two!) basic activities of the spirit: knowledge and love," on the one hand, and "two (and only two!) processions or emanations within God," on the other, Rahner concluded: "We are allowed, then, to combine these two data and to connect, in a special and specific way, the intra-divine procession of the Logos from the Father with God's knowledge, and the procession of the Spirit from the Father through the Son with God's love." This looks scientific, systematic. However, Rahner does not explain how or why we are allowed to do this matching of activities with processions. And the last chapter noted problems for his premises. When, as here, terms such as "all," "only," "never," and "none" play a crucial role, a PRS-type norm, citing the authority of language, is likely to challenge their application. So again, as with regard to the definition of theology, such appeals to the authority of language may appear confining, not allowing due leeway for the development of systematic theology. However, the same illustration can counter this impression.

Recall the last chapter's comments on Rahner's restrictive claim of two and only two basic activities of the spirit. Perhaps, I remarked, amid the welter of interconnecting psychological concepts, some sense of the term *basic* might be discerned that would allow us to identify "knowledge" and "love" as the only two basic psychological concepts, but I doubted it. However, it does not matter. For certainly all other psychological states or activities cannot be reduced to just these two. And if all the rest remain possibilities, then the divine persons and their relationships might be characterized by admiration, awe, generosity, gratitude, joy, interest, respect, compassion, or what have you, alone or variously combined (as for human persons). Or they might be differentiated in transcendent ways for which we have no suitable terms. "System," not language, is the enemy of such openness. So the general lesson I sense, from this example as from this study as a whole, is that, far from being confining, theology within the bounds of language means theology where it belongs: within the broad bounds of mystery.

Thus, this study, which, progressing chapter by chapter through issues of linguistic methodology, has said so little about imagination or creativity in theology, nonetheless makes room for imaginative, creative theology. "How do they know where they are going before they start walking?" asked Koyama. "How can they describe the changing scenery before they see it?" Will methodology teach Paul to conceive the church as the body of Christ, or instruct the author of *Hebrews* to view the crucified one as eternal high priest? Later, with time and new perspectives, will mere methodological reflection lead Augustine to his Trinitarian analogies or suggest to Teilhard his evolutionary, Christ-centered vision of a world on its way to Omega? Surely not. Methodology has its limits; and so, a fortiori, does methodology within the stated focus of this study. Concerned though it is with meaning and truth, the study dictates no specific meaningful, true developments within the bounds it traces so amply and so flexibly.

However, to sense the study's significance as well as its limits, recall the comparison with London. That great metropolis consists of much more than just its streets; yet, for ready communication, a network of alleys, roads, and boulevards traverses its every part—a tangled, irregular, complicated network. Thus, even a sketchy map, though it says nothing about where, when, or how to travel the arteries it traces, can be helpful, even indispensable, in finding one's way about the city. So it is for the vast, complex enterprise of theology, whose linguistic highways and byways pervade it still more thoroughly, still more indispensably, and—as we have seen—still more confusingly. For such a domain, even an imperfect map is better than none.

Notes

Preface

1. Koyama, *Water Buffalo Theology*, x.
2. Hoy and McCarthy, *Critical Theory*, 63. Cf. Føllesdal, "Triangulation," 719: "Philosophers and linguists have always said that language is a social institution. They have, however, immediately forgotten this and have adopted notions of meaning that are not publicly accessible and where it remains unclear how such entities are grasped by us."
3. E.g, *Logic for the Labyrinth: A Guide to Critical Thinking*; *Essentialism: A Wittgensteinian Critique*; *Language and Truth*; *A Middle Way to God*; *Identity and Mystery: Late-Wittgensteinian Perspectives*; *Linguistic Philosophy: The Central Story*.
4. A sampling of books (alphabetically by author): Alston, *Divine Nature and Human Language*; Ayers and Blackstone, *Religious Language and Knowledge*; Boeve and Feyaerts, *Metaphor and God-Talk*; Braaten, *Our Naming of God*; Brown, *Do Religious Claims Make Sense?*; Burke, *The Rhetoric of Religion*; Burrell, *Analogy and Philosophical Language*; Castelli, *L'Analyse du langage théologique*; Charlesworth, *The Problem of Religious Language*; Christian, *Meaning and Truth in Religion*; Clarke, *Language and Natural Theology*; Dewart, *Religion, Language, and Truth*; D'Hert, *Wittgenstein's Relevance for Theology*; Donovan, *Religious Language*; Downey, *Beginning at the Beginning: Wittgenstein and Theological Conversation*; Ebeling, *Introduction to a Theological Theory of Language*; Fawcett, *The Symbolic Language of Religion*; Ferré, *Language, Logic, and God*; Fox, *Mystery and Meaning*; Frankenberry and Penner, *Language, Truth, and Religious Belief*; Gabus, *Critique du discours théologique*; Gilkey, *Naming the Whirlwind*; Grabner-Heider, *Semiotik und Theologie*; High, *New Essays on Religious Language*; Hutchison, *Language and Faith*; Jeffner, *The Study of Religious Language*; Jennings, *Beyond Theism: A Grammar of God-Language*; Kaempfert, *Probleme der religiösen Sprache*; Kerr, *Theology after Wittgenstein*; Kimpel, *Language and Religion*; Kort, *Bound to Differ: The Dynamics of Theological Discourses*; Lundeen, *Risk and Rhetoric in Religion*; Macquarrie, *God-Talk*; Malherbe, *Le langage théologique à l'âge de la science*; Marranzini, *Il linguaggio teologico oggi*; McCutcheon, *Religion within the Limits of Language Alone*; McFague, *Metaphorical Theology* and *Speaking in Parables*; Mertens and Boeve, *Naming God*

Today; Mondin, *Il problema del linguaggio teologico dalle origini ad oggi*; Need, *Human Language and Knowledge in the Light of Chalcedon*; O'Callaghan, *Thomist Realism and the Linguistic Turn*; Palmer, *Analogy: A Study of Qualification and Argument in Theology*; Pastor, *La lógica de lo inefable*; Porter, *The Nature of Religious Language*; Ramsey, *Christian Discourse* and *Religious Language*; Ross, *Portraying Analogy*; Scharlemann, *Naming God*; Sherry, *Religion, Truth, and Language-Games*; Smith, *Speech and Theology*; Soskice, *Metaphor and Religious Language*; TeSelle, *Speaking in Parables*; Tilley, *Talking of God*; Tonkin and Keef, *Language in Religion*; Torrance, *The Ground and Grammar of Theology*; Tracy and Cobb, *Talking about God*; Van Buren, *The Edges of Language: An Essay in the Logic of a Religion*.

5. Wittgenstein, *Philosophical Investigations*, §203.
6. Gasking and Jackson, "Wittgenstein as a Teacher," 51.

Chapter 1. The Terrain Ahead

1. Ford, "Epilogue," 720.
2. Macquarrie, *Principles of Christian Theology*, 1.
3. Nygren, *Meaning and Method*, 2.
4. Pannenberg, *Theology and the Philosophy of Science*, 6.
5. Wittgenstein, *Philosophical Investigations*, §69.
6. Schillebeeckx, *Revelation and Theology*, 93.
7. Kaufman, *An Essay on Theological Method*, ix.
8. Carnes, *Axiomatics and Dogmatics*, 57.
9. Tavard, *La théologie*, 70.
10. Gadamer, *Truth and Method*, 321.
11. Ibid., 432.
12. Gilkey, *Naming the Whirlwind*, 233.
13. Ibid., 234.
14. Fisichella, "Langage théologique," 727.
15. Macquarrie, *God-Talk*, 18–19.
16. Geffré, *The Risk of Interpretation*, 59.
17. Bonhoeffer, *Letters and Papers from Prison*, 161.
18. Ferré, *Language, Logic and God*, 105.
19. Jenson, *Systematic Theology*, vol. 1, 3.
20. O'Collins, *Fundamental Theology*, 15; original emphasis.
21. Labourdette, "Moral Theology," 1123.
22. Ferré, *Basic Modern Philosophy of Religion*, 30; original emphasis.
23. Thomas and Wondra, *Introduction to Theology*, 19.

Chapter 2. Language and Thought

1. Haight, *Dynamics of Theology*, 176.
2. Putnam, "Language and Philosophy," 14.

3. Arnauld, *The Art of Thinking*, 90.
4. Schleiermacher, *Hermeneutics*, 8.
5. Tavard, *La théologie*, 69.
6. Macquarrie, *Thinking about God*, 3.
7. Wittgenstein, *Philosophical Grammar*, 106.
8. Wittgenstein, *Zettel*, §100.
9. Wittgenstein, *Philosophical Investigations*, §329.
10. Moore, *Commonplace Book 1919–1953*, 19; Moore's emphasis.
11. Ibid., 21; Moore's emphasis.
12. Indeed, they would make the existence of such an essence less likely. For then, in order for the word defined to designate an essence, each of the defining expressions would have to do so. Cf. Hallett, *Logic for the Labyrinth*, 25–27.
13. Plato, *Republic*, 596a (Cornford translation).
14. Frege, *Translations*, 174.
15. Wittgenstein, *Philosophical Investigations*, §67.
16. Ibid., §342; Wittgenstein's italics.
17. Quoted in Nouwen, *Seeds of Hope*, 58.
18. Race, *Christians and Religious Pluralism*, 75–76.
19. Descartes, *The Philosophical Works*, 242–43.
20. Jackendoff, *Patterns in the Mind*, 187.
21. Wittgenstein, *Philosophical Investigations*, §66; Wittgenstein's emphasis.

Chapter 3. Linguistic Spectacles

1. Herder, *Fragmente*, 347, quoted in Schaff, *Language and Cognition*, 9.
2. Whorf, *Language, Thought, and Reality*, 213.
3. Sapir, *Selected Writings*, 10–11.
4. Schaff, *Language and Cognition*, 8.
5. Whorf, *Language, Thought, and Reality*, 213, 214.
6. Ibid., 213.
7. Wittgenstein, *Philosophical Investigations*, §104.
8. Ibid., §115; original emphasis.
9. Wittgenstein, *Tractatus Logico-Philosophicus*, 4.5.
10. Wittgenstein, *Philosophical Investigations*, §114.
11. Wittgenstein, *Notebooks 1914–1916*, 39.
12. Wittgenstein, *Philosophical Investigations*, §23.
13. Wittgenstein, *Tractatus Logico-Philosophicus*, 3.323.
14. Ibid., 3.324.
15. Rahner, *Foundations of Christian Faith*, 293; Rahner's emphasis.
16. Kasper, *Jesus the Christ*, 233.
17. Mersch, *The Theology of the Mystical Body*, 320.
18. Mersch, *The Whole Christ*, 36.
19. Mersch, *The Theology of the Mystical Body*, 319.

20. Mersch, *The Whole Christ*, 578.
21. Mersch, *The Theology of the Mystical Body*, 320.
22. Mersch, *The Whole Christ*, 127.
23. For fuller discussion of this example, from which the present treatment is drawn, see Hallett, *Identity and Mystery*, chapters 2 and 3.
24. Hilary, *De Trin.* 10.23 (CCL 62A, 477).
25. Hanson, *Search*, 499–500.
26. Morris, *The Logic of God Incarnate*, 89.
27. Stump, Review, 220.
28. Thomasius, *Christ's Person and Work*, in Welch, *God and Incarnation*, 89.
29. Ibid., 94.
30. Hick, *Disputed Questions*, 66.
31. Cupitt, "The Finality of Christ," 625.
32. Hick, "Jesus and the World Religions," 178. Cf. Hick, "Incarnation and Atonement," 83. C. S. Evans notes: "Hick does not provide any argument for the accusation, and he has in fact recently retreated from the claim that the doctrine of the incarnation is logically incoherent, in favour of the weaker charge that no one has successfully stated a coherent version of the doctrine that is also religiously satisfying" (*The Historical Christ*, 121, citing Hick, *The Metaphor of God Incarnate*, 3–4).
33. Knox, *The Humanity and Divinity of Christ*, 67.
34. McGuckin, *St. Cyril of Alexandria*, 198, citing: "Scholia 9; Letter to the Monks, para. 12; 1st Letter to Succensus; Explanation of the Twelve Chapters (Expln. 3) and passim." See also *In Jo.* (e.g., PG 74, 344B and 737D).
35. For fuller discussion of this analogy, see D. Brown, *The Divine Trinity*, 253–54.
36. See Hallett, *Identity and Mystery*, 25–37.
37. Cf. Hallett, *A Companion to Wittgenstein's "Philosophical Investigations,"* 26–35.
38. Wittgenstein, *Philosophical Investigations*, §66; original emphasis.
39. Ibid., §340; Wittgenstein's italics; paragraph break omitted.
40. Brück, "Contribution," 142.
41. Barnes, *Christian Identity and Religious Pluralism*, 99.
42. Heschel, "A Jewish Response," 81.
43. Hebblethwaite, "Incarnation—The Essence of Christianity?," 3.
44. Rocca, *Speaking the Incomprehensible God*, 344.
45. Schaff, *Language and Cognition*, 9, quoting Herder, *Fragmente über die neue deutsche Literatur*.

Chapter 4. Linguistic Truth

1. James, *Pragmatism*, 96.
2. Austin, "Truth," 111.
3. Ibid., 113–14.

4. Ibid., 116. These conventions are, of course, ones existing at the time of the utterance, not past or future ones.

5. Ibid., footnote 9.

6. Strawson, "Truth," 154.

7. Ibid.

8. Warnock, "Truth and Correspondence," 18.

9. Austin, "Truth," 116; Austin's italics.

10. Hallett, *A Middle Way to God*, 14 (revised from Hallett, *Language and Truth*, 91).

11. In this regard, see Edward Smith, "Three Distinctions," for numerous complications the formula ignores.

12. Keller, "Analytical Philosophy," 82.

13. This chapter draws heavily on chapters 13 and 14 of Hallett, *Linguistic Philosophy*.

14. Davidson, "Truth Rehabilitated," 66.

15. Fergusson, "Meaning, Truth, and Realism," 185.

16. Hunsinger, "Truth as Self-Involving," 41–42.

17. Küng, "Is There One True Religion?," 129.

18. Leaman, "Introduction," 7.

19. Ward, *Religion and Creation*, 131.

Chapter 5. Truth's Norm

1. Hazelton, "Truth in Theology," 772–73.

2. Lewis, *The Four Loves*, 25.

3. Putnam, "Language and Philosophy," 9. Cf. Ayer, *Philosophy and Language*, 7: "It would seem that Moore himself was inclined to reify meanings: the concepts or propositions which philosophers sought to analyse were given the status of non-natural objects. No doubt it was not possible to apprehend them unless one understood the appropriate words, but this applied equally to many of the objects of the sciences . . . just as the mathematician was not concerned with numerals as such but rather with the numbers which they represented, so the philosopher's command of language was merely a necessary means to the investigation of the objective properties of concepts."

4. Dawson, *Religion and Culture*, 25.

5. In Friedl and Reynolds, *Extraordinary Lives*, 44.

6. Mackie, *Contemporary Linguistic Philosophy*, 17.

7. Russell, introduction to Gellner, *Words and Things*, 15.

8. Nygren, *Meaning and Method*, 101.

9. Wittgenstein, *Philosophical Investigations*, §79.

10. Dillistone, *C. H. Dodd*, 166–67; paragraph break omitted.

11. Lewis, *Mere Christianity*, xi.

12. Kelsey, "Paul Tillich," 98.

13. Thiemann, *Revelation and Theology*, 5–6.

14. Brück, "Contribution," 145–46.

Chapter 6. The Norm's Feasibility

1. Wittgenstein, *Tractatus Logico-Philosophicus*, 4.002.
2. Waismann, "Analytic-Synthetic," 122.
3. Strawson, "Truth," 131; original emphasis.
4. Austin, "Truth," 113.
5. For fuller development of the case for statements as bearers of truth, see Knox, "Truth, Correspondence, and Ordinary Language," 520–21, and Hallett, *Language and Truth*, chapter 4.
6. See Hallett, *Language and Truth*, chapter 5.
7. Ebeling, *Introduction*, 178.
8. Ibid., 179–80.
9. Ibid., 121.
10. Wittgenstein, *Philosophical Investigations*, §77.
11. Alfaro, "Faith," 314.
12. Milhaven, "Towards an Epistemology of Ethics," 238.
13. Haight, *Dynamics of Theology*, 7–8.
14. Wittgenstein, *Philosophical Investigations*, §116.
15. Ibid., §79.
16. Maurice Mahoney, in Steinfels, "The Search for an Alternative," 663.
17. P. Ramsey, "Reference Points," 79, on Ashley Montagu.
18. See Hallett, *Logic for the Labyrinth*, 173–75.
19. Chapter 17 of Hallett, *Linguistic Philosophy*, on which the present chapter draws, adds an important thesis that applies to theology as well as to philosophy: "[L]inguistic details of a kind that linguists alone might reliably supply are seldom such as philosophers, let alone less speculative speakers, genuinely need" (153).
20. Moore, *Some Main Problems of Philosophy*, 4; Moore's italics.
21. Noonan, "Responding to Persons," 301–302.
22. Hartshorne, "Concerning Abortion," 44; original emphasis.
23. Veatch, "Death, Determination of," 144.
24. Netland, *Dissonant Voices*, 183.

Chapter 7. Making Sense

1. Nielsen, *Introduction*, 36; Nielsen's italics.
2. Hospers, *An Introduction to Philosophical Analysis*, 97; original emphasis.
3. Smith, *The Analogy of Experience*, 45.
4. Aquinas, *Summa contra gentiles* 1.31.
5. Clarke, "Analogy," 85; Clarke's italics.
6. Robinson, "The Logic of Religious Language," 2.
7. Capon, *Hunting the Divine Fox*, 8–9.

8. Burrell, *Analogy and Philosophical Language*, 168.
9. Cf., e.g., Nielsen, "Talk of God," 40; Pannenberg, *Basic Questions in Theology*, vol. 1, 225.
10. Rocca, *Speaking the Incomprehensible God*, 63.
11. Clarkson et al., eds., *The Church Teaches*, n. 307.
12. Pannenberg, *Basic Questions in Theology*, vol. 1, 211–12.
13. Wiles, *Faith*, 23–24.
14. Power, "Musings," 308.
15. Swinburne, "Analogy, Metaphor, and Religious Language," 72.

Chapter 8. Sense Versus Possibility

1. Nielsen, "Facts," 138; original emphasis.
2. Reichenbach, "Evil," 68. Mackie comments: "This was the central thesis of my 'Evil and Omnipotence' . . . and of A. Flew's 'Divine Omnipotence and Human Freedom' " (*The Miracle of Theism*, 164n).
3. Quote in Pusey, *The Doctrine of the Real Presence*, 12.
4. Swinburne, in Shoemaker and Swinburne, *Personal Identity*, 25.
5. Bouyer, *Dictionary of Theology*, 42.
6. Campbell, "The Nature of Practical Theology," 84.
7. Suárez, *De Incarnatione*, 40.
8. George, *Theology of the Reformers*, 65.
9. Cornman and Lehrer, *Philosophical Problems and Arguments*, 398.
10. Nagel, *The View from Nowhere*, 97–98.
11. Haldane, *Faithful Reason*, 125.

Chapter 9. Inference and Analogy

1. Newman, *University Sermons*, 274.
2. Avis, *The Methods of Modern Theology*, 211–12.
3. Palmer, *Analogy*, 130.
4. Ibid., 83.
5. Kearney, "Analogy and Inference," 132.
6. For much fuller treatment of the same example, in the same vein, see Hallett, *Identity and Mystery*, chapter 5.
7. Rahner, "The Presence of Christ," 297.
8. Zwingli, "On the Lord's Supper," 190–95, 199.
9. Ibid., 194.
10. Ibid., 190–92. Cf. Congar, "*Lutherana*," 173–74: "Karlstadt said he could not admit that Christ is in the sacrament with his height, his size, his length."
11. Zwingli, "On the Lord's Supper," 190.
12. Ibid., 199.
13. Ibid., 192.

14. Fiorenza, *Foundational Theology*, 307.
15. Lonergan, *A Second Collection*, 59.
16. Sesboüé, *Jésus Christ dans la tradition*, 40.
17. Scotus, *Philosophical Writings*, 20.
18. Peterson et al., *Reason and Religious Belief*, 145.
19. H. Brown, *Heresies*, 172.
20. Chenu, *Is Theology a Science?*, 67.
21. Hebblethwaite, *Philosophical Theology and Christian Doctrine*, 68.

Chapter 10. Universal Claims (Factual)

1. Nietzsche, "On Truth and Lie," 46–47.
2. Regarding the difficulties for this classic example, see Hallett, *Logic for the Labyrinth*, 21–23.
3. Johnson, *A Dictionary of the English Language*, fifth page of the preface.
4. Wittgenstein, *Philosophical Investigations*, §128; Wittgenstein's italics.
5. Hutchins, "Toward a Durable Society," 201.
6. Dawson, *Religion*, 25.
7. In Friedl and Reynolds, *Extraordinary Lives*, 44.

Chapter 11. Universal Claims (Moral)

1. Wittgenstein, *Philosophical Investigations*, §96.
2. Hallett, *Language and Truth*, 158–61.
3. Roberti and Palazzini, *Dictionary of Moral Theology*, 1241.
4. Ibid., 805.
5. John Paul II, *Veritatis splendor*, 75.
6. Cf. Hallett, *Christian Moral Reasoning*, 20, 27–28, 85–88, and *Greater Good*, 47–50.
7. St. Augustine, *Contra mendacium* vii, 18.
8. Cathrein, *Philosophia moralis*, 76–77. Cf. Hallett, *Christian Moral Reasoning*, 20–23.
9. Kluge, *The Practice of Death*, 133.
10. Anscombe, "Modern Moral Philosophy," 10.

Chapter 12. Privileged Senses

1. Geach, "The Meaning of 'God,' " 86.
2. Barth, *Church Dogmatics* II/I, 179.
3. Ibid., 183.
4. Ibid., 181.

5. Hick, *Philosophy of Religion*, 70.
6. Hutchison, *Language and Faith*, 10.
7. O'Collins, *Fundamental Theology*, 204.
8. Ratzinger, "Revelation and Tradition," 40.
9. Warnach, "Symbol and Reality," 60.
10. Torrance, *Ground*, 148.
11. Macquarrie, *Thinking about God*, 37.
12. Thomas and Wondra, *Introduction to Theology*, 94.
13. Carnes, *Axiomatics and Dogmatics*, 64.
14. Hospers, *An Introduction to Philosophical Analysis*, 75; original emphasis.
15. Rahner, *Hearer of the Word*, 147.
16. O'Collins, *Fundamental Theology*, 178.
17. Urban, *Language and Reality*, 675.
18. Deutsch, "Holy Otherness," 109.
19. Dulles, *Models of the Church*, 15.
20. Rahner, "The Concept of Mystery," 53.
21. Ibid., 41–42.
22. Barth, *Church Dogmatics*, II/I, 253.
23. Kant, *Critique of Pure Reason*, 314 (A 319/B376).
24. Malcolm, *Ludwig Wittgenstein*, 71.
25. See Hallett, *Language and Truth*, chapter 4.
26. Dulles, *Models of the Church*, 15.
27. O'Collins and Kendall, *The Bible for Theology*, 50.
28. Ambrose, *On the Mysteries*, in the Roman Breviary for Tuesday in the fifteenth week of ordinary time.
29. Basil, *On the Holy Spirit*, 9.22, from the Roman Breviary for Tuesday in the seventh week of Easter.
30. Aquinas, *Summa theologica* 1.33.3.
31. Carnes, *Axiomatics and Dogmatics*, xi.
32. Montagu, *The Meaning of Love*, v.

Chapter 13. Defining and Saying What Things Are

1. To this definition (from *The American Heritage College Dictionary*) I would add that language also serves to direct people, entertain people, elicit information, convey information, and so forth.
2. Chenu, *Is Theology a Science?*, 56.
3. Moore, *Principia Ethica*, 58.
4. Ibid.
5. Ibid., 3 (preface to the projected second edition).
6. For fuller development of this illustration, see Hallett, *Identity and Mystery*, 47–49.
7. Spiro, "Religion," 142. Cf. Clarke and Byrne, *Religion Defined and Explained*, 3–4.

8. Pannenberg, *Theology and the Philosophy of Science*, 6.
9. Lawler, "Family: American and Christian," 20.
10. Ormerod, *Introducing Contemporary Theologies*, 4; original emphasis.
11. Aquinas, *Summa theol.* I–II, q. 90, a. 2, and a. 95, a. 2, c.
12. Devine, "On the Definition of 'Religion,' " 270.
13. Ibid., 271.
14. Ibid., 272.
15. Ibid.
16. Wittgenstein, *Zettel*, §458.
17. Ebeling, *Word and Faith*, 333.
18. Clarke and Byrne, *Religion Defined and Explained*, 3.
19. Cook, "Truth, Mystery and Justice," 245.
20. Haight, *Dynamics of Theology*, 15.
21. Albanese, *America: Religion and Religions*, 3.
22. Dulles, *Revelation Theology*, 9.

Chapter 14. The Need of Examples

1. Wittgenstein, *The Blue and Brown Books*, 17.
2. Lewis, *On the Plurality of Worlds*, 192–93.
3. Augustine, *Serm.* 272 (*PL* 38: 1247), quoted from Powers, *Eucharistic Theology*, 20.
4. Cerfaux, *The Church*, 343.
5. Quoted in TeSelle, *Speaking in Parables*, 3.
6. McFague, *Models of God*, 43–44.
7. Ebeling, *Introduction*, 185.
8. TeSelle, *Speaking in Parables*, 1–2.

Chapter 15. Important Linguistic Distinctions

1. Aquinas, *Summa theol.* 1–2, q.94.a.2c (English Dominican translation).
2. Hallett, *Greater Good*, 57–60.
3. Aquinas, *Summa theol.* 1–2, q.100.a.5.ad4.
4. Grisez, *Contraception and the Natural Law*, 20.
5. Kant, *Critique of Pure Reason*, 106 (A 69/B 94).
6. See Hallett, *Logic for the Labyrinth*, 122–29.
7. Augustine, *Contra mendacium* vii.18 (translation from Augustine, *Treatises on Various Subjects*, 143).
8. Nouwen, *Creative Fidelity*, 22.
9. Lonergan, *Collection*, 207.
10. Rahner, "On the Theology of the Incarnation," 108.

Chapter 16. Verbal Disagreement

1. Lewis, *Mere Christianity*, ix.
2. Ibid., x.
3. Clarkson and others, *The Church Teaches*, 29.
4. Riga, "The Act of Faith," 149.
5. George, *Theology of the Reformers*, 70–71.
6. Haight, *Dynamics of Theology*, 19–20; paragraph division suppressed.
7. Dulles, "Justification in Contemporary Catholic Theology," 266.
8. Christian, *Meaning and Truth in Religion*, 15–16; see ibid., 17, for an alternative verdict.
9. Delhaye, "La mise en cause," 337–38.
10. Price, *Belief*, 19–20.
11. Knitter, *No Other Name?*, 212.
12. Grisez, *Abortion*, 306; paragraph division omitted.

Chapter 17. Verbal Agreement

1. Lindbeck, "Reform and Infallibility," 352.
2. Denziger and Schönmetzer, *Enchiridion*, 389, n. 1652.
3. Leenhardt, "This Is My Body," 48
4. Lindbeck, "A Question of Compatibility," 230.
5. Küng, *Infallible?*, 67.
6. Noonan, *Contraception*, 292.
7. Ibid., 152.
8. Wiles, *The Making of Christian Doctrine*, 8–9.
9. Wiles, *Faith and the Mystery of God*, 6.
10. Eaton, *Descartes Selections*, xxxviii–xxxix.
11. Tillich, *Shaking of the Foundations*, 57.
12. Atkins, "Religious Assertions and Doctrinal Development," 531–32.

Chapter 18. Interfaith Dialogue

1. Wittgenstein, *Philosophical Investigations*, 223.
2. Anne Clifford's summation, in "The Global Horizon of Religious Pluralism," 168. "Among the major representatives of this model," writes Clifford (ibid., 179), "are George Lindbeck, Paul Griffiths and Joseph Augustine DiNoia."
3. Barnes, *Christian Identity and Religious Pluralism*, 121.
4. Ibid., 80.
5. Ibid., 72, on Hick.
6. Lipner, "Truth-Claims and Inter-Religious Dialogue," 226; Lipner's emphasis.

7. Barnes, *Christian Identity and Religious Pluralism*, 114.
8. Silva, *The Problem of the Self*, 9.
9. Siddiqi, "God: A Muslim View," 66.
10. Verheyden, "On the Christian Doctrine," 41–42.
11. Quoted, without exact reference, in Cohn-Sherbok, "Between Christian and Jew," 91.
12. See Hallett, *Identity and Mystery*, chapter 2.
13. D. Brown, *The Divine Trinity*, 223.
14. Cf. Hallett, *Identity and Mystery*, chapter 4.
15. Hick, *Dialogues*, 15.
16. Ibid.
17. Ibid., 16.
18. Ibid., 180.
19. Ibid., 191; italics omitted.
20. Cf. ibid., 133 ("we do not worship the Real in itself but always one or other of its manifestations to humanity"), 200 ("For whilst their theologies are indeed often mutually incompatible, these theologies describe *different* manifestations to humanity of the ultimate divine reality, and so do not conflict with one another"); *Disputed Questions*, 177–78; "Towards a Philosophy of Religious Pluralism," 103; "Response to Mesle," 134. Gordon Kaufman adopts a similar position (*God the Problem*, 86).
21. Hick, *The Rainbow of Faiths*, 69. Earlier, cf. Hick, *God Has Many Names*, 48.
22. Hick, *An Interpretation of Religion*, 350. Cf. Hick, *The Rainbow of Faiths* 60.
23. For this combination, see, for instance, Hick, *Dialogues*, 190–91.
24. Hick, "Do All Religions," 165. Cf. *God and the Universe of Faiths*, 139–40; *God Has Many Names*, 48; *An Interpretation of Religion*, 245.
25. Hick, "Do All Religions," 162. Contrast this with Hick's earlier negative response to this suggestion ("A Religious Understanding of Religion," 25).
26. Manchester, *The Glory and the Dream*, 47–53.
27. Cf., e.g., Eddy, *John Hick's Pluralist Philosophy*, 144, and Clarke and Byrne, *Religion Defined and Explained*, 89 ("how, if the class of religions has no essential unity, can it be the subject of the generalisations that Hick so obviously wants to make about it?").
28. Cf. Mavrodes, "Polytheism," 286: "In the absence of strong reasons to the contrary, it might be wise to proceed on the assumption that we need not say the *same* thing about every case. We ought, for example, to allow the possibility that there may be distinct religions that have the very same god, and others that really do have distinct gods. There might be religions whose gods are purely fictional and imaginary entities, others whose gods are phenomenal beings in some Kantian or quasi-Kantian sense, still others whose gods are substantial creaturely beings, and still others whose god is the Real, the rock-bottom reality who gives the gift of being to everything else that exists."
29. Newbigin, "The Christian Faith and the World Religions," 94.
30. Lindbeck, *The Nature of Doctrine*, 48–49.

31. Grözinger, "Judaism," 45.
32. Barnes, *Christian Identity and Christian Pluralism*, 17.
33. Grözinger, "Judaism," 44.

Chapter 19. Interfaith Identities

1. Byrne, *Prolegomena to Religious Pluralism*, 31. Cf. ibid., 12; also Byrne, "Ward on Revelation," 19, and "It Is Not Reasonable," 204, 206.
2. For full discussion of this ambiguity in Hick, see Netland, *Encountering Religious Pluralism*, 237–43.
3. Wettstein, "Causal Theory of Proper Names," 109.
4. Wittgenstein, *The Blue and Brown Books*, 2.
5. Byrne, "It Is Not Reasonable," 206.
6. Byrne, Response to Joe Houston, 66.
7. Cf. David Wiggins's distinction, in *Sameness and Substance*, 15–16, between a "thesis of the Relativity of Identity" such as he rejects and a "Thesis of the Sortal Dependency of Individuation" such as he accepts. More recently, see Wiggins, "Précis," 442.
8. Cf. N. Griffin, *Relative Identity*, 42 ("It seems to me that the notion of principles of individuation is the most primitive idea on which we can start to build our account of relative identity").
9. For the only earlier treatment I know of, see Hallett, "From Statements to Parables."
10. Lash, *Holiness, Speech and Silence*, 10.
11. Byrne (*Prolegomena to Religious Pluralism*, 23) cites David Pailin's notion of God as that "which is ultimate ontologically, rationally and valuatively," and comments: "The pluralist needs to extend some such definition of a sacred focus across the religions." Despite the extra descriptive expressions, this characterization, too, and any like it, lacks criteria of individuation.
12. Vroom, "How May We Compare," 72. Cf. Vroom, *No Other Gods*, 100, 159; Stump, "The God of Abraham," 96–98, 119; Levenson, "Do Christians and Muslims," 32.
13. Krieger, *The New Universalism*, 2; Krieger's italics.
14. Houston, "William Alston on Referring to God," 46.
15. Levenson, "Do Christians and Muslims," 32.
16. Byrne, "Reply to Yandell," 215; paragraph break omitted.
17. Vroom, *Religions and the Truth*, 97.
18. Pannenberg, "Religious Pluralism," 103.
19. Phillips, *Faith and Philosophical Enquiry*, 4.

Chapter 20. Theological Language

1. Lonergan, *Method in Theology*, 258.
2. Ibid., 260.

3. Thus, elsewhere in *Method* he writes, for example, that "ordinary language" "is transient; it expresses the thought of the moment at the moment for the moment" (71). Clearly, this could not be said of any natural language. The English language, for example, is not momentary. It does not express the thought of the moment at the moment for the moment. Indeed, it does not express any thought whatsoever. It is a medium for expressing whatever thoughts one pleases: occasional, scientific, metaphysical, theological, or other. Thus, in the context of this remark of Lonergan's, "ordinary language" needs to be understood as (a very restricted sampling of) the ordinary use of language and not as the language used.

4. Tavard, *La théologie*, 28.
5. Ibid., 29.
6. Ibid.
7. Ibid.
8. Wittgenstein, *Philosophical Investigations*, §120; Wittgenstein's emphasis.
9. Keller, "Analytical Philosophy," 76.
10. Latourelle, *Theology*, 101.
11. Carnap, "Replies and Systematic Expositions," 933.
12. Ibid., 936.
13. Carnap, *Meaning and Necessity*, 8. For this reason Quine judged the term *explication* unfortunate. In such conceptual restructuring, "We do not expose hidden meanings" (*Word and Object*, 258).
14. Carnap, *Logical Foundations of Probability*, 7; Carnap's italics.
15. For a critique of the best-known philosophical example, Alfred Tarski's explication of "true," see Hallett, *Linguistic Philosophy*, chapter 7.
16. Macquarrie, *Thinking about God*, 13.
17. Foreword to Rocca, *Speaking the Incomprehensible God*, xi.
18. Eddy, *John Hick's Pluralist Philosophy*, 151.
19. Tavard, *La théologie*, 30.
20. Nouwen, *Seeds of Hope*, 109.
21. Kaufman, *An Essay on Theological Method*, 10.

Chapter 21. Metaphor

1. Wiles, *Faith and the Mystery of God*, 24.
2. Black, "Metaphor," 66.
3. Binkley, "On the Truth and Probity," 150.
4. Phillips, "Mystic Analogizing," 129.
5. Pater, "Analogy and Disclosures," 40.
6. Aristotle, *Metaphysics* 9.10.1051b4 (*The Basic Works of Aristotle*, 833).
7. Cohen, *Arguments and Metaphors in Philosophy*, 137.
8. Ibid., 135; original italics.
9. Swinburne, "Analogy, Metaphor, and Religious Language," 69.

10. Johnson, "Introduction," 4.
11. O'Collins and Kendall, *The Bible for Theology*, 83. Cf. Swinburne, "Analogy, Metaphor, and Religious Language," 71 ("Metaphorical sentences may or may not be paraphrasable by other non-metaphorical sentences"); TeSelle, *Speaking in Parables*, 4 ("In metaphor knowledge and its expression are one and the same; there is no way *around* the metaphor, it is not expendable").
12. Alston, *Divine Nature and Human Language*, 27.
13. Ibid., 2.
14. Swinburne, "Analogy, Metaphor, and Religious Language," 74.
15. Johnson, "Introduction," 35.
16. Alston, *Divine Nature and Human Language*, 30.
17. Ibid., 26.
18. Johnson, "Introduction," 7.
19. Ibid. (quoting Aristotle).
20. Ward, *Religion and Creation*, 147.
21. It might be suggested that "rock," "fortress," and "shepherd" are not incompatible expressions, since all three can be applied, without contradiction, to God. This would serve to highlight the fact, left implicit till now, that the incompatibility spoken of by PRS is incompatibility in nonmetaphorical, nonfigurative speech (nothing can, literally, be a rock, a fortress, and a shepherd).
22. Lash, *Holiness, Speech, and Silence*, 16.
23. Lennan, *An Introduction to Catholic Theology*, 124.
24. O'Collins and Kendall, *The Bible for Theology*, 83.
25. Bowman Clarke, *Language and Natural Theology*, 23.
26. Thornhill, *Christian Mystery*, 103.
27. Hazelton, "Theological Analogy and Metaphor," 161.

Chapter 22. Mystery

1. Power, "Musings," 309–10.
2. Kaufman, *In Face of Mystery*, 61.
3. Jones, *Critical Theology*, 137.
4. Ibid.
5. Justin Martyr, *Apology*, from the Roman breviary for Wednesday of the third week of Easter.
6. Augustine, *De doctrina christiana* I, 6.
7. Boeve, "Naming God Today," 14.
8. Plantinga, *Does God Have a Nature?*, 22.
9. Boeve, "Naming God Today," 15.
10. Thornhill, *Christian Mystery*, 99.
11. Capon, *Hunting the Divine Fox*, 8.
12. Burrell, *Analogy and Philosophical Language*, 37.
13. Hallett, *Darkness and Light*, 103.
14. Kant, *Critique of Pure Reason*, 106 (A 69/B 94).

15. Wittgenstein, *Zettel*, §173.
16. Yandell, *The Epistemology of Religious Experience*, 99.
17. Rahner, *The Trinity*, 116.
18. Ibid., 117; Rahner's emphasis. Rahner often stresses the absolute mystery of God, but his theological practice, as here, often gives a different impression.
19. Rahner, "Why Doing Theology Is So Difficult," 216–17.
20. "St Cyril had preferred *hypostasis* over the rival term *prosōpon* (*persona* in Latin) which some theologians of Antioch favoured. *Prosōpon* appeared to be somewhat vague and even to preserve something of its original meaning of 'mask.' Nevertheless, Chalcedon incorporated both *hypostasis* and *prosōpon* into its final text" (O'Collins, *Interpreting Jesus*, 18). "The Fathers did not indicate a definite philosophical sense of the terms.... To future theology was left the task of elaborating concepts in keeping with this new use of the Greek language" (Bordoni, *Gesù di Nazaret*, vol. 3, 835).
21. Ruben, *Explaining Explanation*, 222.
22. Chenu, *Is Theology a Science?*, 57.
23. Gunton, Holmes, and Rae, *The Practice of Theology*, 287.
24. Dupuis, *Toward a Christian Theology*, 271.
25. Stump, "The God of Abraham, Saadia, and Aquinas," 95.
26. Barth, *Church Dogmatics*, II/I, 232.
27. Gleeson, "Seeking Understanding," 114.
28. Matilal, "Mysticism and Ineffability," 145.

Epilog

1. Macquarrie, *Twentieth-Century Religious Thought*, 316.
2. This comparison is sure to provoke the query, "But why is theology (like philosophy) a danger zone, and not chemistry, astronomy, history, or the like?" An adequate reply to this query might require a whole separate work, but the preceding chapters furnish much helpful data toward a response. Think, for instance, of the defining enterprise, so prominent and prized in philosophy and theology but not in those other disciplines. And in this and other philosophical and theological theorizing, think of the absence of empirical controls.
3. Avis, *The Methods of Modern Theology*, 219.
4. Barth, *Church Dogmatics*, quoted in Avis, *The Methods of Modern Theology*, 52, without reference.
5. Avis, ibid.
6. Ibid., 54.
7. Wittgenstein, *Philosophical Investigations*, §119.
8. Avis, *The Methods of Modern Theology*, 125.

Works Cited

Albanese, Catherine. *America: Religions and Religion.* 2nd ed. Belmont, CA: Wadsworth, 1992.
Alfaro, Juan. "Faith, II: Faith." In *Sacramentum Mundi: An Encyclopedia of Theology,* ed. Karl Rahner. Vol. 2, 313–22. New York: Herder and Herder, 1968.
Alston, William. *Divine Nature and Human Language: Essays in Philosophical Theology.* Ithaca: Cornell University Press, 1989.
Anscombe, G. E. M. "Modern Moral Philosophy." *Philosophy* 33 (1958): 1–19.
Aristotle. *The Basic Works of Aristotle.* Ed. Richard McKeon. New York: Random House, 1941.
Arnauld, Antoine. *The Art of Thinking. Port-Royal Logic.* Trans. James Dickoff and Patricia James. Indianapolis: Bobbs-Merrill, 1964.
Atkins, Anselm. "Religious Assertions and Doctrinal Development." *Theological Studies* 27 (1966): 523–52.
Augustine, Saint. *Treatises on Various Subjects.* Trans. Sister Mary Sarah Muldowney et al. Ed. Roy J. Deferrari. New York: Fathers of the Church, 1952.
Austin, J. L. "Truth." *Proceedings of the Aristotelian Society,* supplem. vol. 24 (1950): 111–28.
Avis, Paul. *The Methods of Modern Theology: The Dream of Reason.* Basingstoke, UK: Marshall Morgan and Scott, 1986.
Ayer, A. J. *Philosophy and Language.* Oxford: Clarendon, 1960.
Ayers, Robert H., and William T. Blackstone, eds. *Religious Language and Knowledge.* Athens: University of Georgia Press, 1972.
Barnes, Michael. *Christian Identity and Religious Pluralism: Religions in Conversation.* London: SPCK and Nashville: Abingdon, 1989.
Bartel, T. W., ed. *Comparative Theology: Essays for Keith Ward.* London: SPCK, 2003.
Barth, Karl. *Church Dogmatics.* Edinburgh: T. and T. Clark, 1936–1977.
Binkley, Timothy. "On the Truth and Probity of Metaphor." *Journal of Aesthetics and Art Criticism* 33 (1974): 171–80. Rptd. in *Philosophical Perspectives on Metaphor,* ed. Mark Johnson, 136–53. Minneapolis: University of Minnesota Press, 1981.

Black, Max. "Metaphor." *Proceedings of the Aristotelian Society* 55 (1954–55): 273–94. Rptd. in *Philosophical Perspectives on Metaphor*, ed. Mark Johnson, 63–82. Minneapolis: University of Minnesota Press, 1981.

Boeve, Lieven, "Naming God Today and the Theological Project of Prof. Dr. Benjamin Willaert." In *Naming God Today*, ed. H. E. Mertens and L. Boeve, 14–18. Leuven: Leuven University Press, 1994.

———, and Kurt Feyaerts, eds. *Metaphor and God-Talk*. Bern: Peter Lang, 1999.

Bonhoeffer, Dietrich. *Letters and Papers from Prison*. Trans. Eberhard Bethge. Rev. ed. New York: Macmillan, 1967.

Bordoni, Marcello. *Gesù di Nazaret: Signore e Cristo*. Vol. 3: *Il Cristo annunciato dalla Chiesa*. Rome: Herder and Università Lateranense, 1986.

Bouyer, Louis. *Dictionary of Theology*. Trans. Charles Underhill Quinn. New York: Desclée, 1965.

Braaten, Carl E., ed. *Our Naming of God: Problems and Prospects of God-Talk Today*. Minneapolis: Fortress, 1989.

Brown, David. *The Divine Trinity*. La Salle, IL: Open Court; London: Duckworth, 1985.

Brown, Stuart C. *Do Religious Claims Make Sense?* New York: Macmillan, 1969.

Brück, Michael von. "The Contribution of Religious Studies to the Dialogue of the World Religions." Trans. David W. Lutz. In Koslowski, *Philosophy Bridging the World Religions*, 123–54.

Burke, Kenneth. *The Rhetoric of Religion: Studies in Logology*. Berkeley: University of California Press, 1970.

Burrell, David. *Analogy and Philosophical Language*. New Haven: Yale University Press, 1973.

Byrne, Peter. *Prolegomena to Religious Pluralism: Reference and Realism in Religion*. New York: St. Martin's; Basingstoke, UK: Macmillan, 1995.

———. Response to Joe Houston, "William Alston on Referring to God." In Helm, *Referring to God*, 63–69.

———. "Ward on Revelation: Inclusivism or Pluralism?" In Bartel, *Comparative Theology*, 13–23.

———. "It Is Not Reasonable to Believe That Only One Religion Is True." In Peterson and VanArragon, *Contemporary Debates in Philosophy of Religion*, 201–10.

———. "Reply to Yandell." In Peterson and VanArragon, *Contemporary Debates in Philosophy of Religion*, 215–17.

Campbell, Alastair. "The Nature of Practical Theology." In *The Blackwell Reader in Pastoral and Practical Theology*, ed. James Woodward and Stephen Pattison, 77–88. Oxford and Malden, MA: Blackwell, 2000.

Capon, Robert Farrar. *Hunting the Divine Fox: Images and Mystery in Christian Faith*. New York: Seabury, 1974.

Carnap, Rudolf. *Meaning and Necessity: A Study in Semantics and Modal Logic*. 2nd ed. Chicago: University of Chicago Press, 1956.

———. *Logical Foundations of Probability*. 2nd ed. Chicago: University of Chicago Press, 1962.

———. "Replies and Systematic Expositions." In *The Philosophy of Rudolf Carnap*, ed. Paul Arthur Schilpp, 859–1013. La Salle, IL: Open Court; London: Cambridge University Press, 1963.
Carnes, John R. *Axiomatics and Dogmatics*. New York: Oxford University Press, 1982.
Castelli, Enrico, ed. *L'Analyse du langage théologique: Le nom de Dieu*. Paris: Aubier, 1969.
Cathrein, Viktor. *Philosophia moralis*. 17th ed. Freiburg: B. Herder, 1935.
Cerfaux, L. *The Church in the Theology of St. Paul*. Trans. Geoffrey Webb and Adrian Walker. New York: Herder and Herder, 1959.
Charlesworth, M. J., ed. *The Problem of Religious Language*. Englewood Cliffs, NJ: Prentice-Hall, 1974.
Chenu, M. D. *Is Theology a Science?* Trans. A. H. N. Green-Armytage. New York: Hawthorn Books, 1959.
Christian, William A. *Meaning and Truth in Religion*. Princeton: Princeton University Press, 1964.
Clarke, Bowman L. *Language and Natural Theology*. The Hague: Mouton, 1966.
Clarke, Peter B., and Peter Byrne. *Religion Defined and Explained*. New York: St. Martin's, 1993.
Clarke, W. Norris. "Analogy and the Meaningfulness of Language about God: A Reply to Kai Nielsen." *Thomist* 40 (1976): 61–95.
Clarkson, John F., John H. Edwards, William J. Kelly, and John J. Welch, eds. *The Church Teaches: Documents of the Church in English Translation*. St. Louis and London: B. Herder, 1955.
Clifford, Anne M. "The Global Horizon of Religious Pluralism and Local Dialogue with the Religious-other." In *New Horizons in Theology*, ed. Terrence W. Tilley, 162–81. Maryknoll, NY: Orbis, 2005.
Cohen, Daniel. *Arguments and Metaphors in Philosophy*. Lanham, MD: University Press of America, 2004.
Cohn-Sherbok, Dan. "Between Christian and Jew." *Theology* 83 (1980): 91–97.
Congar, Yves. "*Lutherana:* Théologie de l'eucharistie et christologie chez Luther." *Revue des sciences philosophiques et théologiques* 66 (1982): 169–97.
Cook, E. David. "Truth, Mystery and Justice: Hick and Christianity's Uniqueness." In *One God, One Lord: Christianity in a World of Religious Pluralism*, 2nd ed., ed. Andrew Clarke and Bruce W. Winter, 237–46. Grand Rapids: Baker, 1992.
Cupitt, Don. "The Finality of Christ." *Theology* 78 (1975): 618–28.
Davidson, Donald. "Truth Rehabilitated." In *Rorty and His Critics*, ed. Robert B. Brandom, 65–74. Malden, MA: Blackwell, 2000.
Dawson, Christopher. *Religion and Culture*. New York: Sheed and Ward, 1948.
De Silva, Lynn A. *The Problem of the Self in Buddhism and Christianity*. New York: Barnes and Noble, 1979.
Delhaye, Philippe. "La mise en cause de la spécificité de la morale chrétienne." *Revue Théologique de Louvain* 4 (1973): 308–39.

Denziger, Henry, and Adolf Schönmetzer, eds. *Enchiridion symbolorum definitionum et declarationum de rebus fidei et morum*. 34th ed., rev. Barcelona: Herder, 1967.

Descartes, René. *The Philosophical Works of Descartes*. Trans. Elizabeth S. Haldane and G. R. T. Ross. Vol. 1. Cambridge: Cambridge University Press, 1931.

Deutsch, Eliot. "Holy Otherness: Religious Differences Revisited." In *The Stranger's Religion: Fascination and Fear*, ed. Anna Lännström, 99–112. Notre Dame: University of Notre Dame Press, 2004.

Devine, Philip E. "On the Definition of 'Religion.'" *Faith and Philosophy* 3 (1986): 270–84.

Dewart, Leslie. *Religion, Language and Truth*. New York: Herder and Herder, 1970.

D'hert, Ignace. *Wittgenstein's Relevance for Theology*. Bern: Herbert Lang; Frankfurt/M.: Peter Lang, 1975.

Dillistone, F. W. *C. H. Dodd, Interpreter of the New Testament*. Grand Rapids: Eerdmans, 1977.

Donovan, Peter. *Religious Language*. New York: Hawthorn Books, 1976.

Downey, John K. *Beginning at the Beginning: Wittgenstein and Theological Conversation*. Lanham, MD: University Press of America, 1986.

Dulles, Avery. *Revelation Theology: A History*. New York: Herder and Herder, 1969.

———. *Models of the Church*. Expanded ed. Garden City: Doubleday, 1974.

———. "Justification in Contemporary Catholic Theology." In *Justification by Faith*, ed. H. George Anderson, T. Austin Murphy, and Joseph A. Burgess, 256–77. Minneapolis: Augsburg, 1985.

Dupuis, Jacques. *Toward a Christian Theology of Religious Pluralism*. Maryknoll, NY: Orbis, 1997.

Eaton, Ralph M., ed. *Descartes Selections*. New York: Scribner, 1927.

Ebeling, Gerhard. *Word and Faith*. Trans. James W. Leitch. Philadelphia: Fortress, 1963.

———. *Introduction to a Theological Theory of Language*. Trans. R. A. Wilson. Philadelphia: Fortress, 1973.

Eddy, Paul Rhodes. *John Hick's Pluralist Philosophy of World Religions*. Aldershot, UK, and Burlington, VT: Ashgate, 2002.

Evans, C. Stephen. *The Historical Christ and the Jesus of Faith: The Incarnational Narrative as History*. Oxford: Clarendon, 1996.

Fawcett, Thomas. *The Symbolic Language of Religion*. Minneapolis: Augsburg, 1971.

Fergusson, David. "Meaning, Truth, and Realism in Bultmann and Lindbeck." *Religious Studies* 26 (1990): 183–98.

Ferré, Frederick. *Language, Logic, and God*. New York: Harper, 1961.

———. *Basic Modern Philosophy of Religion*. New York: Charles Scribner's Sons, 1967.

Fiorenza, Francis Schüssler. *Foundational Theology: Jesus and the Church*. New York: Crossroad, 1984.

Fisichella, Rino. "Langage théologique." In *Dictionnaire de théologie fondamentale*, ed. René Latourelle, 725–30. Montreal: Éditions Bellarmin, 1992.
Ford, David F. "Epilogue: Christian Theology at the Turn of the Millennium." In *The Modern Theologians*. 2nd ed., ed. David F. Ford, 720–28. Oxford: Blackwell, 1997.
Fox, Douglas A. *Mystery and Meaning: Personal Logic and the Language of Religion*. Philadelphia: Westminster, 1975.
Frankenberry, Nancy K., and Hans H. Penner, eds. *Language, Truth, and Religious Belief: Studies in Twentieth-Century Theory and Method in Religion*. Atlanta: Scholars, 1999.
Frege, Gottlob. *Translations from the Philosophical Writings of Gottlob Frege*. Ed. P. Geach and M. Black. 3d ed. Totowa, NJ: Rowman and Littlefield, 1980.
Friedl, Francis P., and Rex Reynolds, eds. *Extraordinary Lives: Thirty-Four Priests Tell Their Stories*. Notre Dame, IN: Ave Maria, 1997.
Gabus, Jean-Paul. *Critique du discours théologique*. Neuchatel/Paris: Delachaux et Niestlé, 1977.
Gadamer, Hans-Georg. *Truth and Method*. Translation edited by Garrett Barden and John Cumming. New York: Seabury, 1975.
Gale, Richard M. "Some Difficulties in Theistic Treatments of Evil." In *The Evidential Argument from Evil*, ed. Daniel Howard-Snyder, 206–18. Bloomington: Indiana University Press, 1996.
Gasking, D. A. T., and A. C. Jackson. "Wittgenstein as a Teacher." In *Ludwig Wittgenstein: The Man and His Philosophy*, ed. K. T. Fann, 49–55. New York: Dell, 1967.
Geach, Peter. "The Meaning of 'God.' " In *Religion and Philosophy*, ed. Martin Warner, 85–90. Cambridge: Cambridge University Press, 1992.
Geffré, Claude. *The Risk of Interpretation: On Being Faithful to the Christian Tradition in a Non-Christian Age*. Trans. David Smith. New York: Paulist, 1987.
Gellner, Ernest. *Words and Things: A Critical Account of Linguistic Philosophy and a Study in Ideology*. Boston: Beacon, 1960.
George, Timothy. *Theology of the Reformers*. Nashville: Broadman, 1988.
Gilkey, Langdon. *Naming the Whirlwind: The Renewal of God-Language*. Indianapolis: Bobbs-Merrill, 1969.
Girardin, B. "Le langage et le mythe." *Zeitschrift für Philosophie und Theologie* 13/14 (1966–67): 401–12.
Gleeson, Gerald. "Seeking Understanding." In *An Introduction to Catholic Theology*, ed. Richard Lennan, 107–44. New York: Paulist, 1998.
Grabner-Heider, Anton. *Semiotik und Theologie: Religiöse Rede zwischen analytischer und hermeneutischer Philosophie*. Munich: Kosel, 1973.
Griffin, Nicholas. *Relative Identity*. Oxford: Clarendon, 1977.
Grisez, Germain G. *Contraception and the Natural Law*. Milwaukee: Bruce, 1964.
———. *Abortion: The Myths, the Realities, and the Arguments*. New York: Corpus, 1970.

Grözinger, Karl-Erich. "Judaism: Intra-Religious Plurality as a Chance for Discourse Between Religions." Trans. David W. Lutz. In Koslowski, *Philosophy Bridging the World Religions*, 38–53.
Gunton, Colin E., Stephen R. Holmes, and Murray A. Rae, eds. *The Practice of Theology: A Reader*. London: SCM, 2001.
Haight, Roger. *Dynamics of Theology*. New York: Paulist, 1990.
Haldane, John. *Faithful Reason: Essays Catholic and Philosophical*. London and New York: Routledge, 2004.
Hallett, Garth L. *Darkness and Light: The Analysis of Doctrinal Statements*. New York: Paulist, 1975.
———. *A Companion to Wittgenstein's "Philosophical Investigations."* Ithaca: Cornell University Press, 1977.
———. *Christian Moral Reasoning: An Analytic Guide*. Notre Dame: University of Notre Dame Press, 1983.
———. *Logic for the Labyrinth: A Guide to Critical Thinking*. Lanham, MD: University Press of America, 1984.
———. *Language and Truth*. New Haven: Yale University Press, 1988.
———. *Greater Good: The Case for Proportionalism*. Washington, DC: Georgetown University Press, 1995.
———. *A Middle Way to God*. New York: Oxford University Press, 2000.
———. *Identity and Mystery in Themes of Christian Faith: Late-Wittgensteinian Perspectives*. Aldershot, UK: Ashgate, 2005.
———. "From Statements to Parables: Rethinking Pluralist Identities." *Theological Studies* 68 (2007): 555–71.
———. *Linguistic Philosophy: The Central Story*. Albany: State University of New York Press, 2008.
Hanson, R. P. C. *The Search for the Christian Doctrine of God: The Arian Controversy, 318–381*. Edinburgh: T. and T. Clark, 1988.
Hartshorne, Charles. "Concerning Abortion: An Attempt at a Rational View." *Christian Century* 98 (1981): 42–45.
Hazelton, Roger. "Truth in Theology." *Christian Century* 88 (1971): 772–75.
———. "Theological Analogy and Metaphor." *Semeia* 13 (1978): 155–76.
Hebblethwaite, Brian. "Incarnation—The Essence of Christianity?" *Theology* 80 (1977): 85–91. Rptd. in *The Incarnation: Collected Essays in Christology*. Cambridge: Cambridge University Press, 1987, 1–10.
———. *The Ocean of Truth: A Defence of Objective Theism*. Cambridge: Cambridge University Press, 1988.
———. *Philosophical Theology and Christian Doctrine*. Malden, MA, and Oxford: Blackwell, 2005.
Helm, Paul, ed. *Referring to God: Jewish and Christian Philosophical and Theological Perspectives*. New York: St. Martin's, 2000.
Heschel, Susannah. "A Jewish Response to Muzammil Siddiqi: God: A Muslim View." In Hick and Meltzer, *Three Faiths—One God*, 77–83.
Hick, John. *Philosophy of Religion*. 2nd ed. Englewood Cliffs, NJ: Prentice-Hall, 1973.

———. *God and the Universe of Faiths: Essays in the Philosophy of Religion.* New York: St. Martin's, 1973.
———. "Jesus and the World Religions." In *The Myth of God Incarnate*, ed. John Hick, 167–85. London: SCM, 1977.
———. "Incarnation and Atonement: Evil and Incarnation." In *Incarnation and Myth: The Debate Continued*, ed. Michael Goulder, 77–84. Grand Rapids: William B. Eerdmans, 1979.
———. *God Has Many Names.* London: Macmillan, 1980.
———. "Towards a Philosophy of Religious Pluralism." In *Religious Experience and Religious Belief: Essays in the Epistemology of Religion*, ed. Joseph Runzo and Craig K. Ihara, 99–116. Lanham, MD: University Press of America, 1986.
———. "Response to Mesle." In C. Robert Mesle, *John Hick's Theodicy: A Process Humanist Critique*, 115–34. New York: St. Martin's, 1991.
———. *Disputed Questions in Theology and the Philosophy of Religion.* New Haven: Yale University Press, 1993.
———. "A Religious Understanding of Religion: A Model of the Relationship between Traditions." In *Inter-Religious Models and Criteria*, ed. J. Kellenberger. New York: St. Martin's; London: Macmillan, 1993.
———. *The Rainbow of Faiths: Critical Dialogues on Religious Pluralism.* London: SCM, 1995.
———. *Dialogues in the Philosophy of Religion.* Houndmills, UK, and New York: Palgrave, 2001.
———. "Do All Religions Worship the Same God?" In *Questions about God: Today's Philosophers Ponder the Divine*, ed. Steven M. Cahn and David Shatz, 153–70. Oxford: Oxford University Press, 2002.
———. *An Interpretation of Religion: Human Responses to the Transcendent.* 2nd ed. New Haven: Yale University Press, 2004.
High, Dallas M., ed. *New Essays on Religious Language.* New York: Oxford University Press, 1969.
Hospers, John. *An Introduction to Philosophical Analysis.* New York: Prentice-Hall, 1953.
Houston, Joe. "William Alston on Referring to God." In Helm, *Referring to God*, 41–69.
Hoy, David Couzens, and Thomas McCarthy. *Critical Theory.* Oxford and Cambridge, MA: Blackwell, 1994.
Hunsinger, George. "Truth as Self-Involving: Barth and Lindbeck on the Cognitive and Performative Aspects of Truth in Theological Discourse." *Journal of the American Academy of Religion* 61 (1993): 41–56.
Hutchins, Robert M. "Toward a Durable Society." *Fortune*, June 1943, 159–60, 194–205.
Hutchison, John A. *Language and Faith: Studies in Sign, Symbol, and Meaning.* Philadelphia: Westminster, 1960.
Jackendoff, Ray. *Patterns in the Mind: Language and Human Nature.* New York: Basic Books, 1994.

James, William. *Pragmatism*. 1907. Cambridge: Harvard University Press, 1975.
Jeffner, Anders. *The Study of Religious Language*. London: SCM, 1972.
Jennings, Theodore W., Jr. *Beyond Theism: A Grammar of God-Language*. New York: Oxford University Press, 1985.
Jenson, Robert W. "Karl Barth." In Ford, *The Modern Theologians*, 21–36.
———. *Systematic Theology*. Volume 1: *The Triune God*. Oxford: Oxford University Press, 1997.
Johnson, Mark. "Introduction: Metaphor in the Philosophical Tradition." In *Philosophical Perspectives on Metaphor*, ed. Mark Johnson, 3–47. Minneapolis: University of Minnesota Press, 1981.
Johnson, Samuel. *A Dictionary of the English Language*. Abstracted from the folio edition, by the author. 11th ed. London: for E. Bathurst et al., 1798.
Jones, Gareth. *Critical Theology: Questions of Truth and Method*. New York: Paragon, 1995.
Kaempfert, Manfred. *Probleme der religiösen Sprache*. Darmstadt: Wissenschaftliche Buchgesellschaft, 1983.
Kant, Immanuel. *Critique of Pure Reason*. Trans. Norman Kemp Smith. New York: St. Martin's; Toronto: Macmillan, 1965.
Kasper, Walter. *Jesus the Christ*. Trans. V. Green. New York: Paulist; London: Burns and Oates, 1977.
Kaufman, Gordon D. *God the Problem*. Cambridge: Harvard University Press, 1972.
———. *In Face of Mystery: A Constructive Theology*. Cambridge: Harvard University Press, 1993.
———. *An Essay on Theological Method*. 3rd ed. Atlanta: Scholars Press, 1995.
Kearney, R. J. "Analogy and Inference." *New Scholasticism* 51 (1977): 131–41.
Keller, Albert. "Analytical Philosophy and the Magisterium's Claim to Infallible Authority." *Journal of Ecumenical Studies* 19, no. 2 (1982): 75–91.
Kelsey, David H. "Paul Tillich." In *The Modern Theologians: An Introduction to Christian Theology in the Twentieth Century*. 2nd ed., ed. David F. Ford, 87–102. Cambridge, MA and Oxford: Blackwell, 1997.
Kerr, Fergus. *Theology after Wittgenstein*. Oxford: Basil Blackwell, 1986.
Kimpel, Ben F. *Language and Religion: A Semantic Preface to a Philosophy of Religion*. New York: Philosophical Library, 1957.
Klubertanz, George P. *St. Thomas Aquinas on Analogy: A Textual Analysis and Systematic Synthesis*. Chicago: Loyola University Press, 1960.
Kluge, Eike-Henner W. *The Practice of Death*. New Haven: Yale University Press, 1975.
Knitter, Paul F. *No Other Name? A Critical Survey of Christian Attitudes Toward the World Religions*. Maryknoll, NY: Orbis; London: SCM, 1985.
Knox, John Jr. *The Humanity and Divinity of Christ: A Study of Pattern in Christology*. Cambridge: Cambridge University Press, 1967.
———. "Truth, Correspondence, and Ordinary Language." *Personalist* 52 (1971): 515–34.

Kort, Wesley A. *Bound to Differ: The Dynamics of Theological Discourses.* University Park: The Pennsylvania State University Press, 1992.
Koslowski, Peter, ed. *Philosophy Bridging the World Religions.* Dordrecht and Boston: Kluwer Academic, 2003.
Koyama, Kosuke. *Water Buffalo Theology.* Rev. ed. Maryknoll, NY: Orbis, 1999.
Krieger, David J. *The New Universalism: Foundations for a Global Theology.* Maryknoll, NY: Orbis, 1991.
Küng, Hans. *Infallible? An Inquiry.* Trans. Edward Quinn. Garden City: Doubleday, 1971.
———. "Is There One True Religion? An Essay in Establishing Ecumenical Criteria." In Küng, *Theology for the Third Millennium*, trans. Peter Heinegg. New York: Doubleday, 1988. Rptd. in *Christianity and Other Religions: Selected Readings.* Rev. ed, ed. John Hick and Brian Hebblethwaite, 118–45. Oxford: Oneworld, 2001.
Labourdette, M. M. "Moral Theology, Methodology of." *New Catholic Encyclopedia*, vol. 9. New York and London: McGraw-Hill, 1967, 1123–25.
Lash, Nicholas. *Holiness, Speech and Silence: Reflections on the Question of God.* Aldershot, UK: Ashgate, 2004.
Latourelle, René. *Theology: Science of Salvation.* Trans. Sister Mary Dominic. Staten Island: Alba House, 1969.
Lawler, Michael G. "Family: American and Christian." *America*, 12 August 1995, 20–22.
Leaman, Oliver. "Introduction." In *Referring to God: Jewish and Christian Philosophical and Theological Perspectives*, ed. Paul Helm, 1–14. New York: St. Martin's, 2000.
Leenhardt, F.-J. "This Is My Body." In *Essays on the Lord's Supper*, ed. Oscar Cullmann and F. J. Leenhardt, trans. J. G. Davies, 24–85. Richmond, VA: John Knox, 1958.
Levenson, Jon D. "Do Christians and Muslims Worship the Same God?" *Christian Century*, 20 April 2004, 32–33.
Lewis, C. S. *Mere Christianity.* Rev. ed. New York: Macmillan, 1952.
———. *The Four Loves.* New York: Harcourt, Brace Jovanovich, 1960.
Lewis, David K. *Convention: A Philosophical Study.* Cambridge: Harvard University Press, 1969.
———. *On the Plurality of Worlds.* Oxford: Basil Blackwell, 1986.
Lindbeck, George A. "Reform and Infallibility." *Cross Currents* 11 (1961): 345–56.
———. *The Nature of Doctrine: Religion and Theology in a Postliberal Age.* Philadelphia: Westminster, 1984.
———. "A Question of Compatibility: A Lutheran Reflects on Trent." In *Justification by Faith*, ed. H. George Anderson, T. Austin Murphy, and Joseph A. Burgess, 230–40. Minneapolis: Augsburg, 1985.
Lipner, Julius. "Truth-Claims and Inter-Religious Dialogue." *Religious Studies* 12 (1976): 217–30.
Lonergan, Bernard. *Method in Theology.* New York: Herder and Herder, 1972.

———. *A Second Collection*. Ed. William F. J. Ryan and Bernard J. Tyrrell. Philadelphia: Westminster, 1974.

———. *Collection*. Ed. Frederick E. Crowe and Robert M. Doran. *Collected Works of Bernard Lonergan* 4. Toronto: University of Toronto Press, 1988.

Lundeen, Lyman T. *Risk and Rhetoric in Religion: Whitehead's Theory of Language and the Discourse of Faith*. Philadelphia: Fortress, 1972.

Mackie, J. L. *Contemporary Linguistic Philosophy—Its Strength and Its Weakness*. Dunedin, New Zealand: University of Otago, 1956.

———. *The Miracle of Theism: Arguments for and against the Existence of God*. Oxford: Clarendon, 1982.

Macquarrie, John. *God-Talk: An Examination of the Language and Logic of Theology*. New York: Harper and Row, 1967.

———. *Thinking about God*. New York: Harper and Row, 1975.

———. *Principles of Christian Theology*. 2nd ed. London: SCM; New York: Simon and Schuster, 1977.

———. *Twentieth-Century Religious Thought*. New ed. Harrisburgh, PA: Trinity, 2002.

Malcolm, Norman. *Ludwig Wittgenstein: A Memoir*. London: Oxford University Press, 1962.

Malherbe, Jean-Francois. *Le langage théologique à l'âge de la science: Lecture de Jean Ladrière*. Paris: Cerf, 1985.

Manchester, William. *The Glory and the Dream: A Narrative History of America 1932-1972*. New York: Bantam, 1975.

Marranzini, Alfredo, ed. *Il linguaggio teologico oggi*. Milan: Àncora, 1970.

Matilal, Bimal Krishna. "Mysticism and Ineffability: Some Issues of Logic and Language." In *Mysticism and Language*, ed. Steven T. Katz, 143–57. New York and Oxford: Oxford University Press, 1992.

Mavrodes, George I. "Polytheism." In *The Rationality of Belief and the Plurality of Faith: Essays in Honor of William P. Alston*, ed. Thomas D. Senor, 261–86. Ithaca: Cornell University Press, 1995.

McCutcheon, Felicity. *Religion within the Limits of Language Alone: Wittgenstein on Philosophy and Religion*. Aldershot, UK: Ashgate, 2001.

McFague, Sallie. *Speaking in Parables: A Study in Metaphor and Theology*. Philadelphia: Fortress, 1975.

———. *Metaphorical Theology: Models of God in Religious Language*. Philadelphia: Fortress, 1982.

———. *Models of God: Theology for an Ecological, Nuclear Age*. Philadelphia: Fortress, 1987.

McGuckin, John A. *St. Cyril of Alexandria, the Christological Controversy: Its History, Theology, and Texts*. Leiden: E. J. Brill, 1994.

McKim, Robert. "Could God Have More than One Nature?" *Faith and Philosophy* 5 (1988): 378–98.

Mersch, Emile. *The Whole Christ: The Historical Development of the Doctrine of the Mystical Body in Scripture and Tradition*. Trans. John R. Kelly. Milwaukee: Bruce, 1938.

———. *The Theology of the Mystical Body*. Trans. Cyril Vollert. St. Louis and London: B. Herder, 1951.
Mertens, H.-E., and L. Boeve, eds. *Naming God Today*. Leuven: Leuven University Press and Uitgeverij Peeters, 1994.
Milhaven, John G. "Towards an Epistemology of Ethics." *Theological Studies* 27 (1966): 228–41.
Mondin, Battista. *Il problema del linguaggio teologico dalle origini ad oggi*. Brescia: Queriniana, 1971.
Montagu, Ashley, ed. *The Meaning of Love*. New York: Julian, 1953.
Moore, George Edward. *Some Main Problems of Philosophy*. London: Allen and Unwin, 1953.
———. *Commonplace Book 1919–1953*. Ed. Casimir Lewy. London: Allen and Unwin; New York: Macmillan, 1962.
———. *Principia Ethica*. Rev. ed. Ed. Thomas Baldwin. Cambridge: Cambridge University Press, 1993.
Morris, Thomas V. *The Logic of God Incarnate*. Ithaca: Cornell University Press, 1986.
Nagel, Thomas. *The View from Nowhere*. New York: Oxford University Press, 1986.
Need, Stephen W. *Human Language and Knowledge in the Light of Chalcedon*. New York: Peter Lang, 1996.
Netland, Harold A. *Dissonant Voices: Religious Pluralism and the Question of Truth*. Grand Rapids: William B. Eerdmans; Leicester, UK: Apollos, 1991.
———. *Encountering Religious Pluralism: The Challenge to Christian Faith and Mission*. Downers Grove, IL: InterVarsity, 2001.
Newbigin, Lesslie. "The Christian Faith and the World Religions." In *Christianity and Other Religions: Selected Readings*, ed. John Hick and Brian Hebblethwaite, 88–117. Oxford: Oneworld, 2001.
Newman, John Henry. *Newman's University Sermons*. Ed. D. M. Mackinnon and J. D. Holmes. London: SPCK, 1970.
Nielsen, Kai. "Facts, Factual Statements and Theoretical Terms." *Philosophical Studies* (Dublin) 23 (n.d.): 129–51.
———. "Talk of God and the Doctrine of Analogy." *Thomist* 40 (1976): 32–60.
———. *An Introduction to the Philosophy of Religion*. New York: St. Martin's, 1983.
Nietzsche, Friedrich. "On Truth and Lie in an Extra-Moral Sense." In *The Portable Nietzsche*, ed. Walter Kaufmann, 42–47. New York: Viking, 1954.
Noonan, John T. Jr. *Contraception: A History of Its Treatment by the Catholic Theologians and Canonists*. Cambridge: Harvard University Press, 1966.
———. "Responding to Persons: Methods of Moral Argument in Debate over Abortion." *Theology Digest* 21 (1973): 291–307.
Nouwen, Henri. *Creative Ministry*. Garden City: Doubleday, 1971.
———. *Seeds of Hope: A Henri Nouwen Reader*. 2d ed. Ed. Robert Durback. New York: Doubleday, 1997.

Nygren, Anders. *Meaning and Method: Prolegomena to a Scientific Philosophy of Religion and a Scientific Theology*. Trans. Philip S. Watson. Philadelphia: Fortress, 1972.
O'Callaghan, John P. *Thomist Realism and the Linguistic Turn: Toward a More Perfect Form of Existence*. Notre Dame: University of Notre Dame Press, 2003.
O'Collins, Gerald. *Fundamental Theology*. New York: Paulist, 1981.
———. *Interpreting Jesus*. Ramsey, NJ: Paulist; London: Chapman, 1983.
———, and Daniel Kendall. *The Bible for Theology: Ten Rules for the Theological Use of Scripture*. New York: Paulist, 1997.
Ormerod, Neil. *Introducing Contemporary Theologies: The What and the Who of Theology Today*. Newtown, NSW: E. J. Dwyer, 1990.
Palmer, Humphrey. *Analogy: A Study of Qualification and Argument in Theology*. New York: St. Martin's, 1973.
Pannenberg, Wolfhart. *Basic Questions in Theology: Collected Essays*. 2 vols. Trans. George H. Kehm. Philadelphia: Fortress, 1970–71.
———. *Theology and the Philosophy of Science*. Trans. Francis McDonagh. Philadelphia: Westminster, 1976.
———. "Religious Pluralism and Conflicting Truth Claims: The Problem of a Theology of the World Religions." In *Christian Uniqueness Reconsidered: The Myth of a Pluralistic Theology of Religion*, ed. Gavin D'Costa, 96–106. Maryknoll, NY: Orbis, 1990.
Partee, Barbara H. "Lexical Semantics and Compositionality." In *An Invitation to Cognitive Science*, 2nd ed., volume 1: *Language*, ed. Lila R. Gleitman and Mark Liberman, 311–60. Cambridge: MIT Press, 1995.
Pastor, Félix Alejandro. *La lógica de lo inefable: una teoría teológica sobre el lenguaje del teísmo cristiano*. Rome: Editrice Pontificia Università Gregoriana, 1986.
Pater, Wim A. de. "Analogy and Disclosures: On Religious Language." In *Metaphor and God-Talk*, ed. Lieven Boeve and Kurt Feyaerts, 33–44. Bern: Peter Lang, 1999.
Peterson, Michael L. and Raymond VanArragon, eds. *Contemporary Debates in Philosophy of Religion*. Malden, MA: Blackwell, 2004.
Peterson, Michael L., William Hasker, Bruce Reichenbach, and David Basinger. *Reason and Religious Belief: An Introduction to the Philosophy of Religion*. New York and Oxford: Oxford University Press, 1991.
Phillips, D. Z. *Faith and Philosophical Enquiry*. London: Routledge and Kegan Paul, 1970.
Phillips, Stephen H. "Mystic Analogizing and the 'Peculiarly Mystical.'" In *Mysticism and Language*, ed. Steven T. Katz, 123–42. New York and Oxford: Oxford University Press, 1992.
Plantinga, Alvin. *Does God Have a Nature?* Milwaukee: Marquette University Press, 1980.
Porter, Stanley E., ed. *The Nature of Religious Language: A Colloquium*. Sheffield, UK: Sheffield Academic Press, 1996.

Power, William L. "Musings on the Mystery of God." *International Journal for Philosophy of Religion* 7 (1976): 300–10.
Price, H. H. *Belief.* London: George Allen and Unwin, 1969.
Pusey, E. B. *The Doctrine of the Real Presence.* 1855. London: Walter Smith, 1883.
Putnam, Hilary. "Language and Philosophy." In *Mind, Language and Reality. Philosophical Papers* 2, 1–32. Cambridge: Cambridge University Press, 1975.
Quine, Willard Van Orman. *Word and Object.* Cambridge: MIT Press, 1960.
Quinn, Philip L., and Kevin Meeker, eds. *The Philosophical Challenge of Religious Diversity.* London and New York: Oxford University Press, 2000.
Race, Alan. *Christians and Religious Pluralism: Patterns in the Christian Theology of Religions.* 2nd ed. London: SCM, 1993.
Rahner, Karl. *Theological Investigations* 4. Trans. Kevin Smith. Baltimore: Helicon; London: Darton, Longman and Todd, 1966.
———. "The Concept of Mystery in Catholic Theology." In *Theological Investigations* 4, 36–73.
———. "On the Theology of the Incarnation." In *Theological Investigations*, 4, 105–20.
———. "The Presence of Christ in the Sacrament of the Lord's Supper." In *Theological Investigations* 4, 287–311.
———. *Foundations of Christian Faith: An Introduction to the Idea of Christianity.* Trans. William V. Dych. New York: Seabury, 1978.
———. "Why Doing Theology Is So Difficult." In *Karl Rahner in Dialogue: Conversations and Interviews 1965–1982*, ed. Paul Imhof, Hubert Biallowons, and Harvey Egan, 216–20. New York: Crossroad, 1986.
———. *Hearer of the Word.* Ed. Andrew Tallon. Trans. Joseph Donceel. New York: Continuum, 1994.
———. *The Trinity.* Trans. Joseph Donceel. New York: Crossroad, 1997.
Ramsey, Ian. *Religious Language: An Empirical Placing of Theological Phrases.* London: SCM, 1957.
———. *Christian Discourse: Some Logical Explorations.* London and New York: Oxford University Press, 1965.
Ramsey, Paul. "Reference Points in Deciding about Abortion." In *The Morality of Abortion: Legal and Historical Perspectives*, ed. John Noonan, 60–100. Cambridge: Harvard University Press, 1970.
Ratzinger, Joseph. "Revelation and Tradition." In Karl Rahner and Joseph Ratzinger, *Revelation and Tradition*, trans. W. J. O'Hara, 26–49. New York: Herder and Herder, 1966.
Reichenbach, Bruce R. "Evil and a Reformed View of God." *International Journal for Philosophy of Religion* 24 (1988): 67–85.
Riga, Peter J. "The Act of Faith in Augustine and Aquinas." *Thomist* 35 (1971): 143–74.
Roberti, Francesco, and Pietro Palazzini, eds. *Dictionary of Moral Theology.* Trans. Henry J. Yannone. Westminster, MD: Newman, 1962.

Robinson, N. H. G. "The Logic of Religious Language." In *Talk of God*. Royal Institute of Philosophy Lectures, vol. 2, 1967–68, 1–19. London: Macmillan; New York: St. Martin's, 1969.

Rocca, Gregory P. *Speaking the Incomprehensible God: Thomas Aquinas on the Interplay of Positive and Negative Theology*. Washington, DC: The Catholic University of America Press, 2004.

Ross, J. F. *Portraying Analogy*. Cambridge: Cambridge University Press, 1981.

Ruben, David-Hillel. *Explaining Explanation*. London and New York: Routledge, 1990.

Sapir, Edward. *Selected Writings in Language, Culture and Personality*. Ed. David G. Mandelbaum. Berkeley: University of California Press, 1985.

Schaff, Adam. *Language and Cognition*. Ed. Robert S. Cohen. Trans. Olgierd Wojtasiewicz. New York: McGraw-Hill, 1973.

Scharlemann, Robert P., ed. *Naming God*. New York: Paragon House, 1985.

Schillebeeckx, E. *Revelation and Theology*. Vol. 1. Trans. N. D. Smith. New York: Sheed and Ward, 1967.

Schleiermacher, Friedrich. *Hermeneutics and Criticism and Other Writings*. Trans. and ed. Andrew Bowie. Cambridge: Cambridge University Press, 1998.

Scotus, Duns. *Philosophical Writings*. Ed. and trans. Allan Wolter. Edinburgh: Thomas Nelson and Sons, 1962.

Sesboüé, Bernard. *Jésus-Christ dans la tradition de l'église: Pour une actualisation de la christologie de Chalcédoine*. Paris: Desclée, 1982.

Sherry, Patrick. *Religion, Truth, and Language-Games*. New York: Barnes and Noble, 1977.

Siddiqi, Muzammil. "God: A Muslim View." In *Three Faiths—One God: A Jewish, Christian, and Muslim Encounter*, ed. John Hick and Edmund S. Meltzer, 63–76. Albany: State University of New York Press, 1989.

Smith, Edward E. "Three Distinctions about Concepts and Categorization." *Mind and Language* 4 (1989): 57–61.

Smith, James K. A. *Speech and Theology: Language and the Logic of Incarnation*. London and New York: Routledge, 2002.

Smith, John E. *The Analogy of Experience: An Approach to Understanding Religious Truth*. New York: Harper and Row, 1973.

Soskice, Janet Martin. *Metaphor and Religious Language*. Oxford: Clarendon, 1987.

Sorensen, Roy. "Vagueness and the Desiderata for Definition." In *Definitions and Definability: Philosophical Perspectives*, ed. James H. Fetzer, David Shatz, and George N. Schlesinger, 71–109. Synthese Library 216. Dordrecht: Kluwer, 1991.

Spiro, Melford. "Religion: Problems of Definition and Explanation." In *Language, Truth, and Religious Belief: Studies in Twentieth-Century Theory and Method in Religion*, ed. Nancy K. Frankenberry and Hans H. Penner, 137–75. Atlanta: Scholars, 1999.

Steinfels, Peter. "The Search for an Alternative." *Commonweal*, November 20, 1981, 660–64.

Strawson, P. F. "Truth." *Proceedings of the Aristotelian Society*, supplem. vol. 24 (1950): 129–56.
Stump, Eleonore. Review of *The Logic of God Incarnate*, by Thomas V. Morris. *Faith and Philosophy* 6 (1989): 218–23.
———. "The God of Abraham, Saadia and Aquinas." In Helm, *Referring to God*, 95–119.
Suárez, Francisco. *De incarnatione. Opera omnia*, vol. 17. Paris: Vivès, 1856.
Swinburne, Richard G. "Analogy, Metaphor, and Religious Language." In *Metaphor and God-Talk*, ed. Lieven Boeve and Kurt Feyaerts, 63–74. Bern: Peter Lang, 1999.
Tavard, Georges. *La théologie parmi les sciences humaines: De la méthode en théologie*. Paris: Beauchesne, 1975.
TeSelle, Sallie McFague. *Speaking in Parables: A Study in Metaphor and Theology*. Philadelphia: Fortress, 1975.
Thiemann, Ronald F. *Revelation and Theology: The Gospel as Narrated Promise*. Notre Dame: University of Notre Dame Press, 1985.
Thomas, Owen C., and Ellen K. Wondra. *Introduction to Theology*. 3rd ed. Harrisburgh, PA: Morehouse, 2002.
Thornhill, J. *Christian Mystery in the Secular Age: The Foundation and Task of Theology*. Westminster, MD: Christian Classics, 1991.
Tilley, Terrence. *Talking of God: An Introduction to Philosophical Analysis of Religious Language*. New York: Paulist, 1978.
Tillich, Paul. *Shaking of the Foundations*. New York: Charles Scribner's Sons, 1948.
Tonkin, Humphrey, and Allison Armstrong Keef, eds. *Language in Religion*. Lanham, MD: University Press of America, 1989.
Torrance, Thomas F. *The Ground and Grammar of Theology*. Charlottesville: University Press of Virginia, 1980.
Tracy, David, and John B. Cobb Jr. *Talking about God: Doing Theology in the Context of Modern Pluralism*. New York: Seabury, 1983.
Urban, Wilbur Marshall. *Language and Reality: The Philosophy of Language and the Principles of Symbolism*. New York: Books for Libraries Press, 1939.
Van Buren, Paul M. *The Edges of Language: An Essay in the Logic of a Religion*. New York: Macmillan, 1972.
Veatch, Robert M. "Death, Determination of." In *The Westminster Dictionary of Christian Ethics*, ed. James F. Childress and John Macquarrie. Philadelphia: Westminster, 1986.
Verheyden, Jack. "On the Christian Doctrine of God." In Hick and Meltzer, *Three Faiths—One God*, 41–57.
Vroom, Hendrik M. *Religions and the Truth: Philosophical Reflections and Perspectives*. Grand Rapids: William B. Eerdmans, 1989.
———. *No Other Gods: Christian Belief in Dialogue with Buddhism, Hinduism, and Islam*. Trans. Lucy Jansen. Grand Rapids: William B. Eerdmans, 1996.
———. "How May We Compare Ideas of Transcendence? On the Method of Comparative Theology." In Bartel, *Comparative Theology*, 66–76.

Waismann, Friedrich. "Analytic-Synthetic," IV. *Analysis* 11 (1951): 115–24.
Ward, Keith. *Religion and Creation*. Oxford: Clarendon, 1996.
Warnach, Victor. "Symbol and Reality in the Eucharist." In *Foundations of Theological Study: A Sourcebook*, ed. Richard Viladesau and Mark Massa, 59–64. New York: Paulist, 1991.
Warnock, Geoffrey. "Truth and Correspondence." In *Knowledge and Experience*, ed. C. D. Rollins, 11–20. Pittsburgh: University of Pittsburgh Press, 1962.
Welch, Claude, ed. and trans. *God and Incarnation in Mid-Nineteenth Century German Theology: G. Thomasius, I. A. Dorner, A. E. Biedermann*. New York: Oxford University Press, 1965.
Wettstein, Howard. "Causal Theory of Proper Names." In *The Cambridge Dictionary of Philosophy*, ed. Robert Audi, 109–10. Cambridge: Cambridge University Press, 1995.
Whorf, Benjamin Lee. *Language, Thought, and Reality: Selected Writings*. Ed. John B. Carroll. Cambridge: MIT Press, 1967.
Wiggins, David. *Sameness and Substance*. Cambridge: Harvard University Press, 1980.
———. "Précis of *Sameness and Substance Renewed*." *Philosophy and Phenomenological Research* 71 (2005): 442–48.
Wiles, Maurice. *The Making of Christian Doctrine: A Study in the Principles of Early Doctrinal Development*. Cambridge: Cambridge University Press, 1967.
———. *Faith and the Mystery of God*. Philadelphia: Fortress, 1982.
Wittgenstein, Ludwig. *Philosophical Investigations*. Trans. G. E. M. Anscombe. 2nd ed. Oxford: Basil Blackwell, 1958.
———. *The Blue and Brown Books*. Oxford: Basil Blackwell, 1960.
———. *Notebooks 1914–1916*. Ed. G. H. von Wright and G. E. M. Anscombe. Trans. G. E. M. Anscombe. Oxford: Basil Blackwell, 1961.
———. *Tractatus Logico-Philosophicus*. Trans. D. F. Pears and B. F. McGuinness. New York: Humanities; London: Routledge and Kegan Paul, 1961.
———. *Zettel*. Ed. G. E. M. Anscombe and G. H. von Wright. Trans. G. E. M. Anscombe. Oxford: Basil Blackwell, 1967.
———. *Philosophical Grammar*. Ed. Rush Rhees. Trans. Anthony Kenny. Berkeley: University of California Press, 1974.
Yandell, Keith E. *The Epistemology of Religious Experience*. Cambridge: Cambridge University Press, 1993.
Zwingli, Ulrich. "On the Lord's Supper." In *Zwingli and Bullinger*. Library of Christian Classics, 24, trans. G. W. Bromiley, 185–238. Philadelphia: Westminster, 1953.

Index

"act," 58–60
Albanese, Catherine, 128
Alston, William, 185, 202–03
Ambrose, Saint 114
analogy, 66–70, 81–88. *See also* Principle of Relative Similarity
analysis, 217–18
Anscombe, G. E. M., 103
Aquinas, Saint Thomas: on analogy, 66; on doing good, 214; on law, 125; on names, 114; on natural laws, 140–41; on the supreme moral principle, 138–39
Aristotle, 199
Atkins, Anselm, 163
Augustine, Saint, 134, 143, 159, 211
Austin, John, 34–36, 56–57
Avis, Paul, 82, 222–23
Ayer, A. J., 97, 233

Barnes, Michael, 31, 165–67, 175
Barth, Karl, 110, 220, 223
Basil, Saint, 114
Binkley, Timothy, 199
Black, Max, 198
Bonhoeffer, Dietrich, 8
borderline cases, 60–61
Bouyer, Louis, 150
Brown, David, 170
Brown, Harold, 89–90
Brück, Michael von, 31, 54
Byrne, Peter, 127, 175, 177–78, 185

Capon, Robert, 68

Carnap, Rudolf, 97, 192–93
Carnes, John, 5–6, 114–15
Casti connubii, 158
Cathrein, Viktor, 102–03
Cerfaux, Lucien, 134
Chenu, M. D., 90, 119–20, 218–19
Christian, William, 151
Clark, Bowman, 207
Clarke, Norris, 66
Clarke, Peter, 127
Cohen, Daniel, 199–200
contraception, 158–60
Cook, E. David, 127
Cornman, James, 78
Council of Chalcedon, 218
Council of Florence, 92
Council of Trent 154–56
Cupitt, Don, 28
Cyril of Alexandria, Saint, 28–29, 132

Davidson, Donald, 42–43
Dawson, Christopher, 96
deductive inference, 81–84, 99
definitions: 2–5, 117–27; of faith, 125; of "good," 120–21; of "law," 125; of "person," 119–22; persuasive, 125–26; of religion, 125–26; theoretical, 119; value-driven, 123–26
Delhaye, Philippe, 151–52
Descartes, René, 22
Devine, Philip, 125–26
Di Noia, J. Augustine, 194

dialog (interfaith), 165–73
Dillistone, F.W., 53
disagreement: verbal vs. nonverbal, 145–51, 171–73
distinctions (linguistic), 137–43
Dulles, Avery, 112, 128, 150
Dupuis, Jacques, 220
Durandus, 75–76

Eaton, Ralph, 162
Ebeling, Gerhard, 57–58, 94–95, 106, 127, 135
Eddy, Paul Rhodes, 194
elephant comparison, 147, 172, 183–84
essence(s), 16–17, 48–49, 131
Eucharist, 75–76, 84–88, 94, 154–57
evil, 75, 138–39
examples, need of, 129–36
explication, 192–93

faith, 125, 149–50
Fergusson, David, 43
Ferré, Frederick, 9, 10
fetal status, 60–61, 147–49. *See also* person
Fiorenza, Francis, 88
Fisichella, Rino, 7
Fourth Lateran Council, 70–71
Frege, Gottlob, 16

Gallagher, Charles, 96
"game," 3–4, 30, 93–94
Geach, Peter, 105
Geffré, Claude, 8
Geoffrey, Warnock, 34
George, Timothy, 78
Gilkey, Langdon, 7
Gleeson, Gerald, 220
God, 169–73, 200, 211–13, 217–18
good, 120–21, 138–39, 157–58
Gregory the Great, Saint, 159
Grisez, Germain, 141, 152
Grözinger, Karl-Erich, 174
Gunton, Colin, 219–20

Haight, Roger, 11, 127–28
Haldane, John, 79
Hanson, R. P. C., 27
Hartshorne, Charles, 62–63
Hazelton, Roger, 46, 207
Hebblethwaite, Brian, 31–32, 90
Herder, Johann, 23, 32
Heschel, Susannah, 31
Hick, John, 28, 170–72, 175–77
Hilary, Saint, 26–27
Holmes, Stephen, 219–20
Houston, Joe, 185
Hunsinger, George, 43
Hutchins, Robert, 96

identities, interfaith, 175–85
identity, 25–29, 84–88, 132–34
Incarnation, 132, 217–18. *See also* Jesus
individuation, 178–79
inference, 81–89. *See also* deductive inference
interfaith dialog, 165–73
"is," 25–27, 85–86, 94, 132

Jackendoff, Ray, 22
James, William, 34, 129
Jenson, Robert, 10
Jesus, 26–29, 132, 169–70, 217–18. *See also* Incarnation
Johnson, Mark, 201–03
Johnson, Samuel, 93
Jones, Gareth, 210–11
Justin Martyr, 211

Kant, Immanuel, 110–11, 141–42, 176, 204
Kaufman, Gordon, 5–6, 194–95, 210
Keller, Albert, 190
Kelsey, David, 54
Kendall, Daniel, 112–13, 206–07
Kluge, Eike-Henner, 103
Knitter, Paul, 152
Knox, John, 28
Koyama, Kosuke, vii

Krieger, David, 183–84
Küng, Hans, 43, 157

Labourdette, M., 10
language: competitors for its authority, 49–50; viewed as code, 9, 20–21, 48; invisibility of, 47–48; medium vs. discourse, 7–9, 188; medium of thought, 11–13; mentalistic conception of, 11–14; shapes and sometimes distorts conception of reality, 23–24; technical, 187–93; theological, 187–93; does not translate nonlinguistic thought, 16–18
language's: authority, 133; cognitive content, 15–16; complexity, viii–ix; definition, 2–6; essence, 6–7; flexibility, 53; neutrality, 50–52; normativity, viii; pervasive relevance, vii
Lash, Nicholas, 180, 206
law, 125
Leaman, Oliver, 43
Lehrer, Keith, 78
Lennan, Richard, 206
Levenson, Jon, 185
Lewis, C. S., 47, 53–54, 145–46
Lewis, David, 133
Lindbeck, George, 153–57, 173–74
Lonergan, Bernard, 89, 129, 142–43, 187–88
love, 93–94
Luther, Martin, 86, 149
lying, 98–99

Mackie, John, 50
Macquarrie, John, 2, 7, 12, 194, 222
Malcolm, Norman, 103
Manchester, William, 172
Matilal, Bimal Krishna, 220
Mavrodes, George, 240
McCarthy, Thomas, vii–viii
McFague, Sallie, 135

McGuckin, John, 28
meaningless statements, 214–15
Mersch, Emile, 26
metaphor, 53, 197–206
methodology, 2
Moore, G. E.: on color, 14–15, 24–25, 130; on good, 120–22, 130, 157–58; on minds, 62
moral: statements, 97–101; terms, 97–99, 157–61
Morris, Thomas, 27
mystery, 108–10
mystery, 209–19

Nagel, Thomas, 78–79
"natural," 140–41
Netland, Harold, 63
Newbigin, Lesslie, 173
Newman, J. H., 81
Nielsen, Kai, 65, 73–74, 76–77
Nietzsche, Friedrich, 91
Noonan, John, 62, 158–59
Nouwen, Henry, 142, 194
number, 17
Nygren, Anders, 3, 49, 51

Ockham, William of, 79
O'Collins, Gerald, 10, 112–13, 201–02, 206–07
organ transplants, 99–100
Ormerod, Neil, 124–25, 191

Palmer, Humphrey, 82–84
Pannenberg, Wolfhart, 3, 71, 123, 186
Pater, Wim de, 199
Paul the Apostle, 101, 139–40
person, 60–61, 119–22, 147–48
Peter, Saint, 88
Peterson, Michael, 89
Phillips, D. Z., 186
Phillips, Stephen, 199
Plantinga, Alvin, 212–13
Plato, 16, 142
Port Royal *Logic*, 12

possibility vs. sense, 73–78, 215
Power, William, 71, 210
precision, 190–93, 199–201
Price, H. H., 152
Principle of Relative Similarity, 36–42, 61–70, 74, 146, 148, 197–98, 205–06, 212–13
privileged senses, 105–14
Putnam, Hilary, 11–12

Race, Allan, 21
Rae, Murray, 219–20
Rahner, Karl: on deductive reasoning, 216–17; on the Eucharist, 85–86; the holy, 108–10; on Jesus, 26; mystery, 110, 142–43; on the Trinity, 226
reference, 175–78
"retroductive" arguments, 88
Rocca, Gregory, 32, 70
Russell, Bertrand, 50

Sapir, Edward, 23
Schaff, Adam, 32
Schleiermacher, Friedrich, 12
Schoeneveld, C., 169
Scotus, Duns, 89
sense vs. possibility, 73–78, 215
senses: "original," 109–11; neutral vs. normative, 141–42, 168, 171–73; privileged, 105–14; secondary, 112; "strict," 109–11
Sesboüé, Bernard, 89
similarity, 68–69. *See also* Principle of Relative Similarity
Spiro, Melford, 122
Strawson, Peter, 34, 56–57
Stump, Eleonore, 220
Suárez, Francisco, 78
Swinburne, Richard, 71–72, 201

Tavard, Georges, 12, 188–89, 194
Te Selle, Sallie McFague, 135–36
theology: autonomy of, 223–25; definition of, 225–26; and language, 223–25; recent, 1–2; rival conceptions of, 226–27
Thiemann, Ronald, 54
Thomas, Owen, 10
Thomasius, Gottfried, 27–28
Thornhill, John, 207
thought: language chief medium of, 11–18; nonlinguistic, 18–20; theological, 18
Tillich, Paul, 10, 150, 162
tradition, 153–57
transsubstantiation, 154–57
Trinity, 170
truth, 112
truth: 91, 112; Austin on, 34–35, 56–57; Ebeling on, 57–58; importance of, 46; mental vs. linguistic, 34; and metaphor, 198–99; Strawson on, 56–57; topic for philosophy, 33; Wittgensteinian account of, 36–42. *See also* Principle of Relative Similarity
Twain, Mark, 47
Tzu, Chuang, 21

universal statements: factual, 91–96; moral 97–101

value vs. verdict, 138–40
Vatican Council I, 149
Veatch, Robert, 63
verbal disagreement, 145–51, 168
verbal vs. nonverbal, 141–42, 168, 171–73
verdict vs. value, 138–40
Veritatis splendor, 101
Vroom, Hendrik, 181–82, 185–86

Ward, Keith, 43
Whorf, Benjamin Lee, 23, 24
Wiles, Maurice, 71, 161–62
Wittgenstein, Ludwig: 60, 165; on concepts, 15; on deaf-mute, 18–19; on games, 3–4, 22, 30,

93–94; on numbers, 17; on language, 24–26, 29–31, 55; on meaning, 52, 215; on metaphysics, 127; on method, 130–31; on ostensive definition, 177; on philosophy, 223; on propositions, 25; on teaching philosophy, viii–ix; on theses, 93; on thinking, 12; on words, 30

Wondra, Ellen, 10

Zwingli, Ulrich, 86

www.ingramcontent.com/pod-product-compliance
Lightning Source LLC
Chambersburg PA
CBHW020643230426
43665CB00008B/298